Love, Light & Shadow

Dear Heidi

Blessing to you sister,
as you walk your
healing journey.
May the path be clear
and beautiful
as you dance with
your light & shadow

Love Light & Shadow

Catherine

Written by Catherine Beerda-Basso

Love and Light Publishing, 2017

First Edition

ISBN: 978-0-9959963-0-4

Edited by Heather Dakota
Photographs collected by Debbie Allison
Cover & Layout design: Twozdai Hulse

Love and Light Publishing
Maple Ridge B.C., Canada

www.catherinebeerdabasso.com

*"I will give you a new heart
And put a new spirit in you.
I will remove from you,
Your heart of stone
And give you a heart of flesh."*

Ezekiel 36:26

Contents

And The Great Spirit came to me and said, "Up on your feet! Go to the potter's house. When you get there, I'll tell you what I have to say." So I went to the potter's house, and watched him working away at his wheel. Whenever the pot that the potter was working on did not come to be, as sometimes happens when you are working with clay, the potter would simply start over and use the same clay to make another pot. Upon witnessing this the Spirit's message came to me: "In the same way that this potter works his clay, so do I work you."

I am a clay pot.

Simply formed and intricately made.
Inside me lies the Truths of Lifetimes lived.
Inside me are those things that dazzle like the stars
and shine like the heavens.
Inside me are the mysteries of the dark and the treasures of the
night. There are stories and words. There are images and beauty.
Inside me is where the treasure lies…

…the treasure of redemption, the treasure of forgiveness, the
treasure of rebirth and new life.
Inside me is my story,
One that is one of many.
I am a simple clay pot, a vessel.
I have something to pour out, and my time to do so has come.

The Clay Pot

How many times
How many times can a clay pot be broken?
How many times can you put it back together
With hope of it functioning the same?
Can you fill it as full?
Will what it contains seep out?
Does it not lose it's value?
Does it not lose its beauty?
Really...

...How many times can a clay pot be broken and put back together,
Before it is time to just throw it away?

Coming out of a very difficult month
these are the things I ponder.
Dark days took me and I wondered just how much I could take.
Words whispered
"You're Alone."
"This is Hopeless."
"You can't do this."

They were only lies.

Exhausted, I lay my broken self out
Piece-by-piece
They are all there,
each piece.
I am broken...yes...
but each part of me remains
intact contrary to what the whispering voices
would have me believe.
They would have me convinced
that I am lost or not whole
But clearly...
...Through tear-filled eyes,
I can see all of me,
Every single piece.

I let emotions wave over me
Again, and again, and again.
I will not run from them.

I will not hide.
The worst has already happened.
I am already lying in pieces.
There is nothing more to fear.

What would light be if there were no darkness?
What is it that it should bring such fear?
For is there not beauty found in the night?

The comfort found in a lovers touch,
The quiet breathing of children sleeping,
The stillness of a summer's night,
The showcase of the starry sky,
The brilliance of the waning moon,
The songs of the nighttime creatures,
And the joy of being awake, while the
rest of the world sleeps.

After a hard day,
the darkness can
bring relief
knowing that tomorrow is a new day
and this one is done.
And for now in the dim, we can
Rest,
Reflect,
Rejuvenate,
And restore.

Every piece is there
Each accounted for
And with the help of the Potter,
I place each piece back together,
and they fit perfectly.

How many times can a clay pot be
broken and put back together?
As many times as is needed.

~Catherine Beerda-Basso
May 25th, 2011

In the beginning

In the beginning, I knew God was real. There was no doubt in my mind that there was something bigger than myself. A Divine Source the I was a part of. It was a knowledge with which I was born. It was nothing anyone had to teach me. I was brought up in the Christian Religion, so I was taught the name of that source was "God," and He was my Heavenly Father. Unfortunately, within the confines of organized religion, I was not taught about the fullness, the vastness, and the infinity of God's Love, Divine Love. Instead, I was taught about a God that was an out-of-reach entity who created me. I was taught that I was not worthy of God's love. I learned about a very small god...one contained in a box full of dogma, religious rules, and essentially, control. He was a Father that was happy with me when I was "good," but wrathfully angry with me when I was "bad." And so, in this environment my limited spiritual view was built on a foundation of good and bad, right and wrong, and obedience and sin.

Many, many years ago, during my "coming out" of religion, I was attending a woman's workshop and was asked to describe how I saw God. My girlfriend who was attending the workshop with me gave a great description to which I could relate. She said God was like a Grandfather or Uncle that lived far away and brought presents at Christmas time. That description stayed with me. I felt sure that there were more people who felt as we did. There was a distance between this religious God and the people who gathered in church to worship him.

My own "fire and brimstone" religious upbringing, which was based on obey or burn in hell, only offered a lot of fear and disconnect, and not much clarity, compassion, or love. I tended to live in fear, guilt, and shame. My conclusion about that God was that He was waiting for me to fix my life and myself. Then, maybe then, I would be good enough to be considered worthy. Jesus helped. His compassion and humanity bridged the gap somewhat. If I am totally honest, the guilt and shame of being a sinner seemed to over shadow Jesus's message of Love, who from the story told in the bible, came to eliminate my shame and guilt. I often wonder how he feels, watching us, some thousands of years later still being taught to live within the guilt and shame, and in his name, none-the-less.

My entire life has been a Spiritual Life Journey. Sometimes the journey was more noticeable than other times. The longing, searching, and seeking was always there. I am still on my Spiritual Life Journey. I will be on it until the moment I take my last breath. I know that I do not have all the answers for which you are looking. What I do have are my experiences, my story, and my truth.

This story is not one of someone who has always made the best choices, or was always someone to be proud of. I have made mistakes. I have messed up and made a mess of my life. I have done things in my past that still make my stomach ache. Within all of my imperfections and poor choices was a child, a girl, a woman who longed for more than she was being shown, not for more in the material sense but more in the Divine sense. I longed to know my purpose and the purpose of this life.

I share my story, because Divinity whispered for me to do so. I believe in the power of story. I believe in the power of passing these stories to each other. It is a tradition that has been used since the beginning of time, but one that has been forgotten in our modern world. We tend to embrace autonomy and individuality more than community and learning from each other.

The Source of all Life will hold many different names in this book. The names that I talk about are the names that I knew and understood at the different times. Your names are yours and I honour that. Perhaps you have no names at all. All are welcome. I truly believe that in the end, it is all Love.

I thank Father Sky and Mother Earth for this amazing opportunity and ask for the strength that I need to follow through. My hope and prayer is that this book will bring wisdom and possibility to those who read it. That you find embracing-compassion and deep honour for your humanity, and your divinity. And finally, that you may come to know the abundance of life, the understanding of unending love, and feel Spirit within and around you in a way that resonates with you.

We are all formed by Love; by a Source whose love and peace can often surpass our human understanding. There is a plan for each of us, not only in the human sense but in a spiritual, energetic sense as well. You are more than you know yourself to be. You have been wonderfully and awesomely made! You are meant to be here, in this time and space. You matter.

Thank you for taking this journey with me.
Love, Light and Shadow to you.

"I now see how owning our story and loving
ourselves through that process is the bravest
thing that we will ever do"

~Brene Brown

Dedicated to:

Those of broken spirit
Those who are stumbling in the dark
Those whose voices have been taken
Those who hide their sorrow
Those who have suffered abuse
Physical, Sexual, Mental and Spiritual
I see you

*

And to Calvin
Your death inspired me to step out from behind my shield
and share my story.
I miss you my friend.

"The wound is the place where the Light enters you."
~ Rumi

1
Death

All new life begins with death. This is something that I feel passionately about. In these pages are a few of the truths of how my life began again. They have been laid out in an offering of sharing. I willingly share with you how death became the catalyst for me to begin a journey back to myself. I am sure there are some that would ask, why? Why would I let others into these private places of my life, my heart, and my mind? I do so because I believe in the power of storytelling. I believe that when we share our story with others, we not only bring a deeper healing for ourselves, but we also help others heal. When we see ourselves in each other's stories, we feel less alone and less disconnected. When we feel connected, we live connected. The world becomes a better place for everyone with this feeling of connection. Grace, compassion, and understanding replace the loneliness, disconnection, and isolation that plague our society today.

The journey to get here, to a life filled with joy, contentment, and internal peace, has been nothing short of amazing. It has been filled with loss, heartache, darkness, and confusion, but also includes love, light, joy, and acceptance. I have been truly blessed though I was not always able see that. It is only when I became fully awake and engaged with my life that I could see the truth about it and my place in this world. I have learned that sometimes it takes a jolt, a shock, or a big event to bring us to such an awakening.

When my dad passed away, this was how it was for me. It was 1999 and my dad was facing yet another battle with cancer. He already had three battles with this opponent and won, but this one would prove to be too much for his body. Early in the morning on November 2, 1999, my dad passed into the next life. As his life here ended my renewed life began.

Ours was a complicated relationship. There were times of great joy and equal times of great turmoil. In among the memories of my childhood freedom were numerous moments of uncertainty and fear that were fed by confusion. These things grew inside my little girl heart. I did not understand my father's intense outbursts of anger, or his physical aggression toward my siblings and me. It cut another wound in my heart each time his "corporal punishment" style of discipline left them in tears. And so, the fear continued to grow, as did I. Eventually hatred, contempt, and rebellion grew out of that fear. The offspring of fear would take up residence in my belly and come with me into my adult life. They always eluded me and were never fully resolved.

On the morning of my dad's passing, I grieved deeply. My grief was not because of his death or passing. Instead I grieved for the loss of amends, I grieved for the chance that was no longer, a chance for forgiveness, grace, and understanding. I grieved that I would never know my father's love or acceptance. I would never be able to give the same back to him. At the time, I had no idea that there was always a chance for such things, even when one person no longer walks the earth.

****

In some ways, my dad and I were alike. Even though I was his adopted child, we shared many of the same qualities and personality traits. We were both driven, go-getters, and hard workers. My dad had a love for reading, working with his hands, and being around people. And most people liked him. He was engaging, knowledgeable, and did not shy away from the tougher topics of life, like politics or religion. Like him, I was a headstrong child with a flair for the wild and dramatic. I often found myself in the role of challenging him and his patience. But I also brought an undeniable light to his life. For the most part, I think he appreciated my spirited self.

But my family had a secret. My dad had an explosive temper. You never knew when or where his anger was going to rear its ugly head. Outside we were a well-groomed, put-together, and perfect church-going family. Inside, there were moments of physical outbursts, tears, fear, and confusion. This is when my heart broke. Between watching my siblings being hurt and seeing my mother cry, something deep inside me was taken and broken into pieces. The most painful was watching my siblings being punished. I was of the heart and mind that I would rather it be me instead of them. At a very young age, I already had thoughts of how little I mattered. My parents only fed those thoughts with their behaviour. One of my first memories is of me trying to pull my dad off my older brother, who was being "punished." I was maybe two or three years of age. My dad had my brother pinned in the corner of the kitchen counter as he hit him. I remember seeing it through tear-filled eyes. These outbursts scared me and scarred me.

It would seem to me that my dad had no idea what I was thinking or how I felt. I am sure these were not the ways he planned or wanted to behave. Many of us have behaved in ways without understanding or anticipating that there could be great consequences for our actions, and so it was with my dad. Unfortunately the rift between him and me was laid out. Neither of us was equipped to heal what was broken, or the damage that was done.

Even in the hospital, we fell out with one another. It was October 15th and Dad was in the hospital due to complications from colon cancer, which ended in an emergency surgery. On the 25th, he had an ultrasound done to determine whether they should go in again to operate. The ultrasound showed that the cancer had taken over most of his major organs and operating was no longer an option. Now it was out of the doctor's hands. Everything was at the mercy of time. We were all sitting in the hospital family room when we received this news. My two older brothers, one with his wife and family, and my mom were there. My older sister was the only one who had not yet arrived. She was out of the province at the time. After the doctor gave us the news, he asked whether we wanted to tell Dad ourselves or have the doctor tell him. Without hesitation, we all agreed it would have to be us to tell him.

When a loved one is at Death's door, it is a surreal time. The world around you stops and time stands still. When I left the hospital each day, I was vexed by the fact that outside those hospital walls life continued as if nothing was happening. I wanted to yell and scream at that top of my lungs, "My dad is dying! Do any of you give a shit? STOP! Stop this world from moving. My dad is leaving, and there is so much shit to clean up before he does!" But alas, the world goes on, and you find some kind of normalcy in this place of being caught between worlds.

So, there we were all around his bed about to tell him that there would be no more surgeries or procedures. We were there to tell him that he was dying. My mom stood beside his bed and took his hand. Next to my mom stood my brother, Steven and his wife, Doreen. I stood at the foot of the bed and my oldest brother; Bob was on the other side of the bed. I am not sure who gave dad the news. I think it was probably my mom. I remember it being a moment when all movement left the room. It was a moment that you could hear the air filtering around, and the heat seemed to suck you in like wet wool. It was in this moment that I saw my dad for the first time, as not just my dad. In that one moment, I saw him as a person in pain and a fellow human being whose time had come. I felt a great compassion and empathy for him. I even felt love. I had struggled with loving my dad throughout all my life. And yet, in that moment, when I saw him lying there, looking so tired and so vulnerable, I felt a love for him. As I look back to that moment, I'm amazed at how someone who had so much power over my life and me was reduced to a frail, sick man so quickly.

When my dad heard the news that they were not going to operate, he was relieved.

"Good, good," was his response. He had never fully recovered from an earlier emergency surgery, and his relief of not having another operation was apparent to all of us. But then, my Mom had to tell him the rest of the news. ((state the other news here or delete the previous sentence.)) I am really unable to put words to what that was like. We all held hands, cried, and prayed. Then my dad told us matter-of-factly that he wasn't ready to go yet. It was almost like he hadn't heard his prognosis and thought he was going to walk out of the hospital.

I was crying. I was crying for so many reasons. I was crying for my mom, my brothers, and the person suffering in the bed. There were so much raw emotions sitting in that room with us. So, before I knew what I was doing, I walked over to my dad's bedside and whispered in his ear,

"I love you, Daddy."

"What? What did you say?" he replied.

"I love you."

He pulled himself up and looked at me with a familiar look of anger and disgust on his face. He looked me in the eye and said these words,

"You have a lot of anger that you need to deal with! I wasn't perfect you know!"

His words slapped me across the face and his anger stung. I was not prepared for that reaction. In that instant, I felt a separation from the rest of the people in the room. I stepped back stunned as my oldest brother stepped forward. Faintly I could hear him say,

"We know you weren't perfect, Dad...."

In shock, I stood there for a moment. I felt crushed and defeated. Every doubt, every negative thought, and every dark moment that my dad and I shared came rushing forward from the past. I felt disconnected from the whole situation, like I wasn't supposed to be there. I left the room and walked into the hospital hallway. I stood outside the hospital room along with a thousand voices screaming in my head. Self-doubt set up camp quickly and the assault began. Anger, Contempt, and Rebellion joined in. Then came the pain of them all. The kind of pain that clutches your chest and makes it hard to breathe. It was the kind of pain that seemed to crush anything that was good within. It seeped into my blood and moved through my whole body. Close behind the assault was Panic and Confusion. With them joining the party, I was on my way into that darkness that I knew all too well. This darkness plagued me for most of my life.

Inside my head, the voices were screaming at me,

Who are you Catherine? You are nothing. You are nothing. Your dad is a respected Christian man. People love him. Who are you? You are a bad girl. You made him angry! It is your fault! You mean nothing! You don't matter. What do you matter? He's right. It is all you. It's entirely your fault. He did nothing wrong. It was all you. You are nothing! You are nothing!

The voices screamed in my head. There were so many. Every doubt and insecure thought screamed at me. I used Rebellion to fight back.

Fuck him! That's fine. He will NEVER see me again. If that's how he wants it, then that's how he gets it. I won't come back here. Go ahead and die, see if I care...good riddance!

I was torn apart, hurt, and devastated. My heart shattered into shards of glass inside my chest. But instead of acknowledging my hurt, I used my trusted companions, Contempt, Rebellion, and Anger to cover it up. I had no idea how or even where to begin to express or expose how I felt. I was completely unequipped, and as always, felt very alone within my tortured hell. I was a daughter, a little girl, yet again feeling stung by my dad's anger and dissatisfaction with me. In my own brokenness, all I could see was that even on his deathbed, he couldn't reach out to me. I felt his pride hold him back. His needed to be right, have the last word, and his words were gold, and mine were shit! Thinking these things only made me feel more hate toward him. Yes, I hated him. I swore in that hallway. I hoped he would die without ever seeing me again.

I walked down the hallway to the end and looked out the window. The tears flowed freely and poured out of me. I was in such pain. I wanted to lash out. But inside me an ember glowed. The very ember that had kept me alive and present in this life for almost 32 years. That small glowing ember saved my life over, and over, and over again. It glowed strong and warm. I knew my plan to stay away wasn't the right one. But I was so hurt and angry at the injustice. The voices were pushing me down. I did not know how to navigate through this storm. My vision completely blurred. I had no way out, no answers, and nowhere to go. So, I did the only thing that came to mind. I screamed past the voices in my head. I screamed my way to the heavens.

God, I am in trouble here, deep trouble. My dad is dying. I want to walk away. I know it is the wrong thing to do. I need your help. I can't do this without you. You have to help me. Please God. I need your help. Please, please, please.

I begged and pleaded, and as I did, the voices got louder. A war began in my mind. A war for my heart had started.

Not returning to my dad's room, I left the hospital in complete distress. The voices tormented and taunted me. They consumed my mind, making it impossible for anything to get in or anything to get out. But I kept praying, desperate and ugly prayers. I prayed like a possessed crazy woman. The truth was that I felt possessed. I was desperate, filled with fear and nothing could hide that. I was in the darkness and needed out.

At the time, I was going to a woman's book-study group with a friend so I called her that night confirming that I would be going with her. It was a trick I played on myself knowing that this was a perfect opportunity for me to sink into despair and hide away. I had sense enough to know that by calling and telling her I would be there, I had forced myself to keep moving. I had two days before the woman's group. I don't remember much of those two days, except that I was in the cold darkness of my depression with the voices and me.

On Wednesday morning, October 27th, I got up to go to the study group. The voices came with me. The book we were studying was called, Just Enough Light for the Step I'm On by Stormie Omartian. Considering the darkness I was walking in, the book could not have been more perfect. I can no longer remember which chapter we were covering that morning or the topic. It was all I could do to show up.

And then it happened. There in that all-purpose room, where I heard "The Voice of Love for, what I thought, was the first time." It was a soft, steady, and powerful voice. It was not yelling and screaming like the other voices, yet I heard it clearly above the rest. The voice said to me,

"It's over Catherine. I am going to take care of everything now. You do not have to do anything."

I knew immediately the voice was that of the Source from which I came. God was speaking to me as plainly as anyone had ever spoken to me before. Never had I felt Love's revelation so plainly or directly. In the moment that those words were spoken, all the other voices were silenced, and the battle inside me subsided. When God was done speaking, there was total silence and a peace instantly came within me.

That moment changed my whole direction in life and brought me to the abundant life I now live. It did not happen all at once. After all, the biggest part of life is the journey. It was definitely the beginning of something new and something big. I had been awakened! God, The Universe, or The Great Spirit had spoken to me. I knew exactly what I had to do.

After the study group was over, I went directly to the hospital. I don't mind telling you that I was scared. Truth is I was literally shaking, and my heart was in my throat. However, blanketing those feelings was the feeling of Divine Love carrying me to where I needed to be. I walked into the room. My mom was sitting next to the bed in which my dad laid. He was still alert at this time, meaning still talking and aware of his surroundings.

He was surprised to see me, and not in the "happy to see you" kind of surprised.

"What are you doing here?" He asked me. I looked into his eyes, and I didn't see him. I saw something else looking back at me. All my dad's bitterness was staring me in the face, and it was pissed.

"Andy!" My mom said, surprised by his attitude. "It's Catherine. She has come to see you."

"I don't want her here. Why is she here?" Then he looked back at me, "What are you doing here?"

"I'm here because I love you." I said back to him, my voice shaking.

I stood at the foot of his bed feeling like I was talking to the devil himself. I've never been so scared in all my life. It did not feel like I was talking to my dad. I was talking to the darkness inside of him that hated my light and wanted me gone. Somehow, I knew that I needed to be there for my dad, because he was struggling with his own voices, insecurities, and his own darkness. In that moment, Spirit opened my eyes to see beyond my reality and beyond the world in which I lived. God showed me the "behind the scenes" battle that raged, and it was very, very real.

"You don't love me!" He spat back.

My mom tried to settle him down and scolded him for his behaviour toward me. She told me that it was the medication talking. Her reasoning wasn't convincing. Right then, it wasn't even important. I knew I needed to be there with him, so I stayed. His anger did settle down in time, but his attitude let me know that he was not pleased by my presence. Surprisingly, once I sat down, I felt okay about his displeasure. I was not distracted by his anger. I felt a deep loving peace all around me. It was a peace that passed all understanding. With that loving peace, I was able to be there and remain.

That day I ended up staying with my mom for most of the day. My sister came into town with her new baby, and their arrival was such a blessing. My mom felt that Dad was holding on to see my sister one more time. He was pleased to see her and her new son. It really warmed his heart. At 5:30 that evening, I went home for dinner and felt a pull to go back again. Later that night my husband, Steve, The Young Blood, (my son), and I went for a little visit. We stayed from 8pm to 10pm. There was a lot of family around. Mom had arranged for a couple, gifted with healing hands to sit and pray over my dad that night.

I went home feeling very wired so I went out for a while with a friend for a drink and filled her in on the crazy journey I had gone through that day. She listened and did not say too much. As for me, it felt good to talk to someone about it, even if they did not fully understand, because I didn't either. I just knew that it was real. I was a part of something very important and very big. When I got home, I tossed and turned into the night. Finally, at 1am, I got out of bed and after talking to Steve about it, I left for the hospital in the wee hours of the early morning.

At this point, I have to mention that Steve was a rock and so supportive of this crazy journey I was on. I told him about the wild day and told him that I knew I had to go back to the hospital and be with my dad. Spirit was telling me this, and I wanted to listen. Steve supported me in every way possible. He was truly my stability.

When I arrived at the hospital, my dad was not doing well. He was fighting, not so much for his life but for his soul. The couple tried to comfort him. He flailed around and thrashed about on his bed. I asked them if it was okay for me to be there. They told me to do whatever I felt I had to. (They were so lovely.)

I sat down beside my dad's bed and took his hand tightly. He looked at me. The fear in his eyes was surreal. He did not recognize me right away. I could tell. Then I saw a glimmer of recognition. He looked exhausted and a little crazed. I just held his hand and cried over him and repeated,

"I am your daughter. I am your daughter. I am your daughter."

To this day, I have no idea why I said those words. My thought is that Spirit put those words in my mouth to say to him, because that was what he needed. While this unfolded, I felt strongly that my being there that night was something that he needed to take the next step of his journey. Later I would realize that it was equally as important for me.

That night, I sat with him as he walked through his "Valley of the shadow of death." I knew beyond a doubt that my being there symbolized a starting point for forgiveness and the freedom that it would bring. At that time, he couldn't give me the release that I so desperately wanted, but Love gave me the strength to give him the release that he needed. Even though my dad had hurt those I loved and hurt me, I wanted him to find peace in his passing. When it came down to it, I did not want him to suffer. So I voiced forgiveness to him. I let him know that everything was all right and that there was nothing to fear. After many hours of the off and on outbursts of fear and confusion, my dad finally became peaceful at about 6:30am to 7:00am. It had been a long night, one I will never forget, nor do I ever want to. There had been some deep spiritual happenings going on, and I had witnessed it. Even in my inexperience, I knew everything had transpired as it was meant to be. There was no accident that I was there that night.

October 29, 1999 Friday Diary Entry

My father is dying. I've watched as his life has slowly slipped away. I feel immense compassion and love for a man who one month ago I didn't love. I have seen and felt things I've never felt before and certainly never knew possible. Never ending is the amazing hand of God holding all that is around me. Right now it is 12:00 noon. I have been here since 1:30am to be with my dad. I came yesterday at 12:30pm to 5:00pm. Back at 8:00pm to 10:00pm. And what a day, I probably won't write about it at this moment as I am tired and my thoughts need a rest. I've seen the end of life through my father's eyes, and again I'm reminded that what we do here matters. There is something beyond this life something more than us, something bigger.

This was the last entry in that journal. I did not pick up a pen again for almost a year. I guess my thoughts were indeed, tired. After that night of walking through his valley of death, my dad slipped into a type of coma. He no longer spoke, and his eyes remained closed. He was still aware of us and showed that during my "shift" to sit with him. I was reading to him from the bible, some of my favourite stories. When I stopped reading, he scratched his fingers on the mattress. When I continued reading, the scratching would stop.

My dad passed away a few days later. His laboured breaths came to a stop. He passed over early in the morning with one of his younger sisters and brother-in-law at his side. We all knew he would not have left with Mom there. He loved her so much. They were two peas in a pod—Andy and Ann. Does it get any better than that? Their love for each other was one of the greatest gifts my Dad left me.

There was a deep exhale that happened within my being that morning. Naively, I thought with him gone that my struggles were finally over. I was not aware of all the healing I would need to walk through and that this was my time to begin the greatest, most important journey of my life.

"We do not grow absolutely chronologically. We grow sometimes in one dimension, and not in another; unevenly."
~Anais Nin

2
Before The Death

Do you know what happens to a young girl who believes she is worth nothing? There are two places she can go; retreat inside herself and hide away from everyone and everything, or look outward and begin to search for things that give her a feeling, any feeling, of happy. She seeks out something that will relieve her of the darkness that hovers all around her and interferes with her perspective of herself and her place in the world. She looks for anything that relieves the pain she walks in, even if it is for a moment or two. The darkness is all consuming, so she seeks out moments of relief and suffers through moments of nothingness, deserving nothing, expecting nothing. And so, the cycle goes.

As a teenager, I did both. The pain, the damage, and the dark thoughts about life and myself got stuffed deep inside and planted themselves into the shadows of my heart. When I needed a form of suffering and self-deprecation, they came out of the depths to add to the damage and pain. That was my inner world.

As for my outer world, I searched for things that would relieve the pain of the darkness, that never seemed to leave me. These were the days that I poured every negative aspect of my life into the festering "father wound" in my heart. This is where I blamed everything. Maya Angelo once wrote, "I did then what I knew how to do. Now that I know better, I do better." I did what I knew. As a young child, my dad, or just the thought of him, evoked some of my greatest fears. So, as I grew, if I felt fear, I blamed him. In blaming him, I found a sort of relief. It was a childish sense of justice. Because that is what I was, a child.

The darkness became my companion. It whispered to me of the relief I could find in death, and I believed it. I can remember being a very young child of five or six years of age, and wanting to die. Being brought up in the church, I would hear the stories about how Jesus loved the little children, and how he never turned them away. It was then that I decided that I wanted to die to be with Jesus. Surely, He would love me. I would sit in church and pray that God would take me. Fantasies of sitting on Jesus' lap in heaven played through my little mind. I felt his warm love and acceptance. As a little girl, this thought pattern was relatively harmless. They were merely fantasies and escapes. As I entered puberty, those childlike thoughts, mixed with the emotional turmoil of adolescence and the continued unrest in my soul, began to brew a dangerous cocktail within me.

I smoked, drank, and lived for the party. Growing up in a small town, it was easy to find the party. During the early years, Grades 8, 9, and 10, the drinking often ignited the vulnerability of my hidden depressive and broken state. I usually found myself in tears at some point during the night. I thank those friends who stood by this sad girl. During these days and all through high school, my self-loathing was at a record high. Evidence of this can be found in my high-school notes and letters to and from my girlfriends. I often found myself suicidal and constructed many plans to run away, but could never go through with any of those plans. I knew it would break my mom's heart. At that time, that was not something I was prepared to do.

Instead, I took all the self-loathing thoughts of suicide and running away and turned them on myself. I was bulimic all through high school. I knew full well it was an unhealthy practice. But my thought was that if I got sick enough and ended up in the hospital, my parents would have to love me. I often stood in front of the mirror telling my reflection how much I hated her, how ugly she was, how fat she was, and how much I detested her. It is heart breaking to think back on those days. I am so sad for that girl hiding in the washroom with her sins and shame. It's a place she should never have been.

Often, after heated exchanges with my dad, I crawled into the back of my closet and bashed my head with my fists longing for relief from the pain and confusion in my head.

During these times, it felt that my head would explode with the injustice that was happening in my life. I had no voice that was being heard.

I am not exactly sure when the voices started, but I heard them in the darkness of my closet. They told me how worthless I was and that I was nothing. That is the one I remember the most, "You are nothing." In response, I spewed hatred toward my dad for his anger and toward myself for igniting it. I think my hatred for him and myself was pretty equal at the time, but maybe just a little bit more for him.

I didn't mind school. It was a social gathering and an escape from home for me. School offered me a certain level of belonging, where home offered me a place in which I was reminded of what I was not.

I was involved in many extra-curricular activities, piano, choir, and sports. I had good friends and a part-time job. The job was one that I found by myself, of which I was really proud. I could hold my own in pretty much any situation. At least it appeared that I could. Over all, I painted a pretty good picture of my life. This was what I had been taught and learned to do really well. Appearance seemed to be very important to my parents, something my mother still denies to this day. There was no doubt to my siblings and me that there was an image to uphold, at all cost. This is something I often heard from my peers who were brought up in church. The appearance of perfection for many was just part of their upbringing. The problem for me was that how we looked on the outside was not exactly what was happening within the four walls of our home. It left me very conflicted and confused inside.

At around 14 years old, I began smoking pot. I remember the first time like it was yesterday. I felt abandoned by my two older siblings. They were both out of the house, living their lives. In my rebellious teen mind, they had left me to deal with the skeletons in our family closet. The truth is they did not desert me, they had just moved on. If either of them read these words, they would be very surprised by my feelings. As the youngest of four children, I had looked to and depended on my older siblings for stability and consistency. It often felt like we were "in it together." There was a lot that went on between us without having to say a word. After all, we were all living in the same house, and for the most part, feeling many of the same emotions. When the older two moved out, my sensitive heart grieved; I felt they did not have time for me like they once had. I was completely unable to process my feelings about this in a healthy way, so I did what many rebellious and depressed teens do, find something to relieve the pain. On this day, I decided to take up smoking pot.

Up until this point, I had been adamant about not taking part in this. I had been around it many times, but refused to partake. Apparently, my resolve...resolved, because on that day, I went with a girlfriend to the local pool hall hang out, found a kid I knew who dealt and bought two joints. (At the time, they were $2 each!) Then my girlfriend and I walked into an alley where I proceeded to smoke both of them, by myself. Looking back, it was a seriously extreme "poor me" moment. This practice plummeted me further into my depression. It was an all-consuming blanket of darkness that separated me from myself.

At 15 years old, I made a conscious decision for myself, one that would affect my life journey for many years to come. I decided to "fuck it all." As I saw it, I was giving up and giving in. I was done. I said to myself, "They think I'm bad. I might as well be bad." I stopped trying to please my parents, or seek their approval. This projection was only in my outer world, because in my inner world I still longed for their love and approval. I know that now. I didn't know it then. I also made a contract with myself to "never let them know how much they hurt me." "Them" referred to my parents, but these kinds of contracts have a way of taking on a life of their own, one beyond your control. If we are not aware of the power of these contracts, "them" becomes everyone. My voice was silenced. I was unable to express the pain of my heart in a constructive way or put up healthy boundaries when it came to my own heart's safety.

In these years, there was a trickle of light coming into the darkness in one form or another. I knew there was something bigger than all I was living. That was not a difficult concept for me to wrap my head around. Somehow even in my situation, I knew. And knowing, was enough. This childlike faith brought with it whispers in the dark. These whispers told me to carry on, and let me know that I was not totally alone. These whispers made me feel like I mattered, and they gave me hope. It was a hope that one day my life would be my own, and I would find peace and happiness.

In middle school, I had a girlfriend who attended the Pentecostal Church in town. In my Christian world, Pentecostals were known for their flamboyant worship and unconventional ways. Surprisingly, I was given permission to attend the youth group at her church. I was blown away at the open expression these people had for God. The church services that I attended in my church were more like funerals. The highlight was when the collection plate was passed around, and I was given the ever-coveted peppermint candy to suck on. The celebrating I experienced at the Pentecostal church was not happening at my church. At my friend's church, there was a band playing, lively singing, raising of hands, and altar calls. I was smitten!

It was at one of these youth services that I found my voice and spoke with my girlfriend about the abuse that was happening in my home. This was only the second time in my life that I told my story to another person. The first time was when I was in Grade 6 and came to school with a black eye. I had received it from my dad along with a bloody nose because I had spilled my milk at the breakfast table. He told me I was being too rough. I stood up for myself saying, "No,

I'm not." The truth was I spilled my milk because I was shaking from fear. My dad had just yelled at my brother over something, so much that it made my brother cry. Prompted by my "talking back," dad got up from his chair, came over, and hit me once, hard, in the face. The blood poured over my toast, and I panicked, which made him even angrier. It was a complete shit show to put it plainly. My mom told me to say that I had walked into the fireplace. I had no plan of saying anything but what I was told. However, something happened inside me when a classmate came up to me that morning and asked me what happened. I just could not hold it in. I told her through tears. I remember her reply like it was yesterday, "Your dad hits you?" It was then that I realized not everyone was getting hit in their homes like we were.

The youth gatherings at the Pentecostal church became a place where I could lay down my sorrows. It wasn't so much that I told other people, other than my friend. But I could go up to the front and grieve my heart to a listening God. I could cry and let some of the emotions go that I carried around with me. I felt God was listening. I felt Divine Love coming down on me. Others came up and laid hands on those of us who were praying. I felt loved, accepted, and part of something good and beautiful. These experiences stayed with me and helped me remain somewhat safe on my journey.

There were always good friends around me. I have always been blessed with amazing friends. They were my family. Good people with beautiful souls were brought into my life to help me along the way. There were even some adults whom I could trust. They saw that I was suffering and poured into me in a way in which I did not feel worthy, but I dabbled in it anyway. Yes, I was looking for attention. It was not because I was narcissistic, but because I was a young girl living in the grasp of a dark depression. I was trying to hold on. When I had some love sent my way, it gave me the reason I needed to keep going. Thankfully there was love sent my way. I will be forever grateful to these people. They had no idea that they were actually saving my life.

Please, if there is a young person, or even an older person that seems needy around you, don't brush them off as being annoying or attention seeking. Nine out of ten times, these people have a story of pain and sadness behind their needy ways. You are not being asked to fix their broken heart. You are merely being asked to feed it with a kind word, a gesture of compassion and grace, or a listening ear. We call them "attention seekers" for a reason. Would it be so bad to give them a little of what they are seeking? Would it be so terrible to give them a little positive, loving, and encouraging attention?

When my parents and I moved away from the small hometown in the north to the big city down south and the Lower Mainland of B.C., my teen years were in full swing. If I had really wanted, I was in Grade 12 and could have stayed up north to finish school. Fortunately, I had sense enough to know I was going nowhere fast. Grade 11 was a blur. The drinking and pot smoking was a regular social event in my life. I felt emotionally and mentally spent. It was just too easy to do the "wrong thing." I needed a change.

I looked at this move as a new start. For the most part, that is what it was. However, the tension at home was still present. Of course now, it was mixed with the normal teenage angst. I know my personality challenged my parents. I was one who walked to the beat of her own drum. I was not very good at conforming. I tried, but even through my brokenness, I had a strong sense of self. An ember burned inside of me that I could not ignore. Even when I felt I was at the bottom and ready to end it, there continued to be something inside that told me "Don't do it. Things will get better." That ember, the little light inside me, kept me alive.

At 18, I moved out with my boyfriend with whom I hadn't even been intimate. I was desperate to move out of my parents' home, but too insecure to do it on my own. Of course, the relationship didn't last. I was way too young, and so was he. We both had no idea what we were doing, but it was a step toward building some confidence in myself. I had chosen a person who was not enough for me. To actually realize this was a huge step for a girl who felt she was lucky to have anyone love her. So even though it did not work out in the long term, that relationship became an important step for me to get back to myself.

For the next few years, I lived on my own, splitting myself between two jobs, a full-time hairstylist and a part-time waitress. At night, I lived my life as a club kid, having a specific bar to go to almost every night. Living alone allowed me to continue to indulge my bulimic tendencies, too. I was not practicing this ritual daily, but it was still part of my destructive behaviour and reared its ugly head on a weekly basis. I was always trying to stay a few steps ahead of the darkness. Now and then, it would overtake me. I would find myself cocooning in my apartment, eating bad food, watching bad TV, and sinking into the dark abyss of my depression. I lived in the moment, but not in a healthy kind of way. Each moment was being filtered through the past.

I moved a lot. I think it had to do with that trying to start over feeling I got when my parents moved us. I could be over thinking all that, since I know I have a gypsy heart. I always thought that if I could just start over, things would be better. With each move, I moved ahead, but I couldn't shake the patterns. Partying and all that came with it eventually took over again. I was missing the inner aspect of my life, I was giving my heart and soul minimum attention, and it began to show. I needed to slow down. Even during this time, after a night of clubbing, I could often be found in my parents' church sitting beside them on any given Sunday morning, making them happy. I was there for them not me. It was easy. I knew the drill. I knew what was expected. To keep them happy with me and off my back, I went to church. It was an empty gesture, and I knew it even then. In those days, I saw "God's Love" as a faraway myth for those good enough to earn it, which clearly was not me...or so I thought.

In my early twenties, my life seemed good. I had a good job managing a Hair Salon, had an excellent circle of friends, was independent, and probably the happiest I had ever been; yet the darkness remained. I was in need of.... something. This desire brought me into an organization, which seemed to stand for much of what I believed and to which I wanted to be a part. The structure of this organization was based on the belief that when you start with taking care and balancing yourself, it flows into family, community, town, country, and eventually to the world. This ripple effect of goodness was powerful enough to change the world and its people. This seemed to be a digestible concept to me. It was without the trappings of religion, which was something else I was seeking. While being a part of this organization, you were also part of a smaller group of women who would walk with you on your journey. Along with that came a larger community of men and women, in which we all spoke the same language.

A friend of mine and her husband were involved in this organization. She encouraged me to take part in their woman's weekend. It started out with an introductory party, much like a Jewelry or Tupperware party, (that should have been my first clue). Women who had done the weekend shared their stories and testimonies of their experiences. Those of us interested gave our thoughts on what we hoped to get from the weekend. After an up-and-down process, I attended the weekend, which cost a considerable amount of money. Looking back, it seemed crazy to spend that money, and yet, I realize that it was a worthwhile experience. It was meant to happen as another step in my journey back to myself.

With the women's weekend over and behind me, I went along with the next step of becoming part of the "Family of Women." This entailed being part of a smaller group who met each week to be in relationship and hold each other accountable. None of this appeared to be out of place or contrived to me. In fact, I really thought I had found somewhere to place my desire...for something. These kinds of organizations know how to gather you in on a very wholesome and real premise, only to disappoint in the end. As I got deeper into the organization, I realized that once again I had found a place where people were not living what they believed. The voice of reason inside me opened my eyes to the untruths of which I was a part. The manipulation, the pressure tactics, and the division between men and women all became clearer the more involved I became. We were not encouraged to have freedom of thought and instead taught to conform, "for our own good." The founder himself was going through a bitter divorce, even though the whole view was family first, then community, and then the world. In my heart, I knew this was not the place for me. However, I had seen what happened to those who tried to leave. Quite frankly, I was afraid of the confrontation that would be unleashed. I felt trapped and unsure of what to do. But I was pretty sure that what I was involved in was not actually a "family" at all. I was beginning to believe it was actually a cult.

It was during this time that I became pregnant with my first son, Nathen. I was 23 years old and unmarried. I convinced myself that staying in this organization was a good place for me to be given my new status in life as a unwed mother. What better place than with a huge community of women, who in my mind would walk with me through this season. But I was wrong. Becoming pregnant changed me from the inside out, as it does for many women. Everything was suddenly heightened for me and much more real. I knew that every choice I made would directly affect another life. During the beginning of my pregnancy, I was very ill and exhausted. I did not have the energy to lead the group of squabbling women, that I had been given to lead, so I call my "God Mother" (district leader), stepped down, and just like that it was over.

I would never hear from anyone from that organization again. The fact that no one called or showed up at my door at night was a true miracle and anything but normal. Clearly Divine intervention had swooped in and given me what I needed without me even asking for it. Typically, when someone tried to leave the cult, (let's just call it what it was), it was not a simple process. They were very averse to loosing members. It would start with continual phone calls from those in your group and the district leaders. If that didn't work in bringing you back to the group, then the home visits would begin. This would include a group of "higher ups" coming to your house and pressuring you to come back. It usually took a few visits for those who were resistant and would not succumb to the pressure. These visits often happened late at night, when people were tired and vulnerable from a busy day. At best, this organization had very strong "cult-like" methods. It is still amazing to me how my pregnancy gave me the opening and courage to get out. The woman's aspect of the organization was called, "The Family of Women." I had seen things here that I did not agree with, but also many aspects that deeply resonated with me. Even in the fog the truth was clear to me, being "trapped" is not "family."

Looking back, I can clearly see how Love was walking me through and working in my life. I knew I wanted a deeper Spiritual connection in my life. I knew what we did here on Earth mattered. I knew there was a God of some sort who had created me, this world, and this life, but I was just not clear on what that spirituality really looked like or how I fit into it.

My son's birth caused me to make several more steps forward toward myself. He had a huge impact on my spirit and increased my desire to delve deeper into my spirituality. Parts of my being that had been in a coma were beginning to awaken. Memories of my childhood began creeping into my life ((clarify the ending of previous sentence)). I had to slow down. As a new mom, my life choices started to catch up with me. Nathen's first few years were a time of me learning to depend on myself, and trusting that inside me I had what I needed to make it. The relationship between my son's father and I were tumultuous and uncertain. My mama bear instincts kicked in. In many ways, it became a time of my baby and me against the world.

Becoming a parent changed how I viewed my own parents, especially my dad. When my son was around two years old, I decided it was a good time to confront my dad about the past. I went to him very naïve. I honestly thought he would be ready to hear what I had to say because I was ready to say it. It did not go over as I had envisioned it. I did not have all the communication or boundary skills I needed. I was still emotionally and mentally wounded and had never really tended to any of them. My emotions were tender with these wounds, and I was very easily hurt. He got defensive. I got defensive. Things exploded between us. However, even in the ugliness of this new wounding and not so graceful confrontation, I felt myself take another step forward. It was the first time I stood up for myself and stayed standing. I felt a shift in him that day, ever so small, but a shift all the same. As I left the house that day, I metaphorically gave him the backpack of guilt and shame that was not mine to carry in the first place.

During these years, I was still joining my parents on most Sunday's. It seemed to keep them happy, and it offered me something familiar and a connection to the God that I grew up with. It offered, what I felt was a nurturing place for my son to come. There can be a great sense of community in church. And that was something.

I had always found myself drawn to the world of the Mystic and New Age. Of course, in the view of the church that I was brought up in, these things were "of the devil." Even though there was a part of me that felt I was going to burn in hell for exploring these worlds, I sensed a deep connection to anything spiritual and anything deeper than face value. So, it was not uncommon that I would occasionally visit a psychic or a tarot card reader. In my very early twenties, I even had my past lives charted, which felt very "dangerous." All of these concepts and procedures were very far from the world I knew as a child. However, I found this world fascinating and even familiar. I could not help but think it had something to say about God, too.

In my late twenties, I met my current husband. We joined together and journeyed through the abyss of Spirituality. He had been brought up by hippy parents who had never imposed any belief system on him. He had encountered God while working in a grocery store and felt a deep stirring to find out more. I was trying to find the God outside the religious confines of my upbringing. We were quite the team.

At the time of my father's passing, we were living together, building a life along with my son. We were reading diverse books, such as The Celestine Prophecy and Behold, The Pale Horse. Both of us knew there was "something" bigger than ourselves and realized that there was so much more going on around us than we were told or even able to see for ourselves. We were experiencing encounters with the Spiritual together and on our own. Both of us wanted to find our answers and seek our own truths. Both of us wanted to experience God and this world fully and completely with our eyes wide open. And together, we did just that.

"The hands of time were created *for weaving, healing, and ushering, not pointing out what was missed and where to hurry.*"
~ *Janae Charlotte*

3
The Years that Followed

For the first few years that followed my dad's death, I was numb. A piece of my heart was covered in stone. My heart wasn't gone, but it was overshadowed and dormant. Looking back, I know it was grief that came into my heart, a deep aching grief, not just for my dad's passing but also for all the death within me. I found it hard to watch people dying on TV or in a movie. It was always so beautiful. These people would tell each other how they felt, share emotions, and make beautiful amends in the end. Seeing these scenes on TV shows or the movies usually drove me to the bathroom where I would have a good cry, partly from grief and partly just feeling sorry for myself. Even thought the events of the last days of my dad's life had offered deep insights into myself and the spiritual realm, the truth was, I still felt jilted and ripped off. I often wondered why one of these happy endings could not have been mine. Why was there no peace or apology for me? I did not know it at the time, but my heart was broken. One great big crack right down the middle. The pain was almost more than I could bear.

This season of my life came to be known as the time I entered my Shack. I encountered this term when I read William Young's beautiful, soul-touching book, The Shack. A book I would describe as "written for the broken-hearted." It was a fictional story but infused with Young's real-life pain and experiences. Thus, it was a very powerful read. I had the privilege of seeing him speak in 2008 at Regency College at The University of British Columbia. This is what he said about his book:

"The Shack is a metaphor. This is a fiction story that I wrote for my six children. But inside that story I wrote my pain, and I wrote my process, and I wrote the conversations I had over the years as I unwound all the junk. And I wrote God as good as I know how and all I can tell you is He's better than I wrote him…We think that if we do the right things in the right order in the right amount then we can ask God or tell God what to do and God will do it. Or if we have enough faith, we can get God to do what He wants. We at least want God to be predictable…The Shack represents the place we get stuck. We build our own interior houses and parts of those houses get built for us, especially as children. And the things that get built in it are mostly old cruddy stuff. It's the way we hurt other people.

It's the way we've been hurt and damaged. It's where we store our lies. It's where we store our secrets. And we think that if we can just come up with some sort of understanding of Spirituality, we can get a red or blue pill, and then not have to worry about this process stuff…God comes to that and takes this ball of string that's tied into a billion knots and unties that ball of string without breaking it. He climbs inside our stuff and involves us in a process in which He wants to heal us and in which there is no shame."

The Shack became the metaphorical place where I went to face my demons; a place where I began to unravel all that was done to me and face the things I had done to others and myself. I did not know it then, but looking back I can see that I had entered into my process.

During these early years, I was still attending my mom's church with her. It was the same denomination that I had been brought up in. This church still felt more like hers (and my dad's) than mine, yet I attended because it gave her comfort during these difficult days of loss. It was also the one place where I felt I could pour myself out and be poured back into. It wasn't so much the sermons given from the pulpit, as it was the familiarity of this Holy Place. It was the place where I had first been introduced to God, and I knew and understood the ritual. The music and songs touched me deeply. I expressed my grief through those songs. I would lift up my hands and sing to the heavens, as the tears streamed down my face I prayed that God would hear me.

This became a big part of my grieving ritual that first year. As anyone who has walked closely with death knows, that first year is like no other. Facing all the milestones for the first time, and how it hits you out-of-the-blue that you will never see that person again in this world. It sneaks up on you and without warning it knocks you right on your ass once again. I can remember an incident when we were in a downtown mall, and I walked into a Hallmark store. There was a whole isle of Father's Day cards, as the day was coming up. In that moment, I realized I would never buy another Father's Day card for my dad. The reality of this hit me like a sack of bricks and the tears flowed way beyond my control.

I did not write at all that first year.

Nothing.

Looking back, I was just surviving. I was trying to get used to my new reality, while attempting to assimilate all the emotions that were trying to bubble up. I don't remember much of that first year. I was unable to process anything outside of myself. The whole world looked so different to me.

It was about seven months after my dad's passing that I decided to go to John, my oldest son's father and pour out my heart. It was clear to me that I had moved on and found someone with whom I was building a life, and it looked to me like John had done the same. We had never been married. We were only young and naïve. My hope was that we could salvage what we once shared and begin building something that would honour what we had been to each other. I saw it as a chance to make amends and create a new relationship between us, both as our son's parents and as people who had shared something.

I remember it was a beautiful sunny day as I drove with heart determination to his house to talk with him face-to-face. I am not sure if I had called ahead, but both he and his girlfriend were home. I knocked on the door and his girlfriend answered. I asked her if I could speak with John. When he came to the door, I asked if he and I could talk. We went across the road to the school and sat in the playground. The floodgates opened as I sat in the swing and John stood in front of me. I poured out the story of what transpired between my dad and me in the last days of his life. John was aware of the history with my dad, and he listened intently. I don't remember much of the conversation, but I told John how there were no amends and no forgiveness asked for or given. I said that it had ended badly, and I did not want that to happen to us. I was an emotional mess as I talked. I cried most of the time. I'm not even sure if I was making sense. But I knew I wanted things to be better between John and me. I knew that we had a chance to make amends and build something better than what was currently going on between us. I did not know how this was all going to happen but I did know I wanted it.

I am not sure how long we were out there. I know I cried a lot and John listened. I am sure he was terrified by the raw emotions that poured out of me, ones I had no control over. And maybe it was not the most eloquent of conversations, but something was planted that day. We began to shift in and around our relationship with each other, and began writing a new story of forgiveness and respect. This shift became one of the many gifts that came out of my father's death.

Now years later, we are family, John and me. He has become much like a brother. He is more than the father to The Young Blood. He is someone who has an important place in my family. My youngest, The Ginger, calls him John-dad. He and my husband are friends, good friends, lifelong friends; an odd pair perhaps but something very real grew between them over the years. There is trust and respect for each other. Even now, as The Young Blood grows into adulthood and has moved on to build his own life, John is still an active part of our lives. It is a great blessing and one for which I can, oddly enough, thank my dad.

I wrote in my journal:

Jan.7, 2001
One year two months
Since you left
One year two months
Of tears
One year two months
Facing fears
One year two months
So many things left undone
I stood by you 'til the end
Hopes of bridges that would mend
I'm tired of the tears that roll down my face
I no longer want to be alone in this place
Your gone it is done
The last song is sung
Now it is time to move on

It seems like I'm always holding back...I know on the outside to some I never hold back but that isn't true. There are things I swallow, things so big they scratch and stretch my throat going down. I am unsure if my body will be able to hold them. Maybe it is for these reasons that I am more forthright in other things because of the thing I must hide.

Comments, faces, and words go through my mind. People who just don't understand...can't understand.

I wanted to share my story being the daughter of a righteous man and feeling God's hand guiding me,

Jesus' light showing me the way and the Goddess' love surrounding me.

My dad's death had a profound effect on me- my spirit. It has been difficult in the sense that there is no more chance of amends...no more chance of a storybook ending or happy-ever-after. People have told me that my father loved me, that he knew that he had made mistakes...it is too bad that he couldn't tell me those things himself. I have developed this innate ability to drift off into a deadening thought about him, my life, and the whole ordeal of his death. I can just sit and stare. I'm sure I could for hours but there are many things that need doing and I really don't think it's a healthy practice. Writing has always proven to be much more productive for me and I really had to push myself to start writing again. Take my power back, so to speak.

No one really noticed this all going on of course. My desire to love life far surpasses the disappointment and well, I just can't quit...I have tried, god how I have tried, but it goes completely against my damn nature!

Feb. 7, 2001

Well the ups and downs continue. Memories pop up and things going on around me bring up feelings of hurt, anger, and incredible sadness...

These journal entries about this time of my life are clear reflection of where I was, in most aspects. Mentally, spiritually and emotionally.

It was in this place that I concluded that sometimes there just wasn't a happy ending no matter how much you longed for it. It was a painful realization since I had forever had that warm ember of hope within me, pushing me forward, and giving me strength. Instead, I felt that hope had failed me. I was shutting down, closing up. I felt myself pulling away from people; it became a struggle to be in crowds, and large social settings. My once outgoing personality retreated. I had to push myself to maintain the persona that had once come so easily.

I remember one day I made a house call to perm one of my mom's friend's hair. She talked to me about my dad, how much she missed him, and how wonderful he was to them as a friend. Waves of emotions crashed over me. I could barely keep it together until I entered the safety of my truck. It was there that the floodgates opened and the emotions poured out. I was so broken within my feelings toward my dad. I felt the relief of him being gone along side the torment of there being no resolution. And mixed in and around that was the feeling of guilt and suffering of not being heard.

A year and a half after my dad's death came my wedding engagement to one of my dearest friends, Steve. Even if I was not quite up for the ride, Life was moving on, so I held on with all my might. I engaged fully in my life, to the best of my ability at the time, and it was a good life. But inside me, the ache would not subside.

August 21, 2001

There's more to do than just talk...sometimes you need to walk.

In the silence of my soul, where no words live. just the sound of days gone by and hopes of things to come.

Sometimes words aren't enough, and they can't tell you what you want to hear.

Sometimes it's the wind of the story that slaps you in the face and tells you how it is.

The warmth of the wind that comes...from the depths of one's soul.

The coldness of the fears and losses of those now gone, the damage done, the sadness won.

The silence can be louder than the words. There is no hiding from silence and all that dwells within it. No hiding from the hopes and dreams, the sadness, and fears.

Dec. 1, 2001

Today I am 33 years old.

Today is the first day of the rest of my life.

I must find my inspiration.

I have been empty

A void, a void of darkness and confusion...standing still.

I left myself for a while to take a journey that wasn't mine to take

I've taken myself away from all that I love out of guilt and shame

Things haven't been the same since he left

I looked at it as grief of loss and though that was true on a level it wasn't all it was about.

There were other things

Guilt for the relief I felt when he was gone.

Even if he had stayed, I never would have gotten what I needed and so a part of me has been happy...

Happy not having to deal with him, not having to talk or justify myself, my life.

Walking the straight line isn't for everyone.

In all my guilt and shame I somehow thought my life wasn't good enough and it was my dad's life I should live.

Well I'll tell you what...no surprise...it hasn't worked.

In fact I have been so unhappy. It's time to come back, back to the life I was meant to live. And even in saying that I feel that I was meant to go through all this. I know that I was meant to leave my life for a while just to see it for what it is and for what I actually have. I may not have chosen a path taken by many but I have chosen for the person God made me to be. Always trying to be true to who I am. A life uncommon...

Dec. 5, 2001

My sister called last night. She asked how thing were going. If I was honest I would have told her how hard things have been...How can you love someone so much and tell them so little?

Ironically, within this time of feeling lost, there were many great blessings unfolding within my life. It is amazing as I look back and remember how much I suffered inside and yet, there were also so many beautiful, heart-filling things happening right alongside the grief and sadness. Learning to walk with grief in one hand and love in the other is the Medicine Woman's way. It is the gift this time of my life brought me.

In March of 2002, I was married to one of my best friends. Corny, I know, but that was the truth. Steve had stood with me through so much in our short time together, as a friend does. He saw me and loved me for who I was, as a friend does. He liked me, as a friend does. It was a beautiful day, one of my happiest memories, and I was filled with love, joy, and so much gratitude. I remember clearly the feeling I had when I was walking down the aisle toward my emotion-filled man. It was this overwhelming feeling of home. I wanted to run to him. Even on this beautiful, life-giving day, the heaviness I felt inside would not subside. As I joyfully and eagerly walked towards a future of love, acceptance and commitment, I also held within me the grief and sorrow of a past filled with brokenness, rejection and shame.

I recall the fog that I walked through during the dinner and reception. My heart was heavy, and all I wanted to do was go home to bed. It was a wonderful day, beautiful, one of the best days of my life, but inside things were stone and heavy. I pushed myself, as I had done most of my life, and brushed it off. I told myself I felt this way due to the busyness of the preparations that led up to the wedding. Deep down, I knew it was something more. This heaviness was something so different from what I had carried. I had wrapped itself around my entire being. Infiltrated my blood and contaminated my cells. Everything hurt. I could barely convinced myself that I was managing

Three weeks after our wedding, The Ginger was conceived. With his much-wanted conception came a not-so-wanted difficult pregnancy. It was the type of pregnancy that put me in the hospital on five different occasions due to Hyperemesis Gravidarum. It was something I had with my first pregnancy but not nearly as intense. I felt completely spent and awful for most of the pregnancy. Thankfully, I was overjoyed to be pregnant, which helped me navigate the sickness brought on by the pregnancy more positively. But the seemingly endless nine months of sickness and low energy took a toll on me physically, mentally, and spiritually. I felt very vulnerable and unsafe out in the world, which was something new for me. On one occasion, I came home from a hospital stay and went grocery shopping. Halfway through the shop, Steve realized he had forgotten his wallet. He decided to leave The Young Blood and me, and go back home to retrieve it. A sense of panic came over me. It was a feeling I had never felt before. I did not want him to leave me there. I was nearly in tears begging him not to leave me. It was completely unreasonable, I realized that, but I could not have him leave me there. The feeling was absolutely paralyzing. Even with Steve's gentle coaxing, I could not be convinced that I could stay there on my own. We ended up leaving the grocery cart and going home together to retrieve the wallet.

Looking back, I see this time as a time of breaking open and breaking down. Through this process of involuntary surrender, the burdens and pains of my past were being, quite literally, physically, and spiritually forced out of their hiding places. All the while, the walls that I built because of that (young girl's) pain were breaking down. Apparently, I needed something like a severe nine months of morning sickness to allow this to happen!

Nov.7, 2003...coffee house writings

Many changes in my life. As my new son now sleeps in his stroller beside me I reflect on the very eventful last few years. Death, Love, Romance, Struggle, Marriage, Illness, New Life, New Home.

Welcome to The Ginger...what a gift to all of us. Especially The Young Blood. He has loved becoming a big brother and yet struggles with letting go of the "baby" role.

There have definitely been challenges. But that is one reason why I commit to write, because I want to face these challenges with all the power I have. To be the best mother & wife that I can be.

I have been through so many changes since Steve came into my life.

Starting with the death of my father. What a trip that was. Then on to marring the most amazing man. A truly heart moving connection, I long for that in my relationships, I strive for that. I find as I get older, I want that more and more. I think it's always been there but became more real first with The Young Blood...then Steve and now The Ginger, who I was a little afraid to connect with...it was all getting almost, almost too much. But I have settled in now and allowed the blessings in.

Dec. 5, 2003...coffee house writings

The baby ginger is fast asleep in his stroller so I have some time to write and reflect. Today is a rainy, gray day. A perfect day to be cuddled up relaxing. I am trying to get back to my tranquil self. I am trying to find balance and purpose. It is a difficult thing when you have two children, a house, a business, and a second job. I know that I have my mother purpose, wife purpose, job purpose. Those I have...down pat in fact. But now I need to re-connect with my soul purpose. So important but such a challenge. So, one way is doing this once a week. Getting my thoughts down on paper. I have been struggling lately...not feeling full inside. Just feeling like I am working, working, working but not getting the fulfillment I need. Not exactly sure of what fulfillment I'm needing but something inside isn't settled. Then I feel guilty because I look at all I have and am so, so blessed by it all. Truly beyond my wildest dreams.

I think a part of my problem is that I am so used to climbing, climbing, climbing that I have difficulty sitting. I am used to the struggle. Is it that I create struggle to have it or is it that I am constantly looking, searching always moving down the path of life? Trying to find the "real" truth in all the truths of this world. It is such an amazing journey, and I want it all. I am so happy and yet so sad. Not all the time but there are times when I am very melancholy. This time of year, that seems to be spurred on by my birthday. I've committed to myself that I will send a letter to Victoria to check out my file...to see if there has been any connection or information. My bio-mom is now 59 years old...time is ticking and I need to close that chapter.

A problem that I realize I still have is worrying too much about what right and wrong, what's okay and not. Am I okay? Am I wrong to think that?....that sort of thing. Those are the trappings of my up-bringing...

Along with these sporadic coffee house writings, there were also the pub stool writings. Due to my busy schedule, I did my grocery shopping late at night. After the boys had been tucked into bed and the household put on a low simmer, I found the grocery store even quieter, which was a lovely treat. Every once in a while, if time allowed, I stopped at the pub by the grocery store with journal in hand and had a drink while writing. These writings were often more about the observation of what was going on around me. I took great comfort in the noise and the anonymity that I found in these excursions. They offered me a place to detach, just a little, from the heaviness and grief that continued to grow within my body.

I decided to learn how to live with the heaviness, like a soldier trapped in her foxhole on the front line. ((yes!!! This is the kind of description that needs to go up above)) After all, this dark heaviness wasn't exactly new, it was just much heavier and took up more space in my body. As I had always done in the past, I found ways to "hunker down" and "soldier through." It was what I knew. I was too blinded with the grief of so much within me that I could not see there were other options.

Steve would describe this time as the season in which he felt that any given morning he might just wake up with a fork in his neck. It was funny on one hand but also a tragic reflection of where things were with me. He could tell where I was every morning by what noises came out of the kitchen. If he heard smashing around, he would hide out in bed as long as he could before getting up and meeting the "crazy lady" for the day. We laugh about it now, sometimes I cry, but I am always grateful for his grace and understanding during my time of deep struggle.

Looking back, I can see there was some postpartum depression involved along side the lingering childhood depression. The pregnancy, putting it plainly, had kicked the shit out of me. It took me almost three years to fully recover. I did not have the same instant bonding experience I had with my first son. It had taken a number of weeks before I would allow myself to fall in love with my new baby. I loved him, but that full-on-crazy-love that mothers often feel, took time to ignite. I also felt the need to prove my worth daily to my husband. It was nothing he required. My own crazy making manifested it all. I would make lists of things that I wanted to accomplish during the day and cross them off when I did. When Steve got home from work, I showed him the list and all that I had done. It wasn't something he cared about or needed, I was doing it for myself, to feel worthy.

Pushing myself was nothing new. Working hard and keeping busy with full schedules was the way I operated for much of my life. For three years in row during high school, I received the Most Participation Award, until grade 11, a year I barely remember due to excessive pot smoking and partying. But, yes, I was well-versed in the art of pushing myself. My motto was push through what was in front of you now and worry about the harm it does tomorrow. Little did I know that tomorrow was coming sooner than I thought, and she was not happy.

I had started drinking wine at night, a lot of wine. When I first came home, from the hospital, with The Ginger, it was tea and tea only.

As time went on and the angst within remained, along with the postpartum emotions, I started with a glass here and a glass there. This was not a crime by any means. The problem was that I soon found myself staying up after my husband went to bed, to finish the bottle by myself. Eventually, the time grew longer and the bottles got bigger.

I was self medicating. I stayed up late by myself, because I felt that I needed space. I drank because everything within me hurt. I was unable to express what was going on inside, and unable to put into words what I was feeling. I was holding it together all day, being what I needed to be for those around me. Then at night, I needed to numb out and relieve myself of the pain. Steve noticed the drinking habit and kept a close eye, fully aware that I was going through something he was unable to see.

The "craziness," as I saw it, was all under the surface. During childhood, I learned how to hide what was really happening within and put forth an appealing outer shell. But, one early morning, at 3 AM, my patient and loving husband witnessed and experienced "The Suffering Woman," sitting up in bed, exposed, and weeping hysterically because she had no idea what was "wrong" with her or why with all her blessings, she felt so broken inside.

I was waking up each morning with my fists clenched. During the day, I held my jaw tight. I needed to "just get through" the day and all would be well. I only wrote in my journal twice that year. I couldn't deal with the war I was waging. I could only see what was right in front on me. So I grasped onto whatever I could to keep my head above water and keep myself from drowning. I distracted myself with the life of a mother, wife, friend, and business owner, and it seemed to carry me through.

Steve was walking his own journey. A year prior to this time of our life, he had joined a men's group after attending an Alpha class (Alpha being an introductory class to Christianity) at my mom's church. While attending Alpha, Steve met an outspoken man who was in his group who really intrigued him. This man was part of a men's group run by one of the church pastors. He invited Steve to attend, and he decided to check it out. The group was based on high integrity and accountability. It was challenging, which was totally my husband's speed. The group was somewhat controversial within that church community and some of the men dropped out not quite agreeing with the radical content that was being presented.

Eventually the pastor decided to start a church of his own. Steve, enjoying the men's group, suggested that we should join this new little church.

It was soothing to be part of a smaller group. After service on Sundays, we would commune over lunch as the children played, it was quite lovely. Around this time, Steve began to consider being baptised. Baptism, within the Christian religion is a sacred sacrament, a symbol of admission/adoption into the Christian Church Family. It was a ceremony brought about during the time of Jesus. It was a symbol to the people of his time, of rebirth and of new beginning within their hearts and lives. It was a washing away of the old and coming into the new. Not being brought up in a religious home, Steve had never been baptised.

After much consideration, the discussion changed from him getting baptised to the both of us doing it together, which really resonated to both of us. In the Christian denomination, I was brought up in, I was baptised as an infant. The parents make the choice for the child. The thought was that this mark was placed upon the child so that if the child died, he or she would be recognized by the saints and taken into heaven.

Even though now I feel so far away from this time in my life, it remains a very sacred and pivotal moment in mine and my husband's life, for ourselves and our marriage. This wasn't a day that was so much about the Christianity of "the church." It was the day both of us acknowledged our Creator and our faith in the knowledge of the spirituality that is all around us, and to which we are a part. It was a very sacred ceremony, and the choice to do it together was monumental. On some level, it feels even more important to us than the day we were married.

I remember the day clearly. We invited some people who were near and dear to us, family and friends, and the very small church family. As we drove up to the lake, we both felt the energy and excitement within and between us. When we arrived, everyone was waiting for us by the lake. The sun was shining and a light breeze was blowing across the lake. We walked into the lake hand-in-hand and were fully immersed and symbolically into our new dedication to our life with The Divine. Though much of what was part of our life then has fallen away, that commitment to living a Spirit-based life and acknowledging ourselves as spiritual beings, belonging to something much bigger than ourselves remains within both of us. That event, that ritual set the tone for our marriage. Even though we eventually left that church family, that ceremonial mark remains on our hearts.

I am not sure if it was before or after our baptism that my husband came home with some concerns over some of the literature in our home. For some who were not brought up in a fundamentalist or religious lifestyle, this may sound strange. But for those who have, this will sound familiar. Within the men's group Steve was attending, came the topic of home protection and child protection. Of course, this is something for which most of us naturally strive. Within the fundamentalist way, there are very clear views about literature, music, and television. So, it was no surprise to me when Steve came home and said there were some books that we might want to think about taking out of our home for our own spiritual safety.

A few of the books were mine. These were books on herbal spells, astrology, books considered New Age, and a deck of beautiful Russian fortune-telling cards, which I loved dearly. My husband wanted to honour what he was learning within his group, and the direction they were being guided. He in no way was forcing this on me or demanding anything of me. But we were a team and in the honouring of that, I wanted to fulfill what he deemed at that time, necessary for our spiritual walk. All of this was nothing new to me. I knew well about the "fear of the outside." I knew well that within the Christian faith you are taught that there is only one way to the one true God, and one must rid himself or herself of worldly influences and stay pure enough to be considered acceptable by God. And though I conceded to honour my husband, I felt a conflicted twinge within my heart.

There were some things that were easy to let go of. We burned them in the backyard fire pit, but there were a few items that had come to mean something to me. It was harder to let go of these. I meditated and prayed about it searching my soul for answers. Steve did not push. He understood what these items meant to me and gave me the space to work it out for myself.

I really wanted to honour my husband, but also myself. I went back and forth about the remaining items. Both sides had their arguments and both were going at it in my head. After a couple weeks of going back and forth, I stood in my carport, engaged in yet another conversation with God about what I should do. Within the chaos of my mind, there came a calm steady voice. I knew immediately that it was the voice of Jesus or at least a voice that represented Jesus. (At this time, my comprehension of those who speak to me was limited to what I had been taught.)

He said to me, "All of this is confusing you, Catherine. Instead of this confusion, why don't you put your faith in me and let everything else go, for now."

Within my mind, I wanted to do the "right thing," be the "good girl." In my heart, I knew the power of the items, and the good magic that they held. There was such sadness in letting them go. But when I heard that voice, I knew that in the end none of it mattered. At this fragile point in my life, what was important was that I had peace of mind. I needed to be mindful to take care of my fragile state. So, I trusted what I heard and let the items go. I don't regret it. I know it was all part of the journey I had to walk to get to the places I needed to go and to get to where I am now. I love how I wanted to honour Steve. Even in my brokenness, I ultimately knew what was important: him, the boys, and our little family. I understood that the unity between Steve and me was the backbone of our family. It needed to be strong.

We are still very mindful of what we bring into our home, but it is not out of fear. We believe knowledge is power. We want to expose our boys and ourselves to the many possibilities of this life. I want them to have the option to choose and engage the mindfulness of their hearts. Steve wants them to open their minds to the truth of what lies beyond the immediate, and what we are shown by society and the media.

It is now my thought, experience and belief that there is more than one way to Divine Love. From what I have observed within others and experienced within myself, there are many ways to the same place. Every soul is given the divine freedom to find their own path. Divine Love will come to all in a form recognizable to the individual. This is not a game of hide and seek.

"*Process is more important than outcome. When the outcome drives the process, we will only ever go to where we've already been. If process drives outcome we may not know where we're going, but we will know we want to be there.*"
~ Bruce Mau

4
Decisions and Mirrors

One of my biggest challenges to over come was that I saw myself as damaged goods and worth very little. I lived with the belief that I was lucky to have what I did and so the expectations weren't high. I came to God like the prostitute, who washed Jesus' feet with the expensive perfume. I was on my knees, head bowed low, thinking that I was nothing, and lucky to be in his presence. I was dirty and unclean. I was nothing.

January 4, 2005

My dad died going on 6 years. I sit with the lesson that sometimes there is no happy ending. On this Earth, sometimes there is not the outcome that we long for. A big realization for me has been that this life is but a bus stop for something greater, bigger, and much more important. As humans, we hold onto this life like it is everything. We hold onto it hoping that it will give us all the fulfillment we long for. We must look beyond this life to find our true fulfillment and peace.

I was looking at my situation head on and seeing things as very literal. Inadvertently, I was still trying to change my past. I recognize this same one-dimensional thinking in many of the people I sit with in healing sessions. We do this because we don't know a better way. There is no fluid movement or allowance for ebb and flow. There is the desire to change the old story, but we are not able to understand that the story is what makes us who we are. It is the story that we are living now that needs our attention. Now I know, I had to walk through this process to become the Healer that I am today. It was within my own wounded walk that I found what healing really looked like and what it needed from me.

In life, sometimes, okay, a lot of times, there are events that happen within and around our lives that are unexplainable and in their wake, leave a whole lot of heartache. This is how it was at the beginning of 2005. The year started with death and tragedy both on the personal and world front. We all felt the painful exhale of the tsunami that affected the countries bordering the Indian Ocean taking the lives of more than 230,000 people from fourteen different countries. On a personal level, I was standing by a dear and long-time friend as she had been forced to say an unexpected goodbye to her mother. It brought home the finality of the death of our bodies and a time when our souls must leave those whom we love and those who love us.

Jan. 6, 2005

What can one write when she is about to watch her friend bury yet another parent? The sadness in my heart is almost too much to bear. The hopelessness, the hollow feeling, the heavy heart of watching someone you love dangle by life's delicate string. This past week has been numbing, a reminder of how delicate life is, such loss in the world with the tsunami and in my own life with the passing of a dear friend's mom. Even as I write this, I cannot believe that she is gone from this existence. Logically I know that she is but my heart has not quite accepted it. My heart is with my friend and her family. She has walked a very long road. I ask God to lift her spirit and hold her tight. She really needs a helping hand.

On January 10, I sent out this email to family and friends:

Well the New Year has started and for the world, it has been a rough start. For myself personally, it has, as well. You know there are always these inspirational messages coming across the wires some are so touching they can bring you to tears. I received a beautiful one this morning from my friend, which did just that. Funny how she sent me that particular inspiration today as I had plans of sending some inspiration of my own today, using my own words. What she sent me reaffirmed that I should go ahead and do this. This past Friday, Jan 7, I watched as my very close friend, the godmother of my oldest son said her last goodbyes to her mother. Her mom, 54 years of age, suddenly passed away on New Year's Eve due to unexpected complications after surgery. You all know, that in itself is sad enough. But what makes this story even harder to swallow is the fact that 10 months and 10 days prior to her mom's passing, my friend with her two siblings, said their final goodbyes to their 55-year-old father. He passed away after a long and hard 11-year battle with multiple myeloma, bone marrow cancer. The truth of it is I could go on and on about the ironies of this family, and the path they have been on. I could tell you about how on the 30th, my friend brought her mom in for surgery. It was my friend's 36th birthday. While we stood at her mother's bedside on New Year's Eve, my girlfriend told me that her mother had been in labour with her for 36 hours, and she now had been with her mom for 36 years. I could tell you about how her mom had journaled the last 5 months of her life and had never journaled before, or the amazing doors and windows she opened for those she left behind, because of this journal. I could tell you about the woman I knew. She touched my life in ways I didn't even realize until she was gone. I could tell you of how her gifts of caring and giving joy to others continues as she was able to donate many of her organs for transplant. Most of all, I would like to tell you what I learned. As I stood beside her bed saying my own goodbyes, I had a chance to talk with one of her best friends. She told me that she was not sure how she would move on, and the thought of not having time together was almost too much to bear. But she had no regrets. She told me about how the two of them had never missed an opportunity to let each other know how they felt about each other. I thought that was so beautiful. What a thought! She knew that her friend loved her, and she loved her right back. How many times do we let opportunities pass us by to let someone know that they are loved? We are always in a hurry to "get stuff done," but not so much in a hurry to show love to one another. Two days after her mom's passing, I was talking to my friend's sister. I learned that home is truly where a mother's love lives. What an amazing power of comfort a mother's home holds. To all you mothers, hold fast to that knowledge, and do not take for granted this gift you provide for your children. Give it to them freely so that no matter what, they know that they are loved. I learned that in a blink of an eye things could change. That was something I thought I already knew, and maybe I did. This was another reminder. Watching someone you love say goodbye to someone who is a huge part of their heart can leave you with a great feeling of helplessness. But again, I have learned that all is not lost and out of ashes beauty can rise. I am taking what I learned and sharing it with you because I want to honour my friend and the memory of her mom. She was someone whom I loved and will greatly miss. Life is indeed fragile. When you are going about your busy lives do not forget those you love and those you care about. For without them, we are nothing. Without loved ones, we sail in an empty ship on a lonely sea. My friend's mom was also a woman of faith. I wanted to include a passage from The Bible that was read at her memorial. It is found in the New Testament and it is as follows:

2 Corinthians 4:16-18

"Therefore we do not lose heart. Though outwardly we are wasting away, yet inwardly we are being renewed day by day. For our light and momentary troubles are achieving for us an eternal glory that far outweighs them all. So we fix our eyes not on what is seen, but what is unseen, for what is seen is temporary, but what is unseen is eternal."

This was the passage to which her bible was open. She had suffered both when her husband was sick and when he passed on. I thank you for reading this, I truly hope this finds you all happy, healthy, and living life like there will be no tomorrow...

Sincerely, Catherine

I felt and continue to deeply feel the emotions of these grief seasons. These are the times that mold and influence one's view of life. It is in times like these that we learn to walk lightly and reflect on what it is we have, realizing that everything can change in the blink of an eye. Here in this place of grief, we remember that each moment is precious. This life we desperately cling to will one day come to an end.

Not all grief is held in death. Sometimes is has to do with the well being of a loved one. The sadness you feel when you watch someone, you love, suffer as they navigate who they are in a big world, that is not always kind or understanding.

Feb 3, 2005

I'm worried. I'm worried about The Young Blood. God forgive me. I know that we should not worry. My faith should be in God and for the most part it is. There is a guilt that lingers deep inside my heart and a responsibility that I take on for the Young Blood's life.

So, it would be as signs of warning would come to set up camp with in my little family that brought worry and concern to my mama heart. Anxiety was becoming a part of my oldest son's life along with, as I like to call it, a "fragile eco system." This anxiety brought with it symptoms that caused both Steve and me deep concern for The Young Blood's well-being, emotionally and physically. But that is his story. I want to honour that so I will only touch on it lightly within these pages. I will say this. His journey has not been an easy one emotionally or mentally. Yet he found himself to be gifted musically, creatively, and physically, as it is in the world of extremes. A few times medication was discussed, but we chose to go the holistic route of food, sleep, activity, and environment. We did not want the medication to affect the creativity, which was essentially his true Self. (To utilize medication, or not to, is an extremely personal decision. Each case is specific and needs to be treated as such.)

March 15, 2005

This is my second afternoon in a row, sitting alone in front of our cabin on Mackenzie beach at Tofino! It has been amazing. The beach today is a little quieter than yesterday since it is Monday and not quite as sunny. It is still beautiful but a little overcast. The two days prior there was not a cloud in the sky. We arrived on the 12th, Saturday. It was a bit of a tough start. A few breakdowns occurred before we got on track.

This truly is God's country. I mean all is God's, but here there is more God less man. The untouched beauty is breathtaking.

The Young Blood and Steve are off for the afternoon on a kayaking excursion...very exciting. I pray the Young Blood stays focused and his spirit is filled with God's wonders. He is so in his element out in Nature. I am sure he will love it. He was a little nervous...which is typical, but excited all the same.

Oh, if only I could stay here in this beautiful world of simple living and peace and calm. The land is rough and harsh but there is such a certainty here that is undeniable. I want to stay in this forever. Wrapped in my blanket sipping my wine and writing in my journal.

Life has had some big ups and downs lately within me. Just trying to figure out where I belong, and where I fit in. What does it all mean? What does "wives submit to your husbands" really mean? Does that mean I give up all that I am to follow my husband, live by his callings, and take on his dreams? Isn't compromise on both sides? Don't we come together and decide?

Currently, we are doing a Freedom in Christ series called The Christ Centered Marriage. We are only into Chapter 3, and already there has been a lot learned. I know that my marriage is blessed. I also know that even with such blessings come responsibility and accountability. Both Steve and I want our marriage to mirror Christ and follow God's path laid out before us. That can sometimes seem easier then it actually is. With life's day-to-day pressures, we've lost our way, time and time again, but we keep striving and facing each day.

My own struggle right now lies within. I am not really happy inside with myself. I feel ugly, fat, negative, and angry. That is why I love it here. I don't feel those things right now. I feel rested and at peace. Less pressure. Less pressure.

On the back of this page I wrote these points down:

- *don't know how to handle the intimacy*

- *don't know how to deal with the pain*

- *don't think anyone believes me*

- *don't know how to show myself*

- *afraid*

- *knowing I am not perfect yet striving for that*

I sat in this magical place facing two uncertainties. One around The Young Blood and what his future would hold and the other was around church and faith, and where I stood with each of them. Both uncertainties had one thing in common. They both invoked the invitation for me to listen to, and trust my heart.

I came clean with my husband about something that had been on my heart for a while around the small church that we had been attending. I had held onto my concerns, thoughts, and feelings because I knew he was receiving the accountability and motivation he was looking for within the circle of men that were a part of this church family, and I wanted to remain connected to God. This seemed the most logical way. I held on and held on until the time when the church doctrine was brought out. It was revealed that within this church, women would never hold office, nor would they teach, nor would they have the right to vote. This was not going to work for me at all.

I was raw, beaten down, weak, and broken, but I was no slave! This I knew and my heart reaffirmed it with that tapping of truth. I knew there was no way I would ever sign such a document and become a full member. I had walked enough roads to know this tapping within my heart. The soft voice that said, "there is so much more." Not to mention that every cell in my body was crying out, "this is not where we belong…we will not live and thrive in this environment."

I am grateful I found my courage and my voice that day driving into Tofino as the tears streamed down my face. All I said that day was not news to my husband. I will add, I am grateful for a husband who knows me well and is man enough to hear his wife's words. I let him know I could never be a full member of the church and that my whole being did not agree with the place they gave women. However, if he wanted, I would go with him, but my heart would never fully be there. He heard me and had seen the writing on the wall. Like me, he had his own reasons for not facing the truth of our fate with this church.

It was a great relief for me to let him know what was on my heart and to have it be clearly received by him. I was still learning that this was possible within a healthy relationship. In this beautiful place of The Creator, we came to the mutual agreement that our future was not with this church. We would continue our journey to find our place. We would trust that we would be guided to where we needed to be.

Oct. 14, 2005

Sitting in Starbucks. I am starting a new tradition: Friday morning coffee. The Ginger is now going to my girlfriend's on Fridays. This gives me an entire day to work, work, work. This is the fourth week and it is working out so well. I just finished day 7 of The Purpose Driven Life by Rick Warren. Yes, I am trying to find my purpose. I know the obvious…mother, wife, daughter, and friend but beyond that…? Where does God want me to do my heart work? I am looking for that answer.

This book would mark the beginning of my spiritual journey through literature. I was still strongly held within the confines of my Christian upbringing, but there was a movement happening within these confines. I was getting taken into its flow, a flow that would begin my journey of releasing the confines. I wanted to find my purpose, peace from the voices in my head, and to rid myself of the heaviness in the pit of my stomach. I really wasn't sure that any of this was possible. When I did soul work, I felt lighter and felt relief from the burdens I carried.

While I was reading The Purpose Driven Life that a whole new aspect of God, The Creator, was shown to me. Its words were life-giving water to my parched soul. I was so thirsty for the words of Love this book gave to me. The words resonated with me on a soul-deep level. I learned how God wanted to be my friend, how I was planned for God's pleasure, and how I mattered. This more personal, intimate view of God was new to me, and yet I knew the intimacy was true. I felt it when He first spoke to me so clearly before my dad died, and continued to do so. I felt the warmth, the purity, and the Love that no words can explain. They began to break down some misconceived notions for me, about God and who I was to him. It was in this book that I discovered it was not about me, but it had everything to do with me. It was not others that hindered my life, but in fact, it was I. I began to learn about the spiritual power that I had within my own being, and how I could use it for my own healing.

As I look through that book now, and read the few things I underlined, I realized I am still walking within many of it's words. Only I am sure Mr. Warren had intended the guidance given to remain within the Christian standard and community, but my heart's path and purpose would eventually take me beyond the walls of Christianity. It is a strange yet wonderful irony that this Christian-based book started me on the path that would lead me to leaving the very place it intended me to stay.

Within the unfolding and discovering there still remained the lingering desperate thought for it to all end. I lived with this almost every day. Some days were worse than others, but whatever the degree of intensity, it never left me. It always remained. In October of that same year, I hopped in my car for a weekend visit to a dear friend who lived five hours away. It was a beautiful sunny, fall day. So many of my favourite things! Traveling with me was the deep heaviness within. I thought about Steve and the boys as I drove toward the highway that would take me on my small adventure. Thoughts flooded my mind as to how I saw myself failing them in so many ways. I thought about how I could have more patience and understanding for Nathen and what he was going through. I thought about how Steve deserved to have a wife that was whole and undamaged. I thought about how Aiden in all his brightness deserved a mother who was better. The more I thought about it, the more I felt they would be better without me. I was unable to see how I could change things or be better for them. With a lack of boundaries within myself, the voices overtook my own small meek voice of self-love. I allowed my stories to run free in my mind, dragging me down to the dark depths of my being.

I am not sure how long this went on. It seemed like hours though in reality, it was probably only a few minutes. Then came another voice…a gentle, peaceful voice. The voice was one of Divinity, of God. How did I know? When Divinity speaks, you know. There was something so pure about this voice, so beyond anything I could conjure within my human form. You just know.

God asked me if I truly wanted to leave this life and those I loved. I said yes that I was done. I could not do it any longer. I felt so unstable and untrustworthy inside. I believed I caused pain and suffering in those I loved. I thought that they were feeling the same as I was inside, and this was too great a burden to bear. I truly believed the world, and those I loved would be better off with me gone. God told me that He (the masculine was how I still saw God at the time) could make this happen. But I had to be sure for there would be no turning back. So, to ensure that I was indeed as sure as I thought, I was given a vision and shown how it was to happen.

It would happen that day, as I was driving within the mountains of Manning Park. My car would drive off the road. It would be a severe car crash. None of this was disturbing to me. I was completely okay with what I was being shown. In fact, I felt a relief, until I was taken to what happened after the crash. I did not die right away.

I sustained very serious injuries and was on some form of life support. Steve and the boys were at my bedside. The boys were crying and Steve was distraught. I did not understand this right away, but it seemed that there were so many things my soul had yet to do. My higher self, my soul, my essence was not as ready to leave this life as my fleshy self was. I watched as Steve and the boys stood by my lifeless body. I saw their broken hearts, their confusion, and felt their grief. God said to me, "You must understand that all things must play out as they are meant to. If you desire to leave this life before your time, there will be a price to pay."

The vision of them at my bedside remained clearly in my mind's eye. It was not a vision that I will ever forget. When I "came back," I was at a traffic light, about to get on the very highway that would later that morning change my life forever. It was up to me. I chose to stay. I woke up to the realization that my life was not just about those whom I loved. It was also about those who loved me. And even in all the brokenness and fog I felt inside of me; I knew how I felt about my husband and my boys. My love for them was fierce and their love for me was equally so. I would not leave that love. I would not leave them. I would stay and find my way through this darkness and fog. I had no idea how, but I knew I did not want to leave. I let God know my decision and the presence left me. I drove into a beautiful fall day, taking in the beauty of the earth and enjoying the solitude of the drive. I drove like this for a few hours until I came to a place on the road where there was a deep embankment that went into the marshland below. God again spoke to me here and told me that this was where the accident would have been. As I passed it, something shift within me, small yet powerful and oh so important. I had made a choice to live...to live, love, and maybe even flourish.

Jan. 20, 2006, 12:30am

What is important to God? What makes us stand out to The Creator? Immediately I think of the story of Jesus in the temple watching a rich man give a sack of coins to the church and an older woman giving only a few coins, worth less than a penny.

This story is found in Luke 21: 1-4

"As Jesus looked up, he saw the rich putting their gifts into the temple treasury. He also saw a poor widow put in two very small copper coins. "I tell you the truth," he said, "this poor widow has put in more than all the others. All these people gave their gifts out of their wealth; but she out of her poverty put in all she had to live on."

I feel this story is telling us that this is what God wants from us... whatever it is we have to give. This, of course, can change from day-to-day, season-to-season, and different times of our lives. Each and every day is new and different. There are different battles to fight, different struggles to face, and different challenges to overcome. Sometimes there can be a feeling of not too much left over in the way of giving. If all you can do is muster up a smile to someone walking on the street or a kind word to the checkout girl, then that is enough.

I continue to learn many good teachings in the bible. It has become my map.

I believe the bible, like other holy books, is a connection to our Creator and for which we were truly created. It is a book based on Love's standards.

I recently went through a tough situation where I had to really stand up. A very close and dear friend confided in me that she was seeing someone outside of her marriage, someone with whom she was developing real feelings. Of course, I gave her a listening ear but also pointed out this was probably not the best thing to be doing.

She agreed and said to me that she had broken it off the day before and was never going to see this person again.

I was not alone with this knowledge, thank God…another close friend knew as well. We counseled our friend only to find out she had not been honest with us about cutting things off with this person.

Then came the day when my friend, her husband, and I ended up at church together. This was when I became a warrior. We sat together, her holding his hand, letting him love her like there was nothing else going on. I cried through the whole service. I knew what I had to do. I came home to talk to my husband about it, and he reaffirmed my thoughts.

I prayed on my own, then with my husband, and on my own again…

"Do I really have to do this? Can't you pick someone else? I don't want to be the one who rocks the boat. This is not going to be fun, and I am all about fun!"

Matthew 26:38, 39

"He said to them, "My heart is overwhelmed with sorrow to the point of death. Stay here and watch with me." Going a little further, he fell with his face to the ground and prayed. "My father, if it is possible, may this cup be taken from me. Yet not as I will, but as you will." ~Jesus

No, I wasn't about to be wrongly tried, tortured, and crucified, but all the same it was going to be painful and the risks were great. But I picked up the phone and called my friend.

"Hi, it's Catherine."

"Hi, is everything ok?"

"No, it's not okay."

"What's wrong?"

"This, this is all wrong…either you tell him or I will."

Silence

"There is nothing going on. We haven't done anything."

"You are having an emotional affair."

Silence

"This is none of your business."

"You are making a fool out of someone I love. It is my business."

It wasn't pretty. I gave her a day. I don't believe in wasting time. She ended up telling him, but not everything at first. It is still a huge mess.

After that happened, I remember standing in my laundry room grieving. Grieving for their marriage, grieving for the loss of a friendship, grieving for my lost friend, and just wondering if what I did was the best thing, the right thing...I know that might sound funny, but the world tells us not to get involved. Don't reach out. Take care of your own and the rest can take care of theirs. And for goodness sake DON'T ROCK THE BOAT!!!!! Too late...I think I capsized it.

As I stood there struggling and weeping, for my heart was breaking into a million pieces. God said to me, in peaceful wisdom.

"You are living by my standards, Catherine, not the worlds."

God's standards were placed in each of us when we were created. It is the knowledge of our hearts that should be followed, not the knowledge from the world. That was a big moment for me, one I will not soon forget. I followed my heart and with that knowledge I found peace.

The peace I speak of doesn't mean I don't still grieve and my heart is not broken, but it just means I do have peace in what my part was. I rocked the boat, it capsized, and we all got wet. No one died. We all just became uncomfortable...very uncomfortable.

A pastor once said to me that all the women in the bible that God worked with were not considered the holiest or most desirable of women. God has a purpose for us all, sometimes even without us knowing.

In the book Pilgrims Progress, written by John Bunyan in the 1600s, we meet a man named Christian. A man clothed in rags with a book in his hand and a heavy burden on his back. It is in this book where he discovers the plight of his city and all those in it. He goes on a journey to search for the Celestial City. It is on this journey that he meets characters with names such as Evangelist, Charity, Hypocrisy, Goodwill, Mr. Worldly, and more.

This book is a beautiful allegory about the journey of life. There are many, many things in this book that touch deeply, but one thing that stands out so strongly to me is when Christian comes upon the cross.

He is walking by the wall called Salvation, and his walk turns to a run, though it is very difficult due to the load he is carrying on his back… his burdens.

He runs until he is at the top of a hill where the cross stands. At the foot of a cross is a sepulcher, a grave marker. As he approaches the cross and grave marker, his burden begins to loosen from his back and fall off. It rolls toward the grave marker and falls into a hole and "is not more" …and not only that he is given new clothing for his journey ahead.

It is such a beautiful scene. What strikes me so about all this is that this happens right at the beginning of his journey. He finds the path, enters the gate, and comes upon the Cross. His burden is taken from him right away! He still has the rest of his journey to make.

In this journey, he has demons to fight, meets travelers who deceive, and is even imprisoned, and he messes up! He sleeps when he should be walking. He shares his journey with some he should not and even leaves behind sacred gifts that he's been given. And yet, his burden is released first. It is not what we do on our journey that matters. It is that we take the journey at all. We do not earn love. It is given freely, no matter the mistakes we make or the accomplishments we fulfill.

This reminds me that God knows of our struggles. God knows of our weakness and yet gives us everlasting Divine Love. How amazing is He with his army of angels fighting for us behind the scenes? How many traps are we protected from without our knowledge? How many hardships are deflected? We will never know.

I know this; God is all that is good. He loves us in spite of our weakness and our fallen nature. I believe that God wants to be there for us, it is up to us to open ourselves to that. It is God's standards that matters, not our own, not the worlds, not your parents, and not *your friends. All of your truth is written in your heart. Your Creator knows you...everything about you, and knows what you have to offer. And it is all good.*

This was one of the few things written in 2006. It was the eerie calm before the storm. This year was filled with a lot of break ups and "circle of friends" changes. These kinds of changes have never been easy for me. When it was time to let them go, I tended to hold onto my relationships just a little too long. I had always put a lot of value into my friendships. In my husband's view, he felt I sometimes put in more than I received back. As a teenager, it was my friendships that got me through those dark years. This is why I had put a lot of stock into these kinds of relationships. Friends were family. That meant they walked with you through life until the end. But that was not always meant to be. I was learning this the hard way.

I decided it was time to get busy. I had slowly been taking on more responsibilities at my son's school and in a church-based mom's group called MOPS. We had become part of yet another small new church. We had met a couple through my work. The wife had seen one of my clients out and about and had asked where she got her hair done. My client gave her my card. It was not long before we brought our two families together, and they told us about their plans for a small community church. Both Steve and I felt it was the right place for us to be. They seemed to have a more grass roots approach to church, something a little more organic and real. This appealed to us, so I became part of the singing team and Steve became support and friend to the pastor. Soon our little church community became a huge part of our life.

The busier I was, the less I had to pay attention to what was happening inside me. I could push through to the next event, the next commitment, keep moving forward, and stay a few steps ahead of what was chasing me down. And what was chasing me was the black dog, the darkness of my depression trying to consume me. With this season of busy, I stayed one step ahead of that which I did not want to face. I falsely filled myself with duty.

At this time, I was reading a book called Captivating by John & Staci Eldredge. It was a Christian-based book about God's deep love for women. I think this was the first book...no...actually I know it was the first religious book that I had ever read that placed me, a woman, in high regard as God's created being. After all, as the story goes, it was the woman who ate the fruit of The Tree of Good and Evil. Then tempted Man to do the same. Woman caused the world to fall into sin. Yup, super-proud moment for women all around. And we wonder why we have self-esteem problems!

Though I did minimal marking in Captivating, I do remember how I felt when I read it. I remember the tears, the awakening, and the empowering. You may wonder why I clung to the Christian beliefs even though I was not connecting or being fulfilled by it. First, it was what I knew. Before I could unchain myself from it, I had to know and understand it fully. Sometimes one must know their captor to understand how to escape as safely as possible. There are gifts that I am grateful for that came from the Christian life of which I was a part. I was unable to remain under just that one title "Christian."

Reading Captivating had marked a shift inside me, in which I could see myself as jewel of creation. As John and Staci explained the Christian Creation Story, the woman is the last to be created, the final expression of The Creator, the one that makes it all complete. I had never been taught that view of the story. I had never been told that I was worthy. I never had the creation story presented where women were depicted as worthy, or so treasured by The Creator. Once I read the words, a new world of reality opened up to me, a reality that was waiting for me to discover it.

While on a camping trip that same summer, I had a dream. It was one of those dreams that was so real that you physically feel all that was going on. Each of my senses was awake and experiencing everything.

I was floating above the Pacific Ocean and looking down upon a small, heavily wooded island. It was a beautiful west coast scene. Looking down at the island, I realized that I was not alone. God was there along with a dear girlfriend. They were just hanging out, together, aware of me but not engaging with me. My girlfriend had a cozy jacket on and was looking quite relaxed and content hanging out with God. (Well, I guess hanging out with God would be a chill experience!) Then, I realized I was not feeling content. I was feeling a lot of pain, particularly in my chest. I clutched at my chest and looked over at God and my girlfriend. My girlfriend did not say anything to me, but was looking at me with a smile on her face, and love and compassion in her eyes. I looked to God and said,

"My heart, my heart...it hurts so much."

And God replied, "I know, Catherine that is because I am peeling back the layers of your heart."

I woke up right then to find myself in the Westfalia Camper. It was 6:00 am and my chest was gripped with pain. I sat up feeling like my heart was caught in a vice. It was then that I remembered God's words to me. I laid back down breathing slowly and sinking myself into the pain. Then I surrendered to the rebirth for which my spirit was preparing me. It hurt. But I was ready and tired of fighting it. It was time to open my heart to a new possibility of existence, a new view on life.

As I thought about the dream later that day sitting by the campfire and reflecting on my life, I tried to recognize when there had been other moments of layers being peeled off. I looked back to see when my Spirit had tried to do this before, but I had either resisted, or let the layer be peeled off, only to put it back on. I believe our Spirit, the part of us that has God's love print on it, is constantly trying to refine us back to our centre, our Selves. For it is here that we come back to our original created form of purity and perfection. It reminds me of an old hymn called "Refiners Fire:"

Purify my heart
Let me be as gold and precious silver
Purify my heart
Let me be as gold, pure gold
Refiner's fire
My heart's one desire
Is to be holy
Set apart for You, Lord
I choose to be holy
Set apart for You, my Master
Ready to do Your will
Purify my heart
Cleanse me from within
And make me holy
Purify my heart
Cleanse me from my sin
Deep within

There is a passage in the bible that speaks of this as well. Saying that we will go through the fire so we can become what we were created to be, pure Gold. And it is The Creator's hands that will hold us as we burn through our struggles and walk through our darkness.

Part of being able to let these layers go was to come to an understanding of who I was, especially who I was to my Creator.

At the end of the year, I wrote down some personal goals for myself.

- weight loss = fit lifestyle
- complete my book (this was the year I started writing it)
- peaceful living & simplify
- comfortable with who I am centered with the person God created me to be
- patience with family and self
- re-evaluate my expectations & stay in the moment
- really live in the moment
- surrender to God's plan for me
- honesty, live in honesty

Nov. 16, 2006

Focus on the positive...not the negative *love yourself*
Tough day today
Highs and lows
Very emotional...time to sleep

Nov.20-24, 2006

Had an emotional breakdown this week. Realized I am trying to live up to someone else's expectation thus fighting my true Self. I am so exhausted and want this to be over!

It is amazing to me as I re-read these thoughts and goals. They very much reflect the life I am living right now, eight years later. It is not so much in the context I had envisioned at that time. The intention remains, but not as a list to attain. It is an intention I am living actively on a daily basis.

Going along with the theme of the year, it ended on a very dramatic note. With drama comes refinement, and it would seem God had one bigger layer to peel away before the turning of the year. It happened during an extended family dinner gathering at Christmastime. The incident began when my then two-year-old son accidentally kicked my 25-year-old nephew in the crotch, while they were horsing around on the floor. My nephew's anger exploded, and he picked up my son by the shoulders and proceeded to yell right into his face and shake him. My mom told me later, that his response was because everyone was laughing at what had happened.

Steve pulled the baby away from my nephew, who then wanted to fight Steve. Both of my kids were crying. I just wanted to go home. No one knew what to do. Two more times my nephew tried to physically take Steve outside to fight. Steve just kept telling him to calm down. It was time to leave. I sat on the stairs calming my kids down just enough to be able to walk out of the situation relatively intact. The Ginger still refers to it as the time his cousin threatened him. At two years old, that was how he saw it.

The truth is that incident was not the event that peeled off the layer. I would say it softened and prepared it. But it would be the actions of my mom that would peel the layer off. Because of what happened, we would not be joining in on the family dinner happening at my mom's. I knew this was not going to go over smoothly, so letting my mother know required me to root in deep. I knew it would disappoint her. I took no pleasure in that. What I did not expect was what would come out of that disappointment. She proceeded to tell me that none of what happened would have happened if The Ginger had not kicked my nephew. I reminded her how many times this very thing happened to fathers all over the world when they wrestled with their boys. It had not been done with intent. I also reminded her that The Ginger was two and my nephew was an adult. Her response was that The Ginger was almost three.

Was this really happening? Was this conversation taking place? I looked out my bedroom window, phone against my ear in complete amazement. My Mother was implying that the whole incident and what followed was a toddler's fault. I was in such disbelief that I had to verify with her that was how she saw it. Yes, it was. Not only that, we needed to get over it and stop being ridiculous about not wanting to be around my nephew.

Like a cup of cold water in the face, reality hit me. Something lifted from my eyes, and in that moment, I saw things very clearly. When we were kids and our father lost control, it was never his fault. It was ours. If we had not been bad, none of what happened would have happened. We were bad kids and our behaviour made my dad lose his temper and react in an abusive manner. The lights were on, and I was home!

I remained calm on the phone with my mom. In fact, I surprised myself with how calm I was. I shared with her my disbelief in her attitude toward The Ginger and us. I made it clear, we would not be anywhere my nephew would be until this was talked out. I took a stand. I had to. Being a part of all the drama that was unfolding felt like taking a visit to Crazy Town. I was not into being there. The way I saw it, I had a choice to stay or leave. I chose to leave.

I hung up the phone feeling like the air had been sucked out of me. I felt for my mom. She had been conditioned to protect the offender and not take a stand for the offended. I believe it was unconscious on her part. It was nothing new to me. I had lived that. What was new was the realization of how deep it went and how vastly it affected my family, and its very foundation. It was very different seeing it through my wounded self, and then seeing it now through my adult eyes and filtering it through my spirit being that was waking up. The illness, so to speak, had not only been my father's but my mother's as well.

This peeling away had been painful, and I was unable to see how this could possibly resolve itself. Alongside the pain, there was also a piece of freedom and realization that my mom and I were walking a different road. I was more than okay with that. This unfolding led me to a place where I began to consider that perhaps I did not want that approval. Going deeper, perhaps I did not even need it. I called this new possibility "a painful liberation." It would take me a while to unpackage my feelings around what happened that Christmas of 2006. The residual effects had impacted my heart, my spirit, and my entire being. I was awake.

Grief had woken me up. The grief of death. The grief of uncertainty. The grief of toxic choices. It was both, painful and liberating. My heart was calling me to trust it and forge a new path. Life was giving me the stories that held the mirrors and I was being invited to make the decisions that were for my highest good. I was beginning to see that the choices, were truly mine to make.

"All changes, even the most longed for, have their melancholy; for what we leave behind us is a part of ourselves; we must die to one life before we can enter another"
~Anatole France

5
Break Down

The layers continue to be peeled back, and I am very optimistic about this New Year. I am a little afraid, as I know change is coming, but I am excited about that as well. God has laid some things out for me. Now it is time for me to do the work. This is the year of "Living Free." This is my choice. In making this choice, I will discipline myself to spend time doing those things that keep me at peace and focused on living in God's light. My heart has been broken so many times. It is time for me to take care of it and get rid of that which clouds my heart's light. What transpired over Christmas peeled off a huge layer...it was a painful liberation! Now we are in the New Year. The work to move passed the emotional garbage of 2006 begins.

#1 I will not take my hurt out on my husband.

#2 I will be clear on where my emotions are coming from and what is causing them.

#3 I will not be controlled by the hurt. I will not make decisions based on my heart and let God's light guide me.

Shed the old skin

Become renewed

Today it has snowed and school has been cancelled. Steve has decided to take a snow day as well...all is well at the Basso home.

Ps Had a great talk, as usual, with my girlfriend Sonja this morning...

These are the things that give my heart peace.

Coming into this New Year, along with a new attitude, I chose to put my focus on my body by concentrating on letting go of unneeded weight and exercise. On occasion, I was still indulging in purging, and my body image was still taking a beating. It seemed this was the familiar place to go. Fix the outside and everything else will follow.

Finding it hard to write everyday but feeling really good about my eating habits and exercise.

Looking at my life differently also. Choices are given to us. It is up to us what we do with them. This world does have heartbreak and sorrow, but do we let that control us? NO!...because the blessings far outweigh the sorrows...if we let them.

Attitude
Choices
Faith

I was trying. Though most times, it really felt more like stumbling around in the dark. Even though I still had a feeling of being lost, I continued to show up, trudging through the brokenness that appeared to be my life and acknowledging the pain and sadness of my heart. I attempted to be as honest with myself the best way I knew how, all the while raising my boys, growing a marriage, and nurturing the relationships around me.

As a family, we faced our own challenges. My oldest son, The Young Blood was walking with anxiety and the effects of that. It was painful for both Steve and me to watch him suffer in such a way. It was a day-by-day, breakdown-by-breakdown walk. We faced each situation as a new one and walked alongside him as best we could without him being completely dependant on us. It was a delicate dance to say the least.

We discovered early on that an annual trip to Tofino, a west coast destination, did wonders for The Young Blood. It ended up becoming our place of deep spiritual healing and medicine. The ferry ride over was wrought with anxiety and discomfort, only to have it begin to subside as we drove off the ferry and onto the island. Miraculously it completely evaporated when we hit the Pacific Rim National Park. This was a place where he could breathe, settle his mind, and clearly hear his heart. The ocean calmed him. The forest and mountain fed him. We were so happy to discover this early on. It did not take long to realize that this place did each of us some good.

March 16-2007

My Peace

My God

Is found in the waves of the Pacific Ocean

It is where I go to find the calm of my heart,

And to still my busy mind.

It is in the grandness of the rainforest trees

That I feel The Creator's power

It is in the misty morning

Where I feel The Divine Love

This is my home

With the sounds of roaming waves in my ears

And the smell of seaweed and salt on my skin

I am alive!

My God

My Creator

Speaks to me here

His power and Her stillness

Is shown to me

On the wings of The Eagle

My spirit soars high

Over warm sandy beaches

Dangerous cliff sides

And peaceful rainforests

That live and breathe

As we do.

March 22-2007

Not feeling so great today....feeling a little discouraged about everything. So, I am walking gently through today. Had a good cry this morning. The boys and I took the dog for a walk in the cool spring morning, which felt good. I am getting the laundry done and bought myself a bottle of red wine. Perhaps I will savour a glass this afternoon.

Why am I feeling so sad?

I had the best time with Steve on our little getaway last week. We really are kindred spirits and such good friends. What makes me sad is as soon as we left that environment he feels so distant, like we can't be friends anymore. I feel like other things, job and finances come before our relationship. Now this may not be true. It just feels like that.

March 30-2007

Feeling not so great about myself today, struggling.

Giving it over to God...get me through this day and use me as you see fit.

Today I choose to live freely in God's Light.

To love my children, husband, and friends. To live in peace.

...You see what you want to see

My struggle is deep inside of me...

There were so many entries like these. Pushing and pulling myself through the day, feeling the heaviness within getting heavier all while keeping up with the momentum of life and the commitments I made. I was involved in MOPS-Mothers of Pre-Schoolers, a Christian-based mothers group. I was involved in my little church on the worship team and facilitating women's events. I was running my own successful business. And I was also being a mom, wife, daughter, and friend. All of this kept me busy and on the move. I felt like I was a part of something bigger. The heaviness inside would have to wait.

I gave it attention here and there, but for the most part I hunkered down and soldiered on.

I told myself what I had told myself most of my life, "Just get through it. We will deal with the casualties later…when we have time." But time was running out. The busier I was, the deeper I sank into the abyss of darkness. It was getting harder and harder to move forward. I felt like I was walking in thick mud. All the things I was doing were good things, things that made a difference, things that benefitted my community and others, and things that made the world a better place. But, the one place I needed to put my energy the most was not getting any care or nourishment at all. That place was me, myself, and I.

In the Christian faith, I was taught to be selfless. I was taught to put God first over all things, then others, and then myself. This simple formula was beautiful and made sense. In more common words, it would sound something like this: Let your spiritual practice be the foundation of your life. Look out for and be mindful of those around you. Be a brother or a sister and help those in need, better your communities, and impact the world. Through it all, love yourself, your whole self. For when you love yourself, you honour Creator. When you love yourself, you can more freely love others. When you love yourself, you can love the world with ease. The problem was, where I came from, selflessness meant not thinking of Self at all. I continued to hear that I was nothing without God, that I was a sinner, unclean, and unworthy of God's love. Ultimately, I was inadvertently taught that I could not trust myself. Self-love was not something considered or expressed. The truth was, I was taught the exact opposite.

And so, I began to get tired. I was tired of feeling my body hurt, feeling the heavy sadness, fighting a losing battle, not feeling good enough, running from a broken childhood, and tired of feeling in general. I wanted to disappear. It had moved passed the feeling of wanting death. I did not even want that anymore. I just wanted to disappear, evaporate, and no longer be.

I remember sitting in the front yard with Steve and telling him that I wanted to leave. He thought I meant the marriage at first. I explained to him that I was at the edge of something within me and that my spirit, the energy within, that made me, ME wanted to leave and not do this life anymore. I would still be here physically but the life inside would be dead. What I said scared him. I was scared, too. I had never been to this place before. I needed him to know where I was. I needed to know it mattered to someone that my spirit was dying. As always, he stood by me letting me know he did not fully understand what I was feeling, but that he loved me, was here for me, and did not want me to leave in any capacity.

I heard his words and saw the sincerity and love in his eyes. He was true to his word. I knew that. However, in that moment, it wasn't enough. I think I was already too far gone. I let go. I fell off the cliff, so to speak, and sunk to the bottom of the ocean. What happened in that place of stillness changed my life forever. For it was there, on the deep ocean floor that God/Spirit/Goddess/Divinity/Love met me.

I realize this sounds a little crazy, but it was what I lived. This experience was very real. Within my being, I had let go of what I thought life was. So, I navigated to a place within myself where I could feel nothing. All my life I had felt so much, what felt like too much, and I wanted to feel nothing. Looking back, I realize I wasn't letting go of life, as much as I was letting go of the life I was living. This was my "breakdown."

I had spread myself too thin and was living under a learned notion of doing "God's work," as a way of pleasing Him. So not only had I taken on too much, I was also doing what I was doing within the twisted, very misguided intention of gaining favour with God. I thought I was taking care of what was important in my life, but I was overlooking aspects of my life. I realized that what I saw as success had nothing to do with the spiritually grounded life I was seeking.

Down on the ocean floor within the stillness of my sanctuary, I was met by the most glorious, loving, kindest, most gracious life form ever. And now, because of that encounter, to use the word "God" seems so astronomically small to me. The God I learned about in church was so small, so tiny compared to this force that sat with me. The God I learned about was a boxed God, who sat in the confines of a man-made religion. That was not the God I met at the bottom of the ocean. At the beginning, we just sat in silence, I didn't even care that the Being was there. Yes, I totally disregarded this Divine presence that had come alongside me at the darkest time of my life. And you know what? It was unmoved by my indifference. It was Love, pure Divine Love that sat with me. It needed nothing from me. It wanted nothing from me. It asked for nothing from me. It just was.

Over time a conversation began, a gentle conversation that flowed with the slow current around us. It was here, in this place, that renewal began its slow and gentle process. There was no rush. Love did not push. There were no timelines or what-ifs. There was only the stillness of the ocean and Love, abundant Love. The Voice told me that we could be there as long as I needed. It told me that I was not alone and was already whole. It told me that I was Love, and loved.

Up on the surface, life was still moving as it does. The breakdown had woken up the reality of self-care and nourishment. There remained a strong residue within and around me of the self-loathing actions of my teen years, actions that still plagued me. This residue needed attending. It was time to turn my focus onto myself. This was an uncomfortable thought for someone brought up in an unhealthy world, but even so, I knew what needed to be done. Given the immense love and support I was feeling from The Universe, it was time to attend to the self-abuse of my teen years.

Sept 1-2007

Good morning! We are up in Whistler at John and Carolyn's place to close off the summer. But more importantly today marks the beginning of a 6-month commitment I am making to myself. These next 6 months, I am spending with Spirit and myself. I need to learn to take better care of myself. I am always there for others, but I fear I have neglected part of my own heart and soul. On my walk this morning, I concluded that I had to let go of myself…the person of my past, the child within. I need to let her go so she can be free to enjoy all the joyful childhood times she had…not forever be trapped in the darkness of the disappointments and great sadness' of her life. I want her to be free, feel loved, and be at peace so I can have those things fully – I know I have a blessed full life, but it could be even more, and I want to attain that.

When I have friends in need I give them my all and let them know in no uncertain terms that I am there for them. It is time to do that for myself…to take the time to be in relationship with myself and really peel back the layers of ME.

I am doing this by spending a minimum of one hour a day alone with myself, writing in here, or praying and meditating. I have joined a fitness camp to lose some weight and get fit. I commit to eating clean and to be conscious of what I put into my body. I also will be taking part in a daily meditational devotion called "Breathe... Creating Space for God in a Hectic Life" by Keri Wyatt Kent. I believe that by creating that specific space to do this I am creating space for myself. I will be honest and open with myself through this process.

Oh yeah, and during this time there will be NO over-extending myself for other things!!! And so it begins, here in Whistler, a new relationship with Me!

September 4, 2007

Ok so this new way of life is going to be a challenge to get onboard with daily. For the last two days, I thought about writing in here and truth be told I could have made the time even though we were up in Whistler. I really could have disappeared for an hour to do the writing but I talked my way around it. There is the "self-sabotage." Not to mention I did not eat the best and through both those things, I felt anxious, overwhelmed, and upset with myself. This of course is the worst cycle to set up for myself. I just have to do this...it is time...I feel that strongly.

So, I did the first chapter already in "Breathe," and I am going to review it right now:

The first exercise talks about reviewing the day.

I would like to start my day fresh with meditation and close it the same way, cleaning out what needs to be let go. I have held onto a lot of stuff. These things I have held onto are the things I hope to work through and let go.

Observations:

I get upset if I am forced to wait when I am in a hurry.

Pressure around time is always in the back of my mind.

I don't feel like I have enough time at the end of a workday.

I don't feel like I have enough time during the day.

I like staying on top of things even if I have to push or deprive myself. I have an expectation of myself that I feel I must fulfill. It affects my health when I don't get proper sleep or, have too much caffeine. Raises in my blood pressure lead to high highs and low lows.

I am not patient with my family and shut my husband out.

Spiritually I do not take the time for enough follow-through with my spiritual practice. I touch on things, but I don't go too deep because I think it takes too much time.

When I think about how I feel about my kids, the love overwhelms me. They are the jewels of my life. I feel honoured and blessed to be their mom. They make me laugh, cry, and be a better person. They are a huge source of motivation in my life. Without them, I would not be complete.

When I think that I am loved even more than that, it blows my mind.

To increase the margins of my life, I am doing this meditation, taking up a regular exercise program, eating clean, loving myself, and cleaning myself out emotionally, spiritually, and physically.

It was during this very tender time that I gave up some things and never looked back. I became very mindful about the food I put into my body. I sought ways to eat as simply and organically as possible. I was not stringent about it, but very mindful. Even this subtle shift caused great ripples in my well-being. Coffee was something I chose to eliminate from my life. The detox was not fun. There were headaches for days, but oh so worth it. I have never looked back and continue to avoid things with high caffeine content.

I was walking very gently in those days. I found that I was walking between two worlds. Part of me was walking in the "real time" world, taking part in the day-to-day, and doing what needed to be done for my family and me. The other part of me sat at the bottom of the ocean, in the "underworld," unsure if she would ever want to emerge again. Through all of it, I kept moving forward. It was very slow, but I was moving. This meant making decisions based on where I was at any given moment. These decisions felt very difficult at the time. I knew that some of them would let other people down.

September 8-2007

(Back story: on Sept. 5th we, as a family, drove to Nelson to attend Steve's grandma's, his father's mother's, funeral. After which all of us...his mom and dad, sister and her family, and our family trekked off to Kamloops to spend a day with mom's family.)

Our plan was to go home today, but the kids really wanted to stay another night. It is not often that we are all together here in this way. Steve and I were both undecided due to an "End-of-the-Summer BBQ Bash" at the church we are attending. For myself, the more I think about going home the more I feel the walls close in. It is more to do with the obligations and expectations. I know that we could have pulled it off and it would be fine. But being here with Steve's family feels important, too. Timing might be a little off but I do feel this is a good idea to stay. I also know that I am on the right track with my plan for the next 6 months. There are some things I have been putting off and now is the time to get real, deal, heal, and feel. At the Letting Go Ceremony during the camping trip with "The Moon Sisters," I am going to let go of the pressure that I take on from other people's expectations of me. I am scared of what is going on with me BUT...I also know that this is necessary. This is the time. I am so blessed, and it's time to clean out the inner closet some more and live an even better life of freedom. I want to set that example for my children to take time out in their lives to spend time in spirit, to love and be loved. I am starting to learn to live that way and pray to pass that on to my kids. I no longer want to live in anger and frustration, worry and fear. Those emotions suck the good stuff away. Life will bring tribulations and hard times. I know to embrace these times now that I want to live that knowledge. I know there is a lot of wisdom inside of me. I know that the divine walks with me. It is up to me to share my knowledge with those around me. Sometimes, well more than sometimes, we are confused as to what is productive. We use the human definition of productivity, but what if that is not Spirit's definition. I often go back to the story of the woman in the temple who gave only a few coins equalling less than a penny, while others around her were proudly giving sacks of gold. Jesus said monetarily she gave the least. However, with her heart, she gave the most. Maybe the time has come to evaluate my expectations of myself. Thank you, Creator, for this time. You have richly blessed me. I am forever grateful.

My Purpose:
To let people know
That God/Spirit/The Creator is more than a church,
and more than a religion.
LOVE is purer than all those things.

September 11-2007

Well over a week and it definitely has been a challenge to write in here. Back into real life and feeling overwhelmed, tapped out, and disconnected. Not so good. I went to bed feeling bad and woke up the same way. My heart hurts. I just want to feel better and I just don't have the strength to handle a lot right now. It is so hard to feel so broken down and unable to do just the smallest things.

September 17 -2007

Today was a good day from beginning to end. I started Cardio Boot Camp today and loved it. I was nervous, BTW, I am on a mission for myself—feeling good— that's the goal. Being a calm, centered mom—that's the goal. Today was a good day!

I was beginning a new way of life. I was focused on simplicity and slowing things down, but these things take time to really sink into life. One of my mom friends from MOPS had decided to make a similar change in her life, so I went to speak with her about it and hear her story. This helped me stay the course. Living in a world that was moving quickly around me, was a constant challenge to get off the "crazy train" and just breathe. Looking back now, I see what a one-day-at-a-time these kinds of changes are.

…When I am at peace, it is so easy to see Love and feel it within and around me. I also see now I had to read BREATHE to be able to begin my own book, I pray that my book lets people see the God I know.

I am being called to simplify, without a doubt. Divine love pulls me out of the mire of life that I get myself tangled up in. Giving to others/ loving others is an important part of walking in the Light but it is not the only thing. I realize that on a deep level. I was not giving myself what I needed to be deeply fed. The balance for myself was not there. I guess I had hoped someone would be there to give it to me, but in truth I was, and am, the only one to do that for myself. I have worked hard for things in my life; not material things but emotional things. There has been a lot of success. I feel right now that God has charged me to rest, slow down, take care of some personal things, and enjoy some of the fruits of my labours.

September 25-2007

Yesterday started out well but ended badly. Feeling very overwhelmed. I started sobbing. Steve was at a loss and got frustrated. I became defensive and we argued. Not good.

I just could not get it together. By the end of the day, I was exhausted. Right now, I have to be so careful and diligent to what I eat, drink, and do with my time. I am so fragile and vulnerable. Two things I have a HARD time being. But at the same time I know that this is all happening for a reason. I must surrender to this. I must let go and walk this strange road for the benefit of those around me and myself. I love my family, this much is true. I first and foremost want to be the best I can be for them.

My command is this: "Love each other as I have loved you." ~Jesus

September 29, 2007

Well I am learning to say, "NO." I have turned some new clients away, not taken on a new job with MOPS, and stuck to Boot Camp. Next week I cut out bread. I have cut out coffee, diet pop, and now bread. My whole schedule has changed. I rise early and go to bed early. The road has not been easy. I feel pretty raw and am really facing some heavy stuff.

October 2, 2007

The journey continues to simplify my life. Some days are good... others...not so much. But through it all, I feel blessed, loved, and thankful because I am living a real life, a life of ups and downs, and truly full. Growth is hard and struggle sucks but living a real life makes it worth it all.

These were the hardest months. One day I remember walking with some mom-friends. I was slammed with a feeling of desperation. I buckled over, feeling like I could not take one more step. The tears came. I stood there doubled over until I could pull myself back together. Now, many years later, I realize that much of what was happening was a crumbling of the old. It was a transformation into the new. When I think of transformation of any kind, there are aspects that cannot remain as they are. There must be a death to make way for a new life. I recognized this time as a time of "Hanging on the meat hook" as my teacher, guide, sister, and friend, Pixie Lighthorse speaks of so well in the sanctuary of SouLodge. I will share more about SouLodge later in the book, but for now I will explain. "Hanging on the meat hook" is a metaphor for when you decide to leave all the comfort of what you know to go within and face the demons and dungeons. By doing so you welcome awakening and enlightenment in its truest forms, bringing yourself closer to God, Spirit, the Universe, and Self. This concept is taken from an ancient myth about the goddess Inanna. She decided to leave her world of glory and comfort, a world in which it would seem she had all she could ever want, to take the ultimate journey down into the Under World. It is in this place she comes to face her dark side, which slams up against her with judgement and insult. Even though she had come with protection, it all gets stripped away. She is reduced to a piece of rotting flesh hanging from a meat hook. After three days, which seems more like a lifetime, the restoration cycle begins. Ironically, for myself, it was about three months that I lived in full physical, mental, and emotional pain.

Focus on the blessings that you have
Do not long for what you do not have

Live your value
Live your intent
Live your purpose

During this time, one of the biggest decisions I made was to look for my biological mom one more time. Soon I was going to be 40 years old. It was important to me to put this longing to rest. My motivation had moved beyond a young girl who wanted to know where she came from to that place of a woman and mother who did not want another woman to suffer in guilt for what had transpired so many years ago. When I thought of my biological mom, I felt there was much sadness and grief. I wanted to relieve her of that if I could. So I began the process of sending away for my registration of live birth, not knowing what it would bring.

November 9 -2007

Well the last 36 hours of my life have been, well I cannot even put it into words. On Wednesday, I received my sealed registration of life birth. On it read my given name at birth, my biological mom's full name, and where she lived...This was how the 36 hours kicked off, and it has been a whirlwind ever since...

The whirlwind was due to the "coincidences" that all came to pass because of this one little paper. I was born in a town about 30 minutes away from where I live now. This I did know. But my parents had come down from the north, 15 hours away to pick me up when I was three weeks old. I grew up in the north only to move to the lower mainland with my parents in my 12th year of school. After my dad died, Steve and I moved back to the town my mom was living in. It was the same one we live in now, 30 minutes from where I was born. Through my document of birth, I saw that in fact my biological mom had lived in the very town I now lived in.

I called one of my girlfriends to share the news with her not thinking about the fact that her husband's family had already lived in our town for many generations. After hearing the information, she decided to ask her husband if the name was familiar, who in turn asked his dad. He gave my bio-mom's name to his dad and asked if he recognized it. His dad told him that not only did he recognize it, but also he knew the woman it belonged to because this woman had been his sister's best friend during high school. Later in life, my bio-mom's husband would work for my friend's husband's father. Yes, did you get that? From this place, things unravelled quickly.

Within 36 hours, I knew where my bio-mom had lived with her husband. I learned that they moved away one year before I moved here as a teen. I learned they had eventually divorced, and she was now remarried. And most importantly and amazingly, I found out that I had a sister who was seven years younger than me. As I go over this information, it is still amazing how that one phone call to a friend changed an entire world for me.

My girlfriend's husband became my Private Investigator and found my bio-mom's phone number and address for me. I opted to write a letter first because I had no idea where things were for her, or if her husband or daughter knew about me. I figured that a letter would be a little easier to take than a direct call. Weeks passed. I heard nothing.

Dec 7, 2007

A week has passed. My birthday came and went without any word from my bio-mom. The weekend was lovely all the same, probably one of my best birthdays ever. Very bitter sweet, for though there is this sad situation happening, I am getting stronger and better day-by-day. Healing is happening through all that I am doing, and I feel the shifts and transformations that are happening within and around me. My Private Investigator was even more disappointed! He asked if he could poke around a little more, and I gave him the go ahead. Thank goodness for that! It was through his determination that we found out we had the wrong phone number and address! He found all the right information, passed it onto me, and told me in no uncertain terms, to call her. So, after a quick call to a soul-sister and some encouragement from Steve, I called the number...and for the first time talked to the woman who gave birth to me 39 years ago. It was the craziest and most surreal moment of my life. And the best thing was she was happy, so happy I had called. My bio-mom's mother had forced her to give me up. It was not something she had wanted to do.

It was an exceptional way to end the year. It was a year that had blown my world and my Self wide open. It was a tough year, one of the most difficult, but one that would catapult my journey back to myself. And I finally connected with the woman who gave me life, which would be an important piece to my journey.

"Re-examine all you have been told in school or church or in any book, and dismiss whatever insults your soul; and your very flesh shall be a great poem and have the richest fluency, not only in words, but in the silent lines of its lips and face between the lashes of your eyes, end in every motion and joint of your body."
~ Walt Whitman

6
Inspirations

At the end of the year, I completed *Breathe*. Upon completion, I wrote a mission statement. I took that statement with me into the New Year and held it as my rock. When I wrote it, I used the language of that time in my life.

> *I am to be a light in this world,*
> *A light of God's love.*
> *This light should reflect in the way I parent,*
> *In the type of wife I am,*
> *And in the type of friend.*
> *It should shine in all aspects of my life*
> *Both personal and professional.*

In the language I use today, I would say....

> I am a Light in this world
> A Light of Divine Love
> This Light reflects in all that I do
> And shines in all aspects of my life.

This mission statement did not come from somewhere outside of me. It came from a sacred place within me, a place where Divinity touches lies. It is a place that is within each of us. I still stand with this statement. It has morphed along with me, serving me as I am in every moment.

The year's end had been so much about turning my attention toward Self and my needs. One of the things I brought into my life was joining a book club. I love to read, but I had forgotten this joy. As a young teen I read a lot, going to the library every second Saturday leaving with a stack books. It was my escape. Bringing reading back into my life fed my soul. The literature that was coming my way through my book club was nourishing my mind and heart.

One of my favorite books was *Lessons in Becoming Myself* by Ellen Burstyn. It was a very personal memoir of her life as a child coming out of a severely abusive childhood, her job as an actress, growing older, and her spiritual journey through it all. She shows how we can find the truth of whom we are no matter how our lives begin. Truth has no boundaries and is found within each of us.

This book oozed with richness and wisdom. Thank you, Ms. Burstyn, for writing your heart. I have heard it said that memoirs are a reflection of one's conceit for oneself. It is someone believing his or her story is so important it needs to be in a book. Is this a bad thing? This story affected my life and I am grateful. My thought is that every story is worth a book, or at least to be shared and heard one time. For we all have stories that are wanting and needing to be told. The offering is equally as important as the receiving. I am grateful and in awe of those who have the courage to answer the call to do so.

Another lovely piece of wisdom that Ms. Burnstyn shares in the book is something she gathered from one of her Sufi teachers, Dr. Elahi also known as Shah Bahram. He explained to her, and the group she was studying with, how to recognize a real teacher. He explained that a real teacher is a living example of what he or she is teaching. When a real teacher tells you that you must do something, it is because they themselves are already doing it. And a real teacher's teachings will be evident in the people around them. As Jesus said, 'By his fruits you will know him.'

February was the month I met my biological mom and sister face-to-face for the first time. We were all meeting in Kamloops where my sister lived. Just before we left to drive up there, a huge snowstorm hit the highway we were taking. I did not care. We were getting up there come hell or high water, or in this case high snow. As we drove up, the snowdrifts were six feet plus on either side of the highway, but nothing was keeping me from this meeting. ....

They were waiting for me at my sister's house. Excitement, trembled through my veins as I got ready and the smile would not leave my face. I had carefully picked out clothing that reflected who I was, because I wanted them to know me, to see me. I was feeling nervous. I remember needing to focus on keeping my breath steady as I drove across the bridge, toward my sister's house. Would they like me? Would there be a connection? Would we be alike in anyway? These were some of the questions that I was trying to put at ease. At this point, the truth was it really didn't matter. This was happening. So, I stepped up to the front door, over flowing with emotions and knocked…

When my sister, Rhonda, opened the door, it was love at first sight. We hugged and cried. It was an easy transition into sisterhood for us. It happened in that moment when our eyes met. Stepping into the house, I looked around to see my biological mom, Carol, standing in the middle of the living room watching her daughters embrace for the first time ever. It was clear to see she was frozen in so many of her own emotions so I went to her. We embraced with tears falling down our cheeks. Without a thought I asked her, "Do you feel guilty?" Unable to speak she nodded, yes. I proceeded to tell her that she did not have to feel guilty. It was understood that her choice had been made for her and I was not angry. It was time for the guilt she was carrying to be released.

We sat for hours talking, laughing, crying, and laughing some more. We each took great pleasure in hearing how our laughs were so distinctly alike. There was a lot of howling around that. Questions were asked and stories told. The time of my conception, pregnancy, and birth were a difficult time for Carol. The pain and grief she went through was evident to me and my sister as she shared that time with us.

There is much of that day that will remain private. For this story does not belong to only me. I will tell you that we were so engrossed in storytelling and listening that we completely forgot to go for lunch. I will also say that it was a very positive reunion. We each realized how lucky we were that it had gone so well between the three of us. One thing that stood out to all of us that day, was our personalities. My personality was more like Carol's than Rhonda, even though Carol had raised Rhonda. Indeed, genetics play a huge part in our makeup, and yet, I have qualities from my mom who raised me as well. So there I was, witnessing and living nurture and nature walking together.

A month later was Carol's birthday and a thought came to me, that perhaps she would like to have both of her daughters visit for her birthday. I ran the thought by my sister first, and she thought it was a great idea. We called our mom to let her in on our plan and she was thrilled. Rhonda and I were there for two nights. We enjoyed our uninterrupted time together. Being at Carol's home and a home that Rhonda had lived in allowed me a visual of them that helped me further get to know who they were. I was shown photo albums, pictures on the wall, and told more stories. By the time we drove away, I was filled to overflowing.

After dropping off my sister, I started heading home. I had always thought that if I found my biological family, I would be complete and find a place to belong. Driving home that day, looking at the snow-capped(?) mountains and being bathed in the magnificent sunlight shining down on my path, I had the realization that I already had it all. Finding my bio-mom and sister were really added bonuses in my life. They enriched an already rich life. I already had everything I needed within myself, just as I was. This was an amazing and beautiful realization, so much so I pulled over to the side of the rode to text it to a girlfriend. I already had it all, and it took finding what I thought I needed, to realize that I already had exactly what I needed, because what I needed was in me.

Feb. 28, 2008

At the MOPS leadership meeting, last night, the topic of God speaking to us came up. There seemed to be a frustration with the lack of communication between some of the women and God. I found this interesting and the thought came to mind. Do we have so much distrust in ourselves and have so little self-worth that we do not realize how close we are to God?

Another question that arose was: Are we basing God's desire to have a relationship with us on our own personal human desires?

For example:
*If I lose 10 lbs., I will be happy.

*If I have the right hairstyle I'll be happy.

*If I live in this type of home or in this neighborhood, people will like me.

* I need to make this amount of money to feel successful.

We place conditions on ourselves that are meant to fulfill our happiness or make us worthier. My thought is that God knows us better then we know ourselves, loves the whole of us, and is what I have been experiencing.

"The Lord does not look at the things man looks at. Man looks at the outward appearance but the Lord looks at the heart." 1 Samuel 16:7 The Bible

> *Are we striving to perfect the laws holding us back from that personal one-on-one relationship with The Creator?*

In my experience, the closer I walk with God…Divinity, the more is revealed to me because of our active relationship. As the trust grows, I see God's character more and more; and I see that character growing in me. It has been a steady process and one of great consistency. But like in any relationship, it starts with a choice. This choice is to first create the relationship, and then to commit to it.

"Behold, I stand at the door and knock; if anyone hears my voice and opens the door, I will come in to him." Revelations 3:20 The Bible

God is waiting, patiently.

"The Lord is not slow in keeping his promise, as some understand slowness. He is patient with you, not wanting anyone to perish, but everyone to come to repentance." 2 Peter3:9 The Bible

I am thinking that perhaps God is waiting for us to make the choice to enter into a relationship. And it is here, as in all relationships that Divinity will be revealed, as we too will be revealed. Yes, there will be risk involved, trust issues will arise, and even rebellion when you are not ready to hear about your true character and some of the things that need transforming. Some of it may even be painful. But I have experienced that God's love will never ever let you down. It does not want to take. It only wants to give for my highest good. But I do need to step into the flow of the relationship and become an active part of the exchange….

Another book of inspiration came into my life about this time: The Shack…Where Tragedy confronts Eternity by William P. Young. I mentioned this book earlier, describing it as a book for the broken-hearted, in particular those who have been wounded by religion or the religious way of life.

This book was another stepping stone for me, helping me unravel and identify how I saw my relationship with the Divine, not just with God, The Father, but also Jesus and The Holy Spirit. This was the trinity with which I was brought up. Young presents these three characters in a non-traditional way blowing out all religious stereotypes, and I loved it. God shows up as a heavy-set, nurturing black woman named Elousia. Jesus is an unassuming, quiet Middle Eastern man. The Holy Spirit takes the form of a beautiful Asian woman named Sarayu, who calls herself the "Keeper of the Gardens". I loved Young's representation so much. It was not so much how he saw the Holy Trinity, but how he expressed his vision in the book. It invited me to step into a realm of possibility in which the Spiritual came to me in a way that I recognized. not in the way I was told to see it. That was mind shattering in such a necessary, "break the chains" kind of way.

Young's writings also offered me a place where I could feel safe to express the pains of my past, to speak them and not be judged or shut down. *The Shack* represented a place where I could be *human* and Divinity would be in that place with me. I had already experienced this within my breakdown. Young's own personal story confirmed what I was beginning to believe. It did not matter how messy, dirty, angry, hurt, confused, or unknowledgeable I was. I was loved, and God, Jesus, and the Holy Spirit would, and did, come to me in ways that I could see and feel clearly.

This book also gave me a title for the season I was walking in. I came to call this time in my life "The Time of the Great Sadness." By giving it a name, it felt like it was more containable somehow. Looking back, I also see that naming it as a way of honouring this time. This was a very real and pain-filled time. The "Time of Sadness" helped me hold onto perspective as I traversed an unknown land, while having a piece of me still in the land I knew.

By reading *The Shack,* I rediscovered the characters of Love that where already residing in my being. I discovered that it is not Love that grows within us, but a "knowing of love" that grows. Even when I felt most alone, I learned how Love is with me, and Love means not being alone. I remembered that emotions are the "colours of the soul." Without emotions our world, my world would be dull and colourless. I was not destined for a colourless life.

I read this book several times. Each time, I was gifted a new message or new insight. As it is with good books, one goes back to savour the goodness again and again. When I saw Mr. Young speak at Regency College, the man moved me. He was true to his heart, while being open and honest with his story. He showed an authentic willingness to teach and learn. In my opinion, we need more men like this. Men who are not afraid to lay out their humanness and be honest about their personal journey of life.

Another inspiration that came to me was a woman's workshop called "Hearts Restored" led by a vibrant, passionate woman named Jodie Duek. She was a friend of a friend. A local group of women and I decided to take the journey to attend this Christian, twelve-week workshop. The intention of this workshop was to deepen one's relationship with God and heal the pain of the past through the love of Jesus. It would prove to be the next season of my unravelling.

HEARTS RESTORED…My Journey

Wednesday, April 2:

I was driving through the parking lot at school. Right after dropping off Nathen, a great sorrow came up from inside me, and I began to sob uncontrollably. I couldn't breathe. I couldn't talk. Deep, gut-wrenching sobs with a stream of tears poured down my face. Aiden in the backseat said, "Mommy are those happy tears?" I needed to get out of that parking lot NOW. I called out, "Dangerously on the edge God, dangerously on the edge! Please have someone call me…I am in trouble here." Within seconds my phone rang. It was my dear sweet friend, "Cat are you okay?" I couldn't speak. I could barely breathe. She asked again if I was okay, and I managed to get out a "No." After a deep breath, I was able to say, "Dangerously on the edge, dangerously on the edge!" Then, I burst into tear-filled laughter as I pulled to the side of the road.

Thus, my journey began. It was what happened the day before that brought this on. We had a church meeting. Three ladies, including myself, brought a new idea for a woman's ministry to the group, which was not very welcomed. The resolution was that we would put together a presentation and see if it was something that would "fit" into the plan and direction of the church. The air became very thick. The tension in the room made itself known. This whole situation brought up feelings of self-doubt and no one hearing me. The sorrow that came over me the morning after was a realization and an acknowledgment of the hurt left over from being discarded and unheard as a child.

So as I "go in" and embark on this journey with "Hearts Restored," I'm not cleaning out my closet, which has already been done. No this time I am going for the attic above the closet. In the attic, there is nothing but one cardboard box. In that box is my biggest challenge. It is the challenge of how I feel about myself. I need to apply God's love to my life. I am more than willing to love others, but how I feel about myself stops me from honouring myself. In a practical way, this looks like me looking at myself as a precious Child of God. In the silence of my mind and the deepness of my heart of solitude, I know it…I believe it. I am a precious Child of God.

I am ready to deal with myself. My desire is to peel back layers that keep me from being all that I am meant to be. I am ready to release the masks I wear for protection. I am ready to look within and give my life back to myself in full. Seeing myself not though my scars but through my Creator's eyes. I want to peel off the layers placed on me by others and live free.

In the box, I laid, broken, forgotten, and alone. I am so sad for that part of me, and yet not sad enough to deal with her. I, myself have minimized her feelings, my feelings. "Push on, push through, no time to go there" has been my mantra.

This time has been a reflection of how I am toward others due to "The Great Sadness." I have made myself feel better by making others small. I have been opinionated, judgmental, and full-of-ego. These are the things I wish to shift.

One of the first things we did after writing why we were attending "Hearts Restored" was to go back into our family of origin. This was not a fun task, but I knew it was a necessary one. As I write this, I cannot help but think of the damage secrets and lies do to the soul. The family of secrets was my family. My mom would argue that everyone has secrets, and she would be right. However, that truth does not make secrets right, good, or productive. Especially not when they are accompanied with lies and distorted truths.

My father was abusive in his rage. My hatred and distain for him did not start with his treatment of me. It was in watching him hurt my brothers and sister and making my mother cry. It was terrible. I never hated him for doing it to me. At a young age, I was already inconsequential. I didn't matter. My feelings were null and void. It's so sad to think about how little I thought of myself. My family now is blown apart. Riddled with battle scares and untended wounds.

-Last week's teachings brought out all the different faces of God, and I am still absorbing all the Love.

-I learned that God <u>wants</u> to be there for me. This is "His" desire, not "His" job.

-In my head, I know God's gift of Love for me, but I have yet to completely believe.

-I thought God was waiting for me to fix everything first, before taking me into His family.

-I do not trust God, yet I have felt a Holy presence, thus the confusion.

"I don't want to waste my time living on the outside.
I'm going to live by the inside out."

By choosing to go into the attic of my psyche and open the box that was in there, I unraveled a story of pain that had been neatly tucked away. As hard as it was to do, it was also revealing and freeing. I saw myself now walking my younger-self through the sadness and pain. Now I could be there for me. I could walk myself through it all with the full knowing of the Creator's Love and plan for me. In the safe container of "Hearts Restored," I was restoring my view of God. I was still within the confines of Christianity, but this was very forward-thinking Christianity that allowed me to expand just that much more. I was being taught bible-based truths that were renewing my power and being. These truths were unraveling the lies and mistruths of my childhood teachings one chain at a time.

As I moved forward on my healing journey, the Divine Voice was coming to me more frequently. I was in a store buying some gifts, when my eyes fell on a fridge magnet that read, "Daughter Bless your heart for the happiness you put in mine."

"Buy it" were the words whispered in my ear. I reached out to take it, but told myself, "no." Then I heard it again, *"Buy the magnet. It is how I feel about you. This is a gift to you from me, so you might always know how much I love you."* I was still not sure, but I bought the magnet. The moment I did, I knew the words I heard were true. That magnet still hangs on my fridge, reminding me of the Divine connection that is Love.

Fathers Day, June 15, 2008

On Sunday morning, I did my usual thing of walking up to Starbucks to get a coffee and read my book before meeting with the rest of the band at church for practice. After reading for a while, I called a girlfriend to have a morning chat. It was during this time that "The Voice" told me to tell her about her dad's love for her, regardless of how messed up, dysfunctional, and hurtful his way was. He did love her. He loved her the best he could. This was overwhelming for her to hear, but I had to say it. When we hung up, "The Voice" said to me, "Now say the same thing to yourself," That was a really powerful moment. I never acknowledged my Dad's love for me before. In that moment, I recognized my own walls, my own shack that I had placed around my heart because of the lie that I had believed about not being loved or worthy of love. I believed that my dad did not, in fact, love me. To him, I was a hindrance, a problem. So I believed that it would not be far-fetched for others to feel the same. This was a HUGE moment of awakening.

Forgiveness-that has been a tough one. What does that look like? What does that mean? I had trouble with the difference between forgiveness and validation.

But I see that forgiveness is more than just a feeling. It is a choice.

I forgive those in my life who have hurt me.

Most of all I forgive myself for how hard I've been on myself.

I forgive myself for not accepting myself for who I am.

Forgiveness does set us free.

"Hearts Restored" brought me back to the beginning, before everything went wrong. I went back to the place where I unfolded out of the Creator's hands. In that moment, I looked into Creator's eyes and saw the love and the purpose for my being. Nothing that had happened from that point had taken that love away. The love, admiration, and joy that I saw the day I came into being was all still there. I had just forgotten. I had forgotten that I was blessed, free, a saint, Love's child, established to the end, chosen, raised up with love, and seated in divine places, and that I shall do great things through Love. I forgot that I was beloved.

June 25, 2008

My journey through Hearts Restored has been so, so good. It has been such an awakening and an integration of who I am. I will miss Jodi's teachings and look forward to when I take the course again.

I love my life and those whom God has blessed me with…the darkness is lifting, even from the corners and the secret spots. I am learning to live free in love and light!

My Vision Prayer

I am ready to put all fear aside and do all that you have created me to be.

I will be calm and direct, and Spirit will go before me and guide the way.

You have spoken to me, and I believe in your words.

My longing is to give all the love you have given to me to others.

You have taken me from the darkness and brought me into the light.

I want you to use me to give the same to others to be your vessel, to be your light.

My prayer tonight was a prayer of vision, clarity of vision, and you have brought me to the place of revealing to me the next season of my journey with you, which is to share your love with others.

You have healed me and made me new.

You have taken the old and washed her clean and brought her back to me the beautiful child you created.

I have a peace that surpasses all understanding.

The story is no longer the driving force behind me. Now, it is the love and the light, and the peace that is only found in your Love.

You silently move passed it all but with much intention.

Spirit is ever-moving, ever-changing to enable people to recognize it.

Spirit does not see colour, race, or social status.

Spirit sees a soul in which it can dwell, teach, and guide.

It moves in and out desiring to be one with all creation.

I see a wall of red fire, solid before me.

It is the power of Spirit asking me to step into it,
and though it is red-hot fire

I am not afraid and my flesh does not burn.

Instead I feel the fire of Spirit's power.

I feel the great warmth of love that inflames it.

I am in the middle of the wall, totally surrounded by fire,
and I am still.

The next read was to inspire and open my awareness just that much further: *A New Earth* by Eckhart Tolle. I thoroughly enjoyed my Sunday mornings at Starbucks reading this book. I took my time to absorb each chapter. I savoured every bite and did not rush to chew through the information. So much wisdom sat on my tongue, melting into my taste buds, and becoming a part of me. Truly this book was a buffet for a starving soul, looking for a deeper truth. So much of my gathering had been in the place of the Christian world. I was excited, and oh so ready, to branch passed this institution and learn more of what was beyond its walls.

A New Earth brought with it a language that was familiar to my heart and spirit. When I read Mr. Tolle's wise words, I felt my wings spread. My spirit lifted. There were no chains binding his words, no expectations. He pulled from many different spiritual practices, incorporating them all within his teachings. This opened a new possibility for me, one I was not sure I was "allowed," but felt so called to follow.

July 11, 2008

During the last few weeks, I finished The New Earth. It was an amazing book full of deep spiritual instruction. It is an excellent book, and I would read it again. Now I am beginning to read a book by Sue Monk Kidd, The Dance of the Dissident Daughter and already I am drawn in. For my life, I want my spirit to soar. I want to share that freedom I have found. I recognize that in organized religion, I feel trapped, held down, and oppressed. I am uncertain about my place in my little church. I am feeling more like a traditional Baptized woman serving coffee and meals. Of course there is a time and place for that, but the burning in my heart lends to something more!

Moving from *The New Earth* to *The Dance of the Dissident Daughter* felt like a seamless flow. While Mr. Tolle gave me a masculine voice to learn from, Ms. Monk offered me the feminine. Both offered me spiritual guidance and instruction within their own experiences. This was life giving to my hungry soul.

In *Dance of the Dissident Daughter* Sue Monk Kidd writes about living without inner authority. To me, her meaning allows me to live in the fear of not living up to what others have deemed "proper" behavior for a woman. With that, Ms. Kidd had my attention, my full attention. This book would take me deep into the sacred feminine. What had once been but a weak whisper was now ready and waiting to be awakened. This book would be the book of all books for me. Ms. Kidd's own journey was one to which I could relate. She understood the hold of church and religion, the fears of breaking away, the backs that turn on you, and the judgment. I would later describe it as being forced to leave your tribe. The tribe, the village within which you had grown up, only to be condemned to never return. Once I read this book, there was no going back...ever.

July 27, 2008

As I look over all I have learned in the last year, I see that clearly many spiritual institutions are saying the same things. I know that everyone wants to be right, but honestly does it matter? If we are all striving for the same things, would we not be stronger unified? Would we not honour our Creator and ourselves far more in unity rather than in division? Ultimately the goal is to prepare for the next life, to not get caught up in this one. To live free, walking in Love and Light toward what lies beyond. If we get stuck in being right or being the superior belief, how is that beneficial to our walk? Does God have joy seeing us exclude his other children because we have judged them on culture, race, or religion? Does God take pleasure in seeing us "one up" each other? My thought would be, No.

God has created us each with a universal truth in our hearts. It is up to us to find that truth and live it. The truths may differ. I don't believe God's plan is for everyone to be the same. This is reveled to us through the diversity in creation, nature, and the individuality of people.

What if God wants us to not dominate the world but only to live the truth that has been placed in our hearts when we were created? Something to think about...

July 31, 2008

Today reading Ms. Monks book I realized that "goddess" is just a word. It is a word that describes the divine feminine. My own thought is there are so many things in which I have been looking for permission to believe. These are beliefs that have been written on my heart since the beginning of time. And now, through this book, they have found me once again...or perhaps they have never left. I have simply rediscovered them.

The dreams and visions were increasing. I dreamt of being pregnant with a daughter. In my dream, I was four months pregnant. It was a sister that pointed out I would be "giving birth" around my 40th birthday. I came to the understanding that the baby girl I dreamt about, represented my Self. I was gestating to rebirth another aspect of myself that had been lost and hiding. Now I recognize this process as a kind of soul retrieval. Soul Retrieval is the collecting of the fragments of one's soul that leaves the psyche due to trauma.

Something else had changed as well. The Voice, the Spirit that had come to walk with me, guide me, and council me had revealed her name to me. It was Arlene. It would not be until later that she would reveal her form to me.

I was entering the world of "The Great Mystery."

August 13, 2008

Summer is slowly coming to an end. It has been an amazing summer. When I look at last summer last year, I have truly enjoyed this summer so much more. Last year, I was at the bottom of the ocean and quite content to stay there. It was there that God met me. Now, I realize it was Arlene, my Spirit guide, who met me there. I did not recognize her at the time, but I do now. She came down, met me in that dark, quiet place and has walked me through this last year. Now I am flying. What a miracle, what a rebirth!

Too be a woman is a blessing
To acknowledge the Divinity within is everything
To open my heart
Setting me free
And raising me up
To be all I can be

~Catherine Beerda-Basso August 25-2008

August 26, 2008

The full moon is coming, and I feel tired. Nature is pulling me into her. I feel the need to be by the ocean...Tofino is calling me. I need some time on my own. I manage to grab some moments by reading or writing, but I need more. I need to have a weekend of solitude.

Things were stirring within me and moving more quickly with every turn. Realizations of blockages were coming to the forefront. My divine power had been awakened and was rooting in. There was no doubt that I was on my way and though the path was strange and new, yet familiar in some way. I knew where I was heading. Every step brought me closer to my true nature, the woman I was born to be, myself. My view of a Father God had been healed. Now I was given a view of a Mother God. Possibilities in this new awakening were coming to life. My spiritual perspective grew. These were exciting times.

Alongside my awakening, came the responsibilities of work, home, and family. September brought something new around the house. This was the year we decided to give homeschooling a try for our oldest son. He had been asking for years and even after a successful grade 8 year, he was still asking. I was terrified and excited all in one. I really had no idea what I was doing, but I was willing to give it a try. If it meant he could find some peace with learning and have a chance to explore his strengths and talents, I was in.

School had been a struggle for The Young Blood. We started to see signs of anxiety in grade 3. From there, it just got progressively worse. There was many a dark night that we spent unraveling his anxieties. We had to make many choices for him that did not fit into the norm. We went with him into those dark places and held up the lantern for him to find his way out. We walked a fine line of consequence and understanding for his unique wiring. As he became older, a close yet distant eye was kept on him. I was determined not to be the mother who came home to find her son hanging in the closet, because he could not take it anymore.

When my son and I look back at this adventure of homeschooling, we are surprised we survived without killing one another. We laugh about it often. For him, it was not what he expected. Being away from his friends and stuck at home with his parents all day was not what he thought it would be. There were cherished times and awesome memories of shared time with family, but they were not enough to have him fall in love with homeschooling. He was back in public school for the remainder of his high school career.

As I wrapped up reading *The Dance of the Dissident Daughter*, another book found its way into my hands via my book club. *The Red Tent* by Anita Diamant would be my next inspiration. It was another rich read for wise women everywhere. It delved deep into the ancient, sacred world of women, and the lives they lived. It was so different from the way we conduct ourselves and connect with one another today. A fantastic, mesmerizing read and another place for me to further nurture and embrace the sacred feminine within.

I ended the year reading *The End of Religion* by Bruxy Cavey. This book was not part of the sacred feminine energy of the books I had been reading and because of that I never finished it. What I did read in that book served to enlighten and validate that I was not the only person longing for something more than what religion seemed to offer. Mr. Cavey had the courage to not only say out loud what I felt, but to be so bold as to put these words into print without being struck down by the lightning of God's wrath. Truly, it was a miracle! He used the context of the Bible to support his speculations, which also showed that the slightest shift of perspective in all things could make words look completely different.

Mr. Cavey bravely writes about the religious methods of rules and guilt to keep people burdened with the shame of not being good enough. It is a constant reminder to them of their dirty sinner's status. He also touched on the repeated pattern of "death, divide, and fight." This is the pattern that can be found throughout religious history. There is a disagreement of theology, which causes a death within the existing congregation. That death brings division. Once you divide, you fight those who do not agree with you, and that fight can be both physical and emotional.

These words were the kind of words that fueled an already burning fire within me. This fire burned away notions with which I had been brought up. It allowed me to see with different eyes and enabled me to clearly hear the truth of my heart. It is not an easy thing to go against what you know. It is difficult to not only question, but pull away from what you have been inundated with all your life. But the heart is strong. It's longing is powerful. I was unable to deny the ache of my heart's hidden desire any longer.

When The Young Blood and I had a chance to take a pilgrimage to Medellin Colombia with an organization named Seeds of Love and Hope International Society, it was the greatest inspiration of the year. We helped with the construction of a new community center for one of the ghetto areas of the city. My son was 14 years old. For both of us, it was an eye-opening and heart-opening experience. It was here that I saw the form of Jesus for the first time with my own eyes. I had a clear, vivid vision of him on the hillside surrounded by the children of the community. He looked up at me and said, "Catherine, you can always find me here." I finally realized what he meant by this vision of Love. His purpose was to walk, and stand with the broken. His heart was for those who were discarded, thrown away, and forgotten, just as it was when he walked the earth.

The day we walked through the hillside community, I wept as I saw the homes and brokenness in which these children lived. You can see this on TV as many times as you like, but nothing prepares you for seeing it with your own eyes, smelling the smells, and touching the pain with your own heart. To experience it all with my full senses was nothing I could have anticipated.

When faced with the reality of generational poverty, displacement, and the brokenness of war, perspective comes quickly to one who lives in such obvious privilege. This trip shifted something in me forever. I have returned to the same center many times. The women and children have become my "other" family. They keep me grounded in gratitude for the life I live, and the humbling honour of being a part of their lives.

And so it was, the year ended in the rawness of realization, the realness of urgency, and truths that could no longer be denied. My road was changing drastically in a way that I had not expected. However, I clearly knew, I was accepting it.

· ·

"Today you are not asked to change in order to become a better version of yourself. You are free to simply let go of what isn't You. Free to let go of what isn't magnificent and beautiful. Free to delight in the nakedness of You. The beauty and excellence of You. The fullness of You."
~ Metta Drum

7
Breaking Open

I was leaving my church…. I was leaving *The* church.

After months of struggling with myself, I knew what I had to do. It was a decision I made on my own and for myself. I let Steve decide what he wanted to do. I would honour that decision, as he was honouring mine. During the last six months, or so, there was a lot of unrest within the core group of our little church. A sense of desperation and lack was bubbling to the surface. Numbers and productivity were becoming the focus: how many new members, how many baptisms happening each month, etc. I would describe it as the profits were becoming far more important than the goodness of the product. We were being told that we needed to prove our productivity to our supporters. We needed to look and act a certain way to be acceptable. Over time, we were slowly and subtly moving away from the safe intimacy that this church community once offered. We were heading into a place that felt far away from Love. After much reflection and prayer, a vision came to me. It was one that mirrored the situation of the Titanic. Warnings were made of the trouble ahead, but those warnings were not heeded. The crash inevitably happened. The ship could not sustain the impact and began to sink. The lifeboats were there, to give life and that is what I chose. By making that choice, to have life, I was seen as a traitor. The exact words said to me were, "If you are not with us, you are against us." Enough said.

My experiences in Colombia were momentous. I came home with a feeling to make some drastic changes and one of those changes was for me to step away from the church community. It no longer held the vision it once had and no longer coincided with my heart's desire. I did not want to be part of an institution. I wanted to be part of a thriving community and an ebb and flow way of life. A life where I could walk on a hillside free of the walls of organized religion. This life started within me and flowed out from that sacred God place. The foundations my life had been built on where cracking, breaking, and taking on a new form. I could deny it no longer. I had become weary of trying to pour myself into a mold that clearly was not for me.

I had wanted to...fit in. Fitting in meant "belonging" to me. I had wanted to belong. It seemed that life would be easier if I just fit in. No rocking the boat. No disappointing others, remaining status quo, being a good girl, or being a good sheep blindly following the flock. The truth was that the way of organized religion was not the way of my heart. I would have more situations like this, ones in which I would "sign up" for something only to find out it was not meant for me. It was not until later in my journey that I would discover that I was not created to fit in. By signing up and "failing," I was finding out just who I was. I did not know that back then, but, what I did know was that I had to go where I was being called.

I was being called <u>out</u> of the church.

It was not an easy move to make, and I did not do it lightly. I loved our church family, and the beautiful community we had formed. My family had grown in this place, so many special times and precious memories had been made, along with so much growth. But I could not deny that the tides had changed.

It broke my heart to walk away from something I loved and into which I had invested so much of my time, my energy, and myself. And more over, I was brought deeper into sadness when the reality that my/our friendship with the pastor and his wife would end, too. I had not even considered that this would happen. For me, I was leaving the church, not the love and relationship we shared. They did not feel the same. It would take me quite some time to walk through this confusion and hurt. Even in the face of this discomfort and challenge, I knew I was doing what I needed to for my own journey. I was following the path that had been laid out for me. Perhaps it did not follow a cookie cutter plan, but it was my journey.

On January 29, 2009, I would begin a 40-day and 40-night guided and intentional spiritual journey. I did this with the help of a book that I had been gifted many years before. The time had come to open *One Day my Soul just Opened Up - 40 Days and 40 Nights Toward Spiritual Strength and Personal Growth*...written by Iyanla Vanzant. It must have been seven or eight years earlier that I had been gifted this book. It sat on my shelf until the time was right. It waited patiently for me to be ready; such a reflection of the truth that all things happen when the time is right.

The introduction of the book called me to remain open it and reminded me that there was something bigger than myself that was taking place. That was not hard for me to take in. It was something I had known most of my life. I think what I was facing was more about how to assimilate all I knew, all I thought I knew, all I was taught, and all I had experienced into something tangible. It was a very human need to make sense of things, to label, mark, and compartmentalize.

Independently finding one's truth was not encouraged in the religious world I had been brought up in. In that world, one was not encouraged to think for one's self. My experience was that you were told what to do, and you did it. There was little room for questioning. Occasionally I would come across a teacher or leader who would be comfortable with questions and welcome it. I give gratitude for them. For the most part, questioning or challenging often set off panic and knee-jerk reactions. That of course is the simple version, but that formula was embedded.

During these 40 days and 40 nights, a new thought developed and that was that God does not bless people. This was a challenge to understand. At first, it went against what I had been taught. As I unraveled old teachings, I understood these words more clearly. The thought came that all I need is already there and blessings are not held back for when we are worthy to receive them. Indeed it is not our Creator who measures us on whether we are worthy or not. No, it is we who measure our worthiness. Blessings continually abound, but it is only I who can choose to see them for what they are, or not.

I started focusing on my Trust muscle. Trust was not something that had been given much time in my life. Trust was translated into not asking questions, not challenging, and going along with the status quo. Sacred Trust had been compromised so many times and boundaries had been broken. Those that remained were blurred. Trust was static in my life. It was time to allow it movement once again. It became my work for this season. Rebuilding Divine and Sacred Trust and discovering what that truly meant to me.

I have been confused about trust.

I also realize that in trusting my own intuition I am really putting my trust in Arlene, my angel spirit guide, as it is she who ignites those thoughts. It is she who intuits inside me. I am not working independently when I make decisions based on intuition. In fact, I am trusting my relationship with God, Spirit, my Divine helpers, and their guidance in my life.

Through this 40-day meditation, I was given a fresh look at prayer, meditation, peace, willingness, honour, and divine freedom, among many others things. Ms. Vanzant separates the workbook into Seven Phases:

Phases One: Honour the Divine

Phases Two: Honour Self

Phase Three: Honour Others

Phase Four: Honour What You Feel

Phase Five: Honour Your Process

Phase Six: Honour Life

Phase Seven: Reflections

Within each phase, there were points that took me deeper into specific realms of how I currently honoured, and how I could transform my way of honouring all things. It was meticulous work. It was like placing beads on a tapestry one-by-one. It was a seemingly long and tedious task, but when completed a beautiful work of art emerged. So it was within my Self. Guided by this meditation, I looked at each bead, removed what no longer was true for me and replaced it with the truth of a new day, the truth of unraveling, and the truth of awakening and enlightenment. I began to realize in order for me to obtain the freedom I so desired, I would have to take down some of what was already there in order to rebuild.

To achieve the peace that I would like, I need to BE more peaceful! I see that shift starting. I was unaware how imperative it was. If I want peace, I need to be peace.

Peace. It was something I longed for. Though the voices in my head were not as loud or as large in number, they were still there. The strongest, deepest, and most effective ones had what seemed like, a death grip on me. And with them came the darkness and the deep sadness of depression. At this stage, I could not even consider ridding myself of either of them. I was looking to just quiet the voices and learn to live with the darkness. I was still not of the mindset that I could be free of them, so learning to live with them had become my focus.

There are still things in my own Self that need attending to- (defensiveness, shutting people out, anger)-that are remnants from my childhood. I will continue to work on these...I am willing to face them

Defensiveness. I grew up in a house full of it. Even as I write this, I can't help but think of the defensiveness that will come from what I have written. The thing is, I do not write it as a criticism; I write it as an observation. I fully believe change and healing come only when we choose to acknowledge the things that plague us and bring them to the light.

There is a grief in sharing this truth, as I know the defensiveness came from a place of not feeling enough and a place of fear and inadequacy. My parents have their own stories and lived lives that were very different from mine. War, death, and immigration were all part of a world that was so big and filled with so many unknowns. When my father left his home country of Holland at 18 years old, his thoughts were about how he would never see his parents or homeland again. When the Germans invaded Holland, my toddler mom and my granny went into hiding as my Grandfather had been taken to a work camp from which he escaped. They lived in a barn with other families, sectioned off by hay bales and paying for their keep by my Granny taking on mending for the farmer's wife. War breeds brokenness. This is where my parents, the ones who raised me, came from. I have so much grace and compassion for their story.

Acceptance is recognition. To accept something does not mean I like it. It just means I am accepting it for what it is at the time, knowing in the end all will work out as it is meant to be. I observe myself resisting acceptance of reality when I feel hurt. I tend to go into the fantasy about the situation instead of seeing it for what it really is. Yet in saying that I am able to accept that I am doing the best I can in my life. I am exactly where I need to be at this time. I have the power to accept even the hard things life deals me because it is just part of a bigger journey. I accept that my reaction is within my control.

Accepting always felt like I was saying it was alright. My thought had been as long as I was fighting against something I was not for it. I thought it was within the suffering of the fight that I would overcome that which I was fighting. And if I accepted something, I could no longer fight it and that, to me, represented defeat. Ha! It is amazing how perspectives shift. For sooner than I liked, the warrior within me became tired and worn out, and yet, through all her fighting, she seemed no further ahead. I had to learn that the fight was not so much about the battle itself. It was about all that was happening around the battle, and the wins and losses while the battle rages.

Through my journey, I came to see that accepting was the letting go of control, releasing of ego, and allowing what was meant to be. There is absolutely a time to fight, and sometimes beyond our control, blood is spilled. There is also another side to war and battle, one we do not focus on...the spiritual side. My thought is, if all things are spiritual, which is my practice, then so is war. If I am fleshing out and attempting to control the war, I leave no room for Spirit or any of the other entities of the Divine to come in and heal the situation. For war is not so much about who wins or loses, it is about healing the wound that caused the war in the first place.

I am still struggling with self-affirmations. There was a part of me that was uncomfortable with the self-praise (as I see it)...this I need to work on.

I am still hearing that I am not quite worth it and that I can't do it. This is so much better than it ever had been in my life, but I am aware that it is still a struggle. I haven't taken good enough care of myself. This is when the negative self-talk is harder to deal with. If I am tired, run down, or overwhelmed the negative self-talk is more prevalent. The good things I do know about myself are that I have a big heart. I love big, give big. I am a good friend and a loving parent. My nature is warm. I invest a lot into my relationships. I walk with The Divine every day. I am a daughter to The King and Queen of heaven!

Affirming myself was something I started as a practice during *Hearts Restored*. For almost an entire year, I read a list of affirmations to myself every morning. There were well over 30 bible-based affirmations about who I was as Creator's child. Spiritual Truths had not been specifically taught, and these truths and affirmations helped me undo some of what had been tied up within my being while growing up. It became a very powerful practice for me. In the beginning, it felt a little uncomfortable. As time went on, I found myself focusing more on the words than how I felt. The words held power, as all words do. Saying these affirmations out loud over time began to shift how I saw myself, how I treated myself, and how I loved myself. There had been many events that had contributed to the tearing down of my self-love. The affirmations were key to my progress, and kept me in line with the truth of myself. If I did not know anything else, I knew who I was and that was power.

I still have a lot to learn about boundaries. I have definitely over stepped boundaries and allowed others to step over mine...well let's be honest, I just didn't have any. By not having healthy boundaries, I allow people to go into the places of my life that I do not want them to be and where they have no business being. I have not had clear boundaries because I am always trying to prove myself...prove that I am worthy, prove that I am enough. Today I reflected on boundaries in my life and the lack there of. I thought about my reasons for not having boundaries and how that began. I looked at today as a change of boundaries in my life. I am responsible for myself first, then my marriage, and then my family. I honour myself when I set boundaries.

Boundaries were something that I completely did not understand. I did not know I could.

*I judge my children by my past...I want to prove myself through them...Nathen in particular (because I was an unwed mother), what a terrible mistake. Today I will grow out of that mistake and just be a mother...not a judge.

I am quick to judge myself...a lot. I also find myself judging others when I compare them to the standards to which I was raised. I realize it is easy to suspend judgment when I just let it go and realize there is no right or wrong way. There is only the way that God has placed in your heart.

*When working with my anger, I realize some of my pain that is still in need of healing. My expectations cause disappointment, which causes frustration and can turn into anger. It is the expectations I place on myself that cause the expectations I have for others. Today I am making the choice to forgive myself and be healed of feeling damaged.

*I have definitely felt the "freeze" of guilt. It is something I am working on and breaking out of. I am intrigued by the fact that guilt is a learned behaviour. That gives me hope and allows me to see it in a new way, because there is now a new possibility of un-learning it!

Guilt was something commonly used in my childhood home, perpetuated by a guilt and shame drenched religion.

*I get mixed up in my "games" and lose my authenticity. It is when I am not open with my feeling or my truth that I feel the worst inside. Then I start wondering WHAT IT WRONG WITH ME??!! That's when the negative cycle begins.

To break this negative cycle, I must live my Truth and be willing to accept the ripples or tidal waves that my truth causes—no more games, only truth.

Patience is not exactly what I thought it to be. Equating patience with faith and trust changes everything. I realize that I need to give a lot more patience to myself so my faith can shine. I must live my truth of knowing I am doing my best to set myself free. Patience is a gift I can give to my children and myself.

"Just as the spider unfolds its web from within its own being,

We must unfold divine wisdom, divine joy and the divine potential

Of God from within ourselves.

The moment we stop trying to make God come to us,

We realize that God is already here."

~ Joel Goldsmith

Step-by-step, chapter-by-chapter, and question-by-question, I worked my way through *One Day my Soul just Opened Up*. I received fresh perspectives and sacred confirmations of which I already knew. These were the thoughts that I already had, but was afraid to put to voice. Quite honestly, I was not sure how without causing offence to the God I knew. The greatest gift of this season was waking up and seeing that it was in my brokenness that I am perfect, just the way I am. What a shift of thinking for a woman who saw herself as damaged goods; to find that in that very place of damage and brokenness there was also the beauty of my heart, my soul, and my entire Being. To be given an option to embrace even that which I saw as broken and damaged was new and awakened something inside of me. A seed was planted within me, and it would not take long for it to take root.

I was seeing the world as a brighter place. I was incorporating more personal time for myself out in the vast world of nature. I found myself more and more grabbing my camera and heading outside. My camera had been a companion of mine for most of my life. I still remember clearly the day I went to the local Pharmesave Drug Store and purchased my very first camera with money I had saved up from babysitting.

With the help of my lens, I was slowly opening myself up to the abundance that was and is all around me. I was collecting images in a way I never had before. I was letting my soul guide me, and my heart call out to me as I walked through forest, field, and mountainside. I breathed in what I saw. I could feel what I saw was beginning to change me within my blood and deep within my bones. Mother Nature was coming alive to me. She was healing me.

Going out for a few hours at a time, at least once a week became my practice. I began to see it as a form of therapy. I would always go alone. This was very different from my normal behaviour as I was used to being very social, but solitude was now becoming more and more welcome in my world. "The Mother of All Things" and I were redeveloping an intimacy that we had when I was a child. I began to pour into her. Timidly at first, but soon I began bringing my heart and soul to her, sharing with her "The Great Sadness" that I carried. She soaked up my tears with her rich dark soil and brushed my cheek with her wind. She was always there waiting.

Another blessing was that my husband chose to work his hours so that he would take off every second Friday so we could have a Family Field Trip Day (otherwise known as FFTD). The Young Blood was completing his year in homeschool and our youngest was in kindergarten and had every second Friday off. We took this opportunity to go out as a family and explore our amazing city. These were fun times. It was really special to be out on a day that other families were at work or school. This made the places we visited less busy and much more enjoyable. The Young Blood has an affinity for marine life and anything water so many of our field trips took us to The Vancouver Aquarium where he experienced a session feeding the otters. These were enriching times for our little family. Even through the stress of The Young Blood's anxieties and the burden of my depression, we had these times of reprieve and just enjoyed one another unhindered and free. All the while, we were deepening our family bonds.

There were sacrifices made for these times together, but they became worth it. We saw the benefits as a family. We saw it in our son. I recall a time, a number of years earlier. We were driving The Young blood to an appointment with a holistic child psychologist. It was quite a distance from our home. All the while, he was chatting with and entertaining his toddler brother. When we arrived at our destination and were looking for parking, things got quiet in the backseat. We did not notice at first until a little, soft voice came from behind us saying, "Is there something wrong with me?"

I will never forget that little voice and all the emotions that it held in that moment. My husband and I looked at each other with tears in our eyes. "No honey, there is nothing wrong with you." We went on to explain why we were going to see this man, that he would help him and us know how to walk through the challenges better. We explained this doctor would give him tools to help him with the anxiety attacks and emotional storms that slammed his little body. He sat with our explanation and nodded in innocent acceptance.

It has always been so important that he see himself as whole, instead of broken. He is who he was meant to be and in need of extra tools and help to navigate the path before him. That was all. This time together as family was medicine in itself. It was not always easy to make happen, but important none-the-less.

Something else that shifted was that I was becoming braver in giving myself what I needed. I took my first weekend away for myself, by myself. I hopped into my Westfalia VW van and headed up the mountain, just past Squamish, to camp out for a couple days on my own. This was new. Normally I was the girl who would do such things with a couple of girlfriends or at the least one. But this was what I needed. I did pretty well, though I found myself sending a few text messages. This was what my heart wanted...needed, and so I listened. I am grateful for a husband who supported me. I hiked on my own, sat by the lake on my own, and sat in my campsite and wrote on my own. When the rains came, I went inside and wrote some more. I watched *Chocolat* twice on my laptop, as the rains hit my roof. I felt unsure yet safe in my little world.

These were the stepping stones to getting me where I needed and wanted to go within myself. Looking back, I see the intention that was walking with me. At the time, I did not see it. I was trying to follow the guidance that was coming from within, even though some of it, most of it, felt foreign. I trusted it.

TODAY....Sept. 18, 2009

I took Today

for it was waiting for me

like everyday waits for us

but we are distracted

with thoughts of "should."

We forget to breathe.

We forget to live.

We are consumed

with that which is dead.

Life is alive

and wants us to play.

Life is a gift,

every up and down

is part of Life's gift

to us

to live

a real life

So I took Today

because it was waiting....

Transformation was taking place, subtle but with huge results. I was changing, growing, transforming, and opening up to new ways of thinking, new ways of living, and new possibilities. I was opening up to my Self.

Broken Open by Elizabeth Lesser would be the next impactful book to come my way. It was a book written for "*...those who are willing to enter the woods of self-examination in order to retrieve what was never really lost.*" As Elizabeth herself explained; she felt like she was one who was willing to go into the woods, the deep dark woods. Somewhere inside her, she knew that is was there she would find the answers she was seeking and needing. I felt same.

The breeze at dawn has secrets to tell you

Don't go back to sleep

You must ask for what you really want

Don't go back to sleep

People are going back and forth across the doorsill

Where the two worlds touch

The door is round and open

Don't go back to sleep

~Rumi

Elizabeth's book was rich with insight. She spoke my language, and I loved her for it. I understood being broken open. I knew the pain it brought, the confusion, and the suffering. I also knew what could happen if navigated through and embraced instead of being pushed away and ignored. Right away in the introduction, she spoke about how the simple act of telling our stories to others along our journey was one of the most profound tools we could use for healing.

It is my observation that the honest, life-giving storytelling is a lost art in our society. One only needs to look at the news to see the reflection of what kind of stories we are now telling. We are sitting in the crap of our own stories and/or in the voyeurism of other people's crap stories. We, as a society, do not seem to realize that we don't have to stay there. As my sister Nissa Howard of Soul Craft says in her E-course "Stories of Now," we can rebrand our stories. We have the opportunity to grab hold of our given story plots and transform the storyline into the life we desire, not necessarily the one we were given.

At this time of my life, I would say that *Broken Open* was like a kick in the ass for me. All be it a gentle kick, it was a kick none-the-less. For so long, I was my story. My story branded and marked me, and not in a good way. It was heavy and debilitating. The time had come to find a way to turn that around. I needed to put my Self in the power position, and take the power away from my story. This book gave me the guidance to do just that.

Broken Open also gave me a view and the insight into how I could be the one to remove what was blocking my transformation, growth, and being free. I had been focused too much and for too long on the why of it all. Why me? Why my life? Why? Why? Why? Then, there was all that time and energy spent on looking for the ones to blame, instead of living with the deep truth of it all. The worst had already happened. My life up to this point had already happened. The fear and anguish I felt around the past would and could never be changed in the past. But I could take hold and make a shift and a change for the future.

I needed someone to tell me that this was possible. I needed to read the words I was reading and hear what I was hearing in order to understand that there was another possibility, many other possibilities. As I write this, I recognize that the need to understand that there are possibilities, is part of my reason for sharing my story. For those of you who are seeking but not yet understanding that you have options, perhaps something within my story resonates with your story and deep inside, too. I will say that you have more power over your story than you may think or feel at this moment. One step at a time, one small shift at a time. Know this, shift and transformation are all possible.

Shifts, like the transformation of perspective, around fearlessness. The warrior, the fighter in me saw fearlessness as something that needed armor and a tough exterior. It was something devoid of my sensitive nature. When I read Elizabeth's words that tenderness was behind fearlessness, somehow deep inside me, I knew these words to be true, even though I was completely unsure how to present that logic to my mind.

Broken Open put into words so many of my own feelings and thoughts. This verified that I held the truth within me. I felt myself nodding in agreement. My heart opened to new ways of looking at the struggles in my life. I learned to see them as a way of growing my Self as opposed to a debilitating event in my life.

At this place of looking back at the road/path I have traveled, I had the thought that bibles and holy books are still being written. I have thought that Holy Words are not just reserved for ancient holy books, such as The Bible, The Quran, or The Torah. I believe God, The Universe, The Great Mystery is continually speaking to us, through literature, art, music, and of course creation. During this "Time of Great Sadness" that is how I see most of the literature that found its way to me, and still continues to find its way. To me, without these books and the brave souls of those writing them, there is so much I would still be in the dark about and unsure of. But it has been through other's stories, that I have found mine.

I was beginning to see myself, as a bud that had been held tightly together by fear and uncertainty. Now, after being broken open by death and love, a new life was beginning to trust and open itself up to the light of the sun, moon, and stars. I was beginning to open myself to the possibility of deep joy and contentment. I was opening myself to the Deep Magic, Love and The Great Mystery that was revealing itself to me over, and over, and over again. Finally, as the fog lifted, I was beginning to believe it.

Within the vulnerability of our true human nature lies our greatest strengths. Within the honesty of our humanness, and all that we see as undesirable, lies the divine beauty of who we are. We each have the freedom to walk into the darkness, mine for those treasures, and trust that we will be led out the other side. There is no one healing without going in honestly and naked. We are not called to go in alone. There is more than enough help, and each of us has the ability to seek that out for ourselves. Going in is the way to get out of the chains that bind us to our burdens.

I watched myself as I became bolder and stronger. My voice was taking a new shape, a new tone. I was liking what I was hearing from myself. My Spirit guide, Arlene, was channeling more and more through me.

"May God, the source of HOPE, fill me with all JOY and PEACE by means of my FAITH, so that my HOPE will continue to GROW by the POWER of the HOLY SPIRIT." Romans 15:13

This year ended with me feeling more peaceful than I had ever felt before. I was expanding. I was truly feeling like a bud beginning to bloom into the light. The darkness was not so dark anymore. The burden seemed more manageable. I felt like I was taking hold of the wheel of my life, beginning to understand my responsibility to my Self. I was a newbie in this world of self-worth, crawling along, and learning to walk soon.

"As a child, I walked with noisy fingers along the hemline of so many meadows of back home. Green fabric stretched out, shy earth, shock of sky. I'd sit on logs like pulpits, listen to the sermon of sparrows and find god in simplicity, there amongst the dandelion and thorn."
~ Jewel

8
In the Stillness

January 14, 2010

This is a year of stillness for me. That was the only thing that came to mind. No resolutions, no goals, no plans. Just to be still and allow whatever is meant to be to be. Already I have seen and felt the benefits of this new way of walking through my life. Time seems to be more abundant without me having to "fight" for downtime. I feel more at ease when there are sudden pattern changes. I can let go of things much easier that usually would get me "hot." My prayer is to take this through not just this year but for the rest of my life. It is not always easy to change our patterns yet I have found this quite easy, telling me that I am in the right place.

At the end of previous year in my book club, we read *Lovely Bones* by Alice Sebold. This brought me to Alice's gritty memoir *Lucky*. In fact, it was while she was writing *Lucky* that *Lovely Bones* was birthed. *Lucky* is an intensely inspirational reflection of Sebold's experience of being raped while attending university. This memoir rocked me deep. The courage this author showed, on so many fronts inspired me. Her determination to not be shamed or shut away had me digging in my heels for my own voice to come forward to tell my story.

I wanted to be like her, speaking my truth, solely because that is what it was, the truth. It caused me to reflect on what I had written so far of my story. I needed to make some changes, open it up, and bring it closer to my heart. This process would happen several times as I opened further and healed deeper through future years. But for now, in this place, I still felt the slight grip of the past. Untangling the doctrine of my childhood and the religious constraints was taking time, more time than I thought it would. This left me feeling frustrated, angry, and disheartened, but I kept moving forward. Through it all, the messages where coming, the signs were being shown, and life was transforming.

At this point in my life, I could feel four distinct energies where before there were only two. Now alongside the darkness and the deep sadness, there was love and light. And all four stood together equally.

An opportunity came my way in late January to interview a woman in hospice. Death had never been something that scared me. The truth of it is, I was interested in talking to those closest to it, because my thought was and still is, that they are that much closer to The Mystery. I wanted to hear what they had to say, if anything. Death is a topic that remains virtually untouched in our North American White culture, and yet, we will all face it more than once in our lives. We face the death of those we love, and at some point, we face our own death. We live in a culture that is surprised and even offended when death or grief happens. I find this interesting, as it reflects a wounded story that lives within each of us. So, when this exceptional opportunity was presented, I accepted with much gratitude.

January 26, 2010

R....her story

9:57AM I call R and let her know who I am and ask her if it would be all right if I came to see her. (We have a mutual friend who asked R if it would be all right for me to talk with her about her journey for my book) I ask her if today or tomorrow would work better. She says that she may not be here tomorrow, so today is good. Yes...that is the truth, plain and simple.

10:15AM As I get ready, my heart beats fast. I know I am going to leave with more than I came in with....

She is skin and bones, and yet she radiates peace. R is 48 and beautiful. This is my thought as I walk into her room. As I enter the room, she is looking for "The Lord's Prayer" in her Bible. The room is bright and full of peace. There is even a hint of cheeriness lingering. That is something I did not expect. Now that I am in it with her, it makes sense. I feel Angels. I feel Light and Death. We've met before, Death and I, but in this room Death is not an evil or angry energy skulking in the corners. In this room, Death is a gentle friend waiting patiently for R to be ready to, as R saw it, go home.

She starts right away by telling me about her relationship with God. How their relationship began in 1994. The relationship soon became everything to her. Throughout her life she had lacked guidance and lived with a lot of internal struggle. Her life had not been easy, but her realization of God's love had made it better. She was now a single mother, the father long gone, to a young daughter who she loved beyond words. She was coming to terms with the fact that she was leaving her. It had not been easy, but she felt confident about with whom her child would be growing up. Above all, she felt confident that God was and would continue to watch over her daughter in her absence.

-R has just had another shot of morphine and slips in and out of consciousness. I sit with her because it is where I need to be right now. In this reality of the thin veil between life and death, the room is peaceful and bright. There is no fear here. R told me that every day brings her closer to God and with that she has great peace. Right now she sleeps. I'm left pondering what she told me before about a time she had become angry at her body and at her life because of the cancer. She was having a hard time with her daughter and had to send her to the washroom for a time out. R was feeling exhausted and began to kick and scream, which turned into crying. Her daughter watched this from the cracked opening of the bathroom door. The next thing R knew her daughter had come in and was wiping her eyes with tissue to dry her mom's tears.

(-R wakes to ask me if I want something to drink. I let her know that I am fine.

The thought crosses my mind that she is dying with such grace.)

After her daughter wipes R's eyes for the second time, she goes back into the washroom for her time out. R is moved by her little girl's actions and realized that she is a special child. R tells me it was then she should have given up control but still was not able. The cancer had control of her body, and she still wanted control of it. It was not until later that she fully turned herself, her body, and her illness over to God.

I had no idea how this was going to look today, given R's condition. She is dying of cancer. But as I sit by her bed, I feel a wonderful peace. I feel an escape from the world of busy pressure. It is here that I feel a place of divine stillness where everything matters and yet nothing does.

-R wakes to tell me about her experience in Cuba, where she was healed.

She had gone to Cuba with her little girl and a friend. At this time, she was very sick, but had heard of dramatic healings that were happening at a church on the island and wanted to take her chances.

(It is during this time that she tells me that throughout most of her life she had felt a spiritual oppression that she just could not shake). Once in Cuba things begin to fall apart. A conflict ensues with her friend. She is unclear as to what is really going on. The friend says that she should have brought her husband with her, and she wants to go home. R feels that the friend is also frustrated with the daughter being along on the trip. R is too weak and distracted to deal with this and tries to keep it together. She needs her friend's help and knows she cannot do this without her. As they wait for the day the church is open for healing, she does what she can to appease her friend . She has one mission and that is to get to the church as she still holds onto hope that the cancer can be cured. The day comes that they need to go to the church. It is a slow walk to where they need to go. The day is very hot and R needs to make several stops to rest, as a result her friend becomes impatient with her, (and in my opinion behaves in a way that clearly is not friendly)! But R is patient, and knowing her friend's story, she gives her grace. When they arrive at the church, the service has already started so they sit in the back. R is exhausted at this point, but then the singing begins. She tells me how it carried her away in an altered state. When the singing ends, she begins to feel like she is having a seizure. The pastor acknowledges that someone is in the crowd that is in need of a deep healing and has come a long way to receive it. He acknowledges that it is R, and begins to pray for her at the front of the church. Now she is lying on the floor with her muscles in spasm. She feels as though something is leaving her body. Then she is brought up to the front of the church for prayers. All the while, her daughter was watching. What stood out to R during all of this was that her daughter was not afraid. She observed but was at peace about everything. R came back from that trip letting everyone know she had been healed. Yes, she was still dying of cancer, but she had been healed. She had been healed of that which blocked her from trusting and told her she needed to remain in control. She was healed of all the wounds, pain, and scars of her life. So yes, she told me, she was indeed healed. The cancer was inconsequential. The healing of her heart and soul far outweighed the healing of her body. Yes, she was sad beyond words to leave her daughter. Through her spiritual healing, she was able to see that was the plan. It is difficult to understand in the flesh but the plan none-the-less. She knew that if she had not had the spiritual healing, her death would be one of fear and darkness, but now it was one of surrender and peace. R felt that was far more important for her daughter to experience.

She was tired.

I felt that I had all I had come for and more.

It was time to leave. While looking deep into her eyes, I thanked her deeply, so that she could see me...and she did.

R spoke the plain truth to me that day. I heard her and all those who were in that room with us. All flesh dies. The body returns to the earth. It is our soul and the essence of us that goes on. We are called to take care of our body. Healing is all relative to the one who is healed. R's story taught me that. She showed me how healing in the flesh and healing in spirit looked in comparison to each other. She showed me, which one was more important in the end.

I will not forget the gift of that afternoon. I will not forget R. As I sit finishing this story, it has been five years since her passing. She left this Earth about a week after I saw her. And as heart wrenching as it all was, I also witnessed the beauty of death. It was a much different experience from the one I had with my father. That was good for me. Thank you R, wherever you are. A humble bow of gratitude for you and the afternoon we shared. I would dare say you are dancing among the stars, free and healed.

The Lord's Prayer

(Traditional)

Our Father, which art in heaven,
Hallowed be thy Name.
Thy Kingdom come.
Thy will be done on earth,
As it is in heaven.
Give us this day our daily bread.
And forgive us our trespasses,
As we forgive those who trespass against us.
And lead us not into temptation,
But deliver us from evil.
For thine is the kingdom,
The power, and the glory,
Forever and ever.

Amen.

(non-traditional)

Ground of all Being
Mother of Life, Father of the Universe
You name is sacred and beyond speaking.

May we know your presence.

May your longings be our longings in heart and in action
May there be food for the whole Earth community
Forgive us our falseness of what we have done
as we forgive those who are untrue to us
Do not forsake us in our time of conflict,
but lead us into new beginnings.

For the light of life, the vitality of life, and the glory of life
Are yours now and forever Amen

~Philip Newell

Another Sue Monk Kidd book had come my way through the book club: *Traveling with Pomegranates*. This non-fiction book was co-written with her daughter, Ann Kidd Taylor, following their Pilgrimage of Personal Discoveries around the Divine Feminine and what they discovered together.

January 21, 2010

Re-opening the feminine
within
When I feel a disconnect
I retreat
From exactly what it is
I need
Living with so many men
and needing
the feminine so much
Therein lies my life's work
But not work in
a labouring kind of way
No...instead
A joy-filled work of

the Soul to keep
stretching and moving
forward
to remain true to the
woman inside of me...

-Catherine Beerda-Basso

I wrote this in the back of Sue Monk Kidd's book. With each step, it felt like I was going back...not backward...but back to sacred truth, truth before it was corrupted. There had to be a voice for women in the spiritual realm. How could a masculine only creator create the feminine? Maybe that question is too simple or maybe we make it complicated for our own agendas. Inside and around me, a whole other aspect of "God" was emerging. The feminine side, the "Goddess", among others was showing up. Writers like Sue Monk Kidd were offering a place for me to learn more about this sacred feminine.

Scribbled on the bottom of one of the pages in *Traveling with Pomegranates*, I wrote the following: *If we deny the existence of "Mary" as a feminine aspect of God, is it we who leave her impoverished and quarantined? In fact, is this not our feminist calling... to release the feminine divine to bring balance to our souls?* Really? I wrote that? I had to recheck and recheck to be sure. But yes it would seem those were my words.

Like Sue I wanted to behave like a finder as much as a seeker. For most of my life, it felt like I was looking for a place to belong and seeking truth. However, I was done with seeking, I wanted to find the truth and that was exactly what was happening. I did not see it clearly at the time. It felt so new and tender, but looking back I can see that I was finding my truth, my path, and a bigger, broader, and a more connected God. A few other players had also been held in the shadows too long. There was another coming out of the shadows, and that other was me. The timing of this emerging could not have been more perfect.

Earlier, I briefly mentioned the challenges that the Young Blood faced. These coming days as he grew into a teenager would prove to be challenging for all of us. I regularly blogged about those days. Blogging was an outlet for me, a way to "lay it down," and receive support without judgment. It gave the story a voice, so it would not be trapped in the walls of our home.

May 2-2010... Blog writing

Digging Deeper: Gardening with a Spiritual Edge

Two weeks ago, the week started with a broken chair, foul words and the Young Blood walking out of the house, never wanting to return. That same weekend ended with a broken dresser and a mother with a broken heart. The truth is that mother was brought to her knees asking, "How did I get here?"

It is my children that seem to teach me the biggest lessons of my life. A young man struggling with anxiety that at times consumes him, leaving him afraid and unsure.

What is it I need to be doing for him as his mother?

What is it that I do that only adds to his exasperation?

What feelings does his behaviour evoke in me that I am reacting to?

For a long time, I thought to write about my Young Blood. I thought I would share about how he has low serotonin. And I would tell you that serotonin is an essential hormone found in the pineal gland, blood platelets, the digestive tract, and the brain. The main function of the serotonin is to control sleep patterns and stress. It is a messenger between the nerve cells, which transmits the chemical messages between the nerves. When the normal levels of serotonin are not available in the body, the results can be several disorders, which range from mild to severe in their consequences. The Young Blood faces things like: anxiety, panic attacks, fears, and phobias, a tense state of mind, suicidal tendency, OCD, anger and aggression, insomnia, craving for sugar, pessimism, and depression. He told me once that his thoughts were like being in a room with everyone but there is a glass wall stopping you from getting to everyone else.

But this post is not about my Young Blood. I wanted to share a little so you could get a picture of the world my son lives in. If you met him, you would have no idea. I have been blessed to meet more and more mothers who have children like my Young Blood. We all share the same story: "Unless you became a part of the child's world, you would never know."

As I have said, this is not about him...it is about me, his mother, and what I had to learn, and where I had to grow, and am still growing, because of him and who he is.

In the early years, I spent a lot of time trying to "fix" him, seeking out vitamin treatments, and finding the right diet, professionals to speak with him and us, and on, and on. Of course, this was not all bad as we have been able to avoid medication and have come to understand the important needs that always must be met to maintain balance. No, it hasn't all been for not, but my motivation was always to "fix."

When high school came, we went through a very dark time, and it was in the darkness that God came and spoke to me after I tried to strike a bargain in order to get The Young Blood "fixed." God told me plainly that there was nothing to fix and that my Young Blood was exactly who he was meant to be. Through God's eyes, there was nothing that needed fixing. Oh how I cried. It was time for me to let go of my fears and control. God proceeded to show me all the wonderful things that came from who he was, including his deep creativity, immense talent in music, empathy that was way beyond his years, and his complete inability to hold onto anything for too long. With him, there was never any guessing as to how he was feeling. And so I let my fear go, or so I thought.

What happened last week showed me that a shift was needed again, not within him but within me. It was all spiritual. The Young Blood was reacting to a big change that was happening. He was doing what he always does. But me, I was reacting fearfully. I was not being what he needed me to be. I needed to be hit across the head twice. The broken chair was not enough. I needed a broken dresser, too. I needed to be in a place of being stripped of everything and fully exposed. I needed to stand in his room totally and completely at a loss and have no answers to finally realize that I was in the way. I needed to surrender to his journey, his path of life.

I drove him to work silently crying the whole way. As the tears streamed down my face, I thought of things to say, but I remained silent and sat in my pain and brokenness. Poor kid, that was the only bad thing about it all. Imagine sitting with your quietly crying mom as she drives you to your new job. Yup it was a moment. On the way, the song "Shadow Proves the Sunshine" by Switchfoot came on the radio. As I drove, I prayed for clarity, forgiveness, and a shift within me, so I could move past wherever it was that was keeping me from being what my Young Blood needed me to be. And God answered. When I dropped him off our eyes met. Me: "I love you" — forgiveness. Him: "I'm sorry."— everything will be okay.

God, "The Great Gardener" is getting me ready for a new season. Spring has sprung in my heart. The long, trying winter is over. It is time to ready myself for all the new things that are about to grow within me. Some things are already growing as we speak, good, healthy, nourishing things. But there are also weeds. Weeds that can choke me with the fear of the unknown. I want control, so I don't feel fear and yet it is in that control that I find only fear. It is time to do some weeding. I say to myself that I am not afraid to get my hands dirty. I am not afraid to have my brow sweat. I will work hard and pull all I can.

But "The Great Gardener" says, "No, you do not have to work hard. It is not necessary for your brow to sweat."

Be still.

Be still.

Be still.

My Spirit reminds me that "The Great Gardner" has given me the right tools to use. These tools were given to me at birth. They are given to each of us.

"One at a time," my Spirit tells me... "One at a time."

It is not about FIXING. It is about removing to make room for new growth. So here I am back at this place again. At first, it feels discouraging, but then I remember GRACE and give that to myself. I am reminded of a letter I wrote to a dear friend a while back.

Fear will always be with us, tripping us up. We just need to learn how to USE it, instead of IT using us. Learn from your fears, figure out the ROOT, and tend to that. Like a weed in the garden, it does not help if you just pull the weed. One must get down on his or her knees, get close to the earth, and dig down into the dirt, and dig out the ROOT. Sometimes you don't get it all on the first go, because it goes so, so deep. You try again and again, and each time you see a sprout you go back and get more of the root. One day, it will be gone.

It is my journey to deal with these ROOTS and DIG DEEPER. There are already some lovely colours happening in the garden of my heart. I wait in stillness to see what other colours "The Great Gardener" has planned for me.

May 6, 2010…Blog writing

A shift is happening. An old root found. Time to go farther.

A few things came my way in the last little while to help me along this journey of digging deeper. Ironically or not, the calendar challenger for May is: THINK THE BEST.

"Think the best of everyone and everything. See the good in all circumstances and in the people in your life."

Thanks to the lovely Dee Sullivan for her Monthly Challenge Calendar. This month's challenge had certainly set the tone for my path.

Another medium that has come into my life is the book, Women, Food, and God by Geneen Roth.

This book came to me by a mama friend of mine whom I trust immensely, and whose opinion I value. Even though I do not eat beef, I find myself dining on prime steak every time I read a portion of this book. And, for me, that is exactly how I have to read it…a portion at a time.

My main killer weed is SELF-DOUBT… you may be familiar? It has a way of sneaking into my garden. Years ago, it over took my garden. Some days, I could barely tell the difference between the flowers and the weeds. I had allowed self-doubt to slowly take over as I walked around with the core belief that I was DAMAGED GOODS. This was the perfect condition for Self-Doubt to flourish.

In her book, Geneen writes about the belief that you are damaged goods, and how that influences your walk in life. This belief calls you to walk in shame, and continually strive to make up for everything that you seemingly lack. It causes you to doubt yourself and sends you to constantly look outward for guidance, instead of inward for the real treasures.

Yup, chew on that one for a moment…or 5…no, no, no, don't worry… take your time…I am still chewing, too.

This book is not about diets, weight loss, or weight gain. It is not about finding your inner child or healing your painful past. It is a book about the way you eat and how that reflects your core, spiritual beliefs. Women, Food and God brings a light to our relationship with food and how it mirrors our feelings about love, fear, anger, meaning, transformation, and God. Geneen believes that our relationship with food is the doorway to freedom.

My own Self-Doubt came from a valid place. It always does. The point is how do I react or respond to it now? I have tended my garden better than I ever have in the past. There is always a new season that brings new gardening work.

If my seeds are starting to sprout, how does this affect my ability to deal with my Young Blood and his particular needs? If I am dealing with his needs while being choked by my weeds, what is left for The Ginger (my youngest son), and The Horticulturalist (my husband)?

Reading this book is re-establishing some "gardening techniques" and is introducing me to new ones that will work for me.

During this time, I was amazed at how something so beautiful could grow out of something so difficult and rough. Like the beautiful, delicate flowers that grow through the pavement or from underneath rock beds. This was a time of shifting perspectives. The rocks and struggles were there. The tough stuff seemed to always be there for me to face. BUT beauty was showing up in spite of the challenge. Peace was still a strong presence and revealing itself as Divine Truth. My heart was beginning to really believe it.

May 17, 2010

This weekend was spent out in the garden. The Horticulturalist and I were working together, one in the front and one in the back, and sometimes side-by-side. We were encouraging each other as we went, patting each other on the back, while keeping The Ginger busy at the same time. I found this work very reflective of the work that we do in our family and our marriage. This journey I am on has brought me to an interesting place of seeing our "roles" for the first time with new eyes.

Like my garden, I need a little work done.

There are those things, like the sweet buttercups, that seem so innocent and non-invasive. But before you know it, they have taken over and are choking the life out of others. You do one of two things: Ignore it or deal with it.

I see myself mostly as a "deal with it" kind of person.

Get Real.

Deal.

Heal…so you can once again…Feel.

During a time of crisis in our lives, this was something a girlfriend and I came up with. I like it and use it often.

So I am in there and getting to work with more digging, more reflection, and more surrender. That is what last week was all about. I listened to my body and felt every emotion instead of avoiding, bolting, or covering. I am really seeing the weeds for what they are. Have you ever done that? I just stopped in the middle of an emotional outburst and just felt it. I was in it, looked at it, and saw the roots that were connected to it.

Amazing things happen when you do this work. Then you control your emotions. Your emotions no longer control you. When you control your emotions, and I do not mean in the way of "control freak" but more like a "managing control." You start to understand the emotions and see them for what they are.

I am a person who feels her emotions, and it shows. I have been called sensitive more than once, and most times it was meant as a criticism and not a compliment. I live with my heart wide-open. I see this as a good thing.

What I do not see as a good thing is living with a wound wide-open.

In Women, Food, and God, Geneen Roth talks about our bodies as a piece of the universe that we have been given. We don't see our bodies as the gift that it is, the vessel in which we enjoy this human experience. These days we live separate from our bodies, sometimes because we do not want to feel the disappointments, the pains and sufferings of life and want to avoid it all. However, our bodies don't lie. They hold the story in every cell, in our blood, and in our bones. Our mind jumbles things up, makes up stories, twists events, and covers things up. Our bodies always respond to what we are going through, honestly.

In the past week as I was stopping in my emotions and feeling them, I discovered some things. Some of my reactions to The Young Blood have more to do with my father (how cliché, I know) than him. As a child, I felt that my family life was dictated by my father's mood, and I resented that.

In a similar vein I sometimes I feel that what hijacks us, as a family, is what is going on with The Young Blood. I feel the root of resentment. This root has to do with a little girl and her father, not a mother and her son. It is an old root that is brought to life by a current situation that seems familiar and yet is not.

My son is a child...my child...and he is who he is. I am no longer a child in a hopeless situation. I am a mother who can and does love her child through the winding terrain he is sometimes thrown into often by things that he has yet to master. It's a huge root, but I am working on getting it pulled up.

And here is the GREAT news it can be done. It can be done!

Feeling the emotions and listening to my body gave me great insight and left me feeling secure instead of insecure. This knowing left me feeling like no matter what, things WILL be okay. In fact, life will be wonderful because this is a real life. There is no light without darkness, and no joy without sorrow. To truly live, we must embrace and walk between two worlds, equally acknowledging both.

This weekend as I drove The Young Blood to work, I held his hand, and he let me. That is what works for him...I am listening. The week still had its ups and downs, but I was not so taken in by the emotions, as much as I was taken in by my love for my child, my family, and my home. It is a choice. Every day I am free to make the choice...and I do.

I will forever see The Young Blood as one of my greatest teachers. Simply by being who he is, he offered me an opportunity to grow, transform, and expand my vision of being a better mom to him. By doing so, I became a better woman for my Self. He brought me, and continues to bring me, to places I do not think I would go for many other people. I thank him for that. Humbly and Deeply, I thank him.

Things were now moving, within me, at a more rapid pace. At the time, I did not "feel" it so much. It's like when you are hiking a new trail and have no idea your position in relation to the end of the trail, so you keep moving forward, knowing and trusting that you'll eventually reach the end. Looking back and bearing witness to what I was writing, I can see there was noticeable movement. The excitement of healing was gathering within me. I wanted to shout it out to everyone. I could never have imagined or even hoped for the shifts that were happening within and around me. I was becoming bolder with my story and with in my way of living. I felt the excitement of it all. Yet even in the excitement of this movement, the pain of the past still reared its head now and again.

When you are brought up in a place of secrets, they become your stories. You hold things close. Even writing this book, there was a certain amount of apprehension that came with it. Shame and Guilt played around in my mind. BUT in order to move through these emotions, stories need to be told and shared for the wisdom that they hold. This I believe.

About this time, I was becoming connected with other bloggers, and creating and growing friendships and sisterhood. It was in one of these realms that I stepped out from behind the veil of secrets to share my story with another woman who was struggling with the circumstances of how she came into this world. She was trying to reconcile her beginnings to the woman she was now and hoped to be. Her story and the responses from the other women in our group lingered with me. I could feel her struggle, her grief, and her desire to move forward and not feeling clear as to how to do that.

Reading her story and the comments reflected back to me my own life, feelings, hurt, and how that hurt and pain was transformed into a renewed life. I shared with her my history and some stories. Most importantly, I shared with her the renewed perspective that I had about all of those stories and the healing path I was on.

June 12, 2015...a letter for Gail...

...it was a number of years ago during my own journey of healing that I realized that my father was mentally ill. That realization did not take all of the darkness of the past away, but it did help me to understand. Even as I write down those few things, my heart pounds for that little girl. But that little girl and I have been on an amazing journey together. It was one of redemption, forgiveness and freedom; the only kind of journey that one can go on with a Spiritual Guide, with a Creator God that is so huge and unexplainable!

You wondered if you would ever feel okay about your beginnings.

I want you to know, Gail, you will come to a place of peace about your beginnings. I promise you, my friend.

If someone had told me I would feel as I do today about my past, well let's just say, I would have called bullshit quickly.

But it is true. It is a journey, but there is freedom to be had, too.

I am grateful for the life I have had.

Crazy...I know.

But everything I have, everything I am is because of those very things that cut so deep. I would not be me if I had not had the life I have had. I would not be where I am now nor love where I am right now. I would not change a thing. My garden is an amazing mix of what may look like weeds, but if you look closer there is a beauty and a pattern to the way they grow. It is home to me.

You will find your way, too, Gail. You will find your peace, in which you can grieve, celebrate, laugh, cry, and feel joy about this life you have been given. There is nothing that separates us from our Creator and everything in our life has God's loving, wise print on it. God wanted everything for you, Gail. Though it did not happen then, it is happening for you now...just for you. You are precious.

I hope this gives you hope....

The more the healing unfolded, the more I was guided to look inward and outward at myself. I started a new blog in which I was holding myself accountable for how I was viewing and taking care of my body, both physically and spiritually. After years and years of abuse and loathing, it was time to undo all that had been done and learn to see myself and my body through my healed eyes.

Sept. 17, 2010...Blog writing

I am doing this for ME!

"I cannot compete with the pain of your past."

I had to say this to someone close to me recently as we were working out our relationship. I think it is something I should say to myself as well. There is a story of my past, of course there is. I mean, who doesn't have a story right? But that story is over. It is done. Now it is just about me...& me. That is what this is about. I have a lot of reasons that brought me here. BUT those reasons no longer exist. Why do I choose to be held captive by those reasons? Am I not worth it?

There have been so many times that I have gone down this road for the wrong reasons whether it be 5 pounds, 10 pounds, or whatever. The amount is irrelevant. What is relevant is the reason why. I don't want to do it for those empty reasons. It's not to be prettier, have guys notice me, to feel like I matter, but because I want to do it for me. That is all. For me...because I like me...and it is time I feel good about me...all-the-time.

I happen to know that the greatest gift I've been given is the freedom of choice, the freedom to live my own life, the freedom to fall on my face, and get back up again. I don't want to waste that gift. I want to be whole. I choose to be whole.

I cannot compete with the pains of my past, so I choose to live free of them!

Oh yeah! It's on!

For the followers of my blog, I posted daily my uncensored feelings about my body, and the emotions that were bubbling up as I went through this process. I had a small following of on lookers and supporters. One particular sister-friend was the one who inspired me to take this journey. She called herself "Amy the Free." I had followed her on her journey and was so touched by her honesty and openness as she exposed those darker corners of herself, not only to her Self but also to us, her readers. I fell in love with her heart and took a cue from her to do the same for myself. I am forever grateful for sisters like Amy, courageous enough to go out on that limb where it bears fruit. And by doing so, they inspire others to do the same. We all have a story of pain and sorrow.

September 22, 2010...Blog writing

Dear Catherine,

I am sorry that I have not always been there for you the way I was meant to. And I am sorry for all the times I pushed you beyond your limit. It was not my intention to hurt you or not take care of you. In fact, you just seemed so strong to me, so able, that I didn't take the time to think that the things I was doing to you could hurt you down the road.

I know there were times in the past when I did hurt you, thinking it would get me a much needed result. For that I am truly sorry, I know it was wrong. I thought I could sacrifice you for the love I so wanted. But I was wrong. I only hurt you and alienated the ones from whom I needed the love.

I haven't always thought highly of you, in fact there were times when I cut you down to dirt. For that I am sorry. I see that it was only the lies that cause me to do such things. I only wish I hadn't believed them. The last several years have been awesome! We are learning to love each other again, like when we were kids…remember? What a time of freedom that was. We were so carefree, so full of love, light, and life…I loved you then, without thought, without question, without insecurities confusing my mind.

I know we can't go back, but in the last few years, we have been finding our way back to each other. For that, I am ever so grateful. I realize it was me who pushed you over the edge. I know. Again I am sorry. I thought you could handle it ALL. But I pushed too hard, hard enough for you to fall.

I realized then that you had reached your end. There was no more rope to hold onto, and together we fell down to the bottom of the ocean. There we sat. Until He/She came and stayed with us, until we were ready to come back to the surface.

And we have been rebuilding haven't we? You, me, and Them. Thank you for giving me another chance. I don't want to lose you. I want us to live. I want to live in the light and love that is ours. You mean more to me than words can say. I promise…I PROMISE never to push you, like that, again. I promise to do the best for you always, and to remind you daily of how much I love you and what you mean to me. The poison we were given is gone and out of our systems. Now we must live like it is. You are worth this. You are worth living for, loving, and standing by. I hope you can forgive me for letting you down in the past. I was lost, dear friend. I was lost.

With all I have
I embrace you with Love and Light

Cat

Oct. 1, 2010…Blog writing

Dear Cat

Thank you for your lovely letter. It touched me deeply.

But I have to tell you, that you are apologizing for something that was not for you to apologize. Remember....I was there. It is okay. Anything that needed to be forgiven was done so long ago. You did what you knew. You did your best. Yes, sometimes your choices did hurt us, but in the end...Well look at us now! Look how far we have come!

Now is not the time to feel sorrow for the past. Now is the time to celebrate our today! We have so much to be grateful for, so much to rejoice in. Let's do that. Let's sing and dance in the Love that we have been given so abundantly, so freely.

You lived in the now and responded to it. You have always given what you had. Through it all, I knew that you loved me. I saw through the crap, all the distraction, and all the drama.

I always saw you.

I always knew your heart.

I know you...I trust you...I love you.

Nothing will ever change that.

You seem to forget that I saw all that you took on to protect me, to keep me from the pain you did not want me to feel.

I saw the sacrifices you made.

I saw your struggles.

I saw how you suffered to protect me. Don't think I didn't see that.

Don't think that I have forgotten.

It is as much a part of me as it is you.

Be at peace with the love you showed me. Be at peace and know that I saw it all...everything.

You are my best friend.

You have an amazing heart.

You have passion that cannot be contained.

You love so fiercely.

You go so deep.

You rock my world.

There is no need to hang your head low. Be proud of you. Be proud of me. Be proud of us.

We have come out the other side and will continue to do so, because you know the One we are following. There is no doubt for you, and I admire and need that. Without you and all your bigness, I could not be me.

So thank you! Thank you for all that you give, all that you are, and all that you are going to be,

With deepest love and adoration

Catherine

Alongside this journey of "exposed writing," I once again felt called to enter into the 12-week intensive of "Hearts Restored." I was still unraveling the religious chains around my heart and continuing that unraveling was an important part of my freedom. There were many perspectives that still needed to be undone. So many feared-based teachings that had been placed on my heart that needed to be eradicated and replaced. I saw this as "the need to change." I felt that I needed to change and be changed. Within the first few weeks of this intentional and intensive journey, I realized it was not change I was seeking...it was *Transformation*.

Sept. 30, 2010...Blog writing

"You offer me sacrifice, but it's your heart that I want."

These were the words sung in song tonight. So much of the teaching I was brought up with had been about what I need to do for God, what I needed to give up for Him, what I needed to suffer through for Him, and yet, all God wanted from me was the love of my heart. Simple.

We start at the beginning...Genesis 1:26...God makes man in His image and with a distinct purpose.

What if every person in the world knew without a doubt that they were made for a purpose. A simple thought, yes? And how powerful! It is so beyond religious label, denomination, the church you attend or don't attend, beyond your status, your geographical location, and beyond your disappointments to know that you were created with purpose. That is something to feel joy-filled about!

When used correctly, The Bible is a foundation of life skills and information. It is like a map for our lives. A place to be encouraged, guided, and nurtured. Tonight we went through a long list of verses that verified out identities in Jesus. There has been a long oppression in the church where we have missed the point that we are already free. What Jesus did through his life and death has freed us of the old law leaving only two to remain.

Love God.

Love your neighbour as yourself…The Law of Love

God loves everyone. Everyone matters.

My guru Jesus said this: "The Lord's Spirit has come to me because God has chosen me to tell the good news to the poor. God has sent me to announce freedom for prisoners, to give sight to the blind, to free everyone who suffers."

What does this mean to me?

I am not judged by what I have done or by what I do, whether it be "good" or "bad." I am already free. God wants to have my love and give me Divine love with no strings attached. There is nothing I can do to have God love me more, and there is nothing I can do to have God love me less. God is not interested in me being lost in guilt and shame.

When I get confused or the ugly head of religion muddies the waters, I go back to the relationship that I have with my children. How far would I go for them? Is there a limit to my forgiveness when they make a mistake? Is there a limit to my grace? Do I wake up some days and just not love them? No, NO, and NO! I can't NOT love them. And so it is with God times a million, and on.

This night, I received a message from Arlene, my Spirit guide;
Believe & Lead.

Oct.6, 2010

Intention for this session of Hearts Restored

This will be my second round at HR. This time, I've come to reconnect and confirm my place in the world with Jesus.

I want to love myself completely as God does and walk free of fears that hold me back from being all God created me to be.

I come here for myself, not my marriage, my children nor my extended family. I come here for me and me alone. Because I know that when I am right with myself...ALL my other relationships will benefit.

Halfway into the course, I received an important message from Arlene... *"So Catherine, there is not a microwave remedy for any of the things you long, hunger, or thirst for...everything that matters to you takes time, ebbs and flows, shifts and reshapes. The things you hold dear take commitment, discipline, and work on your part. You need to remain focused on what you consider "The Prize." And only YOU can do this. You will not find your way anywhere else, but within you. God created you with all the answers already inside, for He/She knew what it was you were going to ask. Have the courage to find the answers and really <u>LIVE </u>them. You will do these things over, and over, and over again. You will pour out your life again, and again, and again. It is the life we live on Earth. Know this. Live this. Be at peace with this. Over, and over, and over again does not mean failure. It means living, and living a real life that needs constant tending. You know you do not do this alone. Utilize all that has been given, and you will teach your children the best thing you possibly can. Live with your heart wide-open and without fear, for God stands holding you in the storm...I love you, you are amazing."*

This year of Stillness brought me to a place of deep listening, something I now call "sacred listening." It was in the stillness that I could hear Spirit's voice. The veil was thinning. It was in the Stillness that life slowed. It slowed down enough for me to catch up with myself. Pieces of me came back, one piece at a time.

Being Still

This is the week for being still.

I feel it in my bones. My bones say slow down.

It is that time of the month. My moon is upon me. There was a time when that did not dictate anything to me other than I better pack along the necessary items as I went about my day. But, after reading The Red Tent by Anita Diamant a while back and becoming older, I have started to rethink this whole time of the month. I decided this year...the year of Being Still...that when this time of the month came I would cease rigorous exercise, meaning no running, no torture chamber, and more going into my Spirit, more reflective activity.

I want to bask in the amazing beauty of this place.

Did you take a look around?

Isn't it amazing?

As there are seasons, so there are times for all the cycles of life.

So today...

I sit in a stillness of joy, gratitude, and amazement...a love I cannot put into words.

I sit in the stillness of memories of a friend gone to soon.

I sit in the stillness of dear friends who are struggling.

I sit in the stillness of Freedom.

I sit in the stillness of knowing who I am.

It is not the food I eat.

It is not the body I wear

It is not the stories of my life.

I am a new creation.

I am a temple where Spirit dwells.

I am blessed.

I am a Saint.

I am Holy and without blame before my Creator...in Love.

I am victorious.

I am an overcomer.

I am set free.

I am strong in Love.

I am more than a conqueror.

I am complete.

I am alive.

I am free from condemnation.

I am the light of the world.

I am the salt of the earth.

I am chosen.

I am God's workmanship, created in Love to do good works.

I am beloved.

I have the Peace that transcends human understanding.

I am clothed with Glory and Honour, and all things are put under my feet.

I am firmly rooted, established in my faith and overflowing with gratefulness and thankfulness!

"You do not have to be good. You do not have to walk on your knees for a hundred miles through the desert repenting. You only have to let the

soft animal of your body love what it loves."
~Mary Oliver

9
Returning to LOVE ... Part One

This year was "The Year of Owl." She had come to visit me in my backyard toward the end of 2010 and infused her medicine into my being. This year would be the year I would need vision in the dark. I would need to take in all that was "bad" or "scary" and transform it into something life-giving. I would need to dig deep for wisdom. This year, I would need Owl by my side to allow the death that was needed to bring in new life. It was Owl who told me this was so, and I believed her.

For most of my life, I had seen myself as damaged goods. But I was already on the road of healing and Owl's presence was affirmation that I was on the right road. My thought is that we are all created whole. The brokenness we feel is a state of mind. Our spiritual purpose here on earth is to find our way back to our wholeness. When we see ourselves as whole, we live accordingly. Thus, we love those around us, as well as ourselves, that much more. This allows us to commune with Spirit, others, and ourselves in a cleaner, clearer way. I have found that the wholeness that I speak of can be found among the wounds and scars of our stories.

It is in this place of communing and love where the spirituality of life comes into play. It is where the energy of God is present. The truths of our wholeness remain the same whether we are able to see it or not, whether we self-medicate or not, and whether we show up or not. The Great Mystery doesn't need us to make it exist. Love was and always will be. We can choose to engage, believe, and live in the Spirit. There will always be things to distract us from engaging with Spirit. It does not mean that God is not there or that time will run out for us.

I was returning to myself, coming home. I liked the way that sounded and felt in my being. I could not have known how challenging and beautiful the road would be for my return home, and how much I would need Love to get there.

The Greatest Is Love:

What if I could speak all languages of humans and angels?

If I did not love another I would be nothing more than a noisy gong

or a clanging cymbal

What if I could prophesy and understand all secrets and all knowledge?

And what if I had faith that moved mountains?

I would be nothing unless I loved others.

What if I gave away all that I owned and let myself be burned alive?

I would gain nothing. Unless I loved others.

Love is kind and patient

Never jealous, boastful, proud or rude.

Love isn't selfish or quick tempered.

It doesn't keep a record of wrongs that others do.

Love isn't selfish or quick tempered.

It doesn't keep a record of wrongs that others do.

Love rejoices in the truth, but no in evil.

Love is always supportive, loyal, hopeful and trusting.

***

For now there are faith, hope and love.

But of these three

The greatest

is

Love

I Corinthians 13:1-7,13

January 20, 2011...Blog writing

The Season of the Storm-Part 1

"Learning to weather the Storm"

~ a story of a mother's journey to be her son's light

We've been in "The Storm Season" for awhile now. It has been a time of unsteady seas, dark courses, and uncharted waters. It has not been easy, so I hold onto the Truth that nothing worth having comes easy. During this time, you might think my outlook and vision was like this:

Colourless
Mute
Grey
Cold
Wet
Void of life
Empty

But I have to tell you something so amazing. Though I have fleeting moments of feeling those things and walking on that bridge with the emptiness trying to consume me, there is something greater that carries me away and brings me peace.

Even as I grieve, I walk in the brightness of Life, Love, and Light.

This post has been a long-time coming. Until today, life has not offered a place for me to come and write these memories down. I write this for myself and for my son, whom I love more than life itself, and for anyone who wants to know the Truth. I write this to honour The Great Spirit from which all good flows, and who holds the essence of Love...True Love...Agape Love.

The storms started just before Christmas when my Young Blood decided to leave home. With this choice came chaos and fear. They brought with them a tornado of emotions, both positive and negative. The Storms came because of Truth. The Truth was painful for the Young Blood to face and because of that pain fear overtook him.

The Young Blood has a good heart. He does not long for chaos or fear. The Storms take a lot out of him, but they need to come to balance nature. Sometimes these storms have to come to clear the vision.

To see my child broken and emotionally stripped was a shock to me. It was so clearly reflective of where he was in his life. You'll understand why I speak as I do. I must respect the delicacy of the matter. What I can tell you is that this has everything to do with what goes on in my son's head and heart, and how those two entities battle within him. This is a situation of pure emotions and self-love...or in this case, the lack there of.

No one likes his or her "dirty laundry" to be exposed, and the Young Blood was no exception. As a child, he reacted as a child. He was scared, confused, and used his anger to cover it all.

He left.

Unable to face what needed to be faced.

He left.

My mother's heart broke. I was broken in a way I have never had it broken before, and I wept.

For two days I grieved. It was a deep grief within. It was overwhelming, pain-filled, and broken. In this place of great sadness and as The Storm raged, the Light of Love came to me with so much to tell me.

Grief is good.

Grief is a reflection of Love.

I needed to allow myself to grieve, allow myself to feel the hurt, and allow myself to see through the hurt to the great and amazing gift of Light within the Darkness. In this Darkness, I allowed Love to carry me and show me all the beauty of this place that I found myself in. It was tremendous.

I was given the gift of deeper understanding for my son. I was given an invitation to stand with him in the storm. I was given an invitation to own my feelings, embrace them (even the prickly ones), and see them as a reflection of a real life filled with the ebb and flow of nature. Grief and Joy can exist side-by-side and that is the amazing place of Life in The Spirit. In this place, all balance, as we know it, is unbalanced. This is where things that don't seem possible are commonplace. This is where the answers are plain and simply placed before us.

It was in this place that I made a decision to surrender to The Storm and all that it brought. I surrendered to the fact that this storm would not blow over quickly. This Season would cover a lot of time. And this was all okay. That is the way of Nature. Even though this time is difficult, unpredictable, and chaotic, we are also in a time of great beauty. This is the time where the whisper of God's voice is heard the loudest, where the arms of Love hold me tight, and where my eyes are opened to all the good that lies within this time and place. Here is where I am alive, breathing, feeling, and living with every obstacle and blessing that crosses my path.

I had a dream that my Spirit Guide came to me while I was in my Grief and showed me the Light that lives in my heart for my son. Right now, he was unable to access his own light, and I must shine mine for him. I must be the Light that he is unable to be.

She showed me a vision of my chest. My hands were forming a heart over it. Through the heart shape a light shined that came from within me. There was no other light in this place, only the warm light that was coming from within me. My hands enabled the light to go farther out and diffuse the darkness. The light was not super-bright. It was just bright enough and very warm and comforting.

This is the "Season of The Storm." In Storm Season, you do what you need to do to weather it and also live in it.

(The Young Blood did eventually come back home. Thankfully he had another home that he went to. These two homes worked together. I'm so grateful for this.)

January 30, 2011 The Season of The Storm- Part 2

"Warrior Mother"

~A mother's personal journey of choosing to stay in The Storm with everything that she is.

Last Monday, I caught up with one of my besties. She asked how my weekend had been. I paused and thought about my answer for a moment. I wanted my answer to be said in a way that I would be speaking of life and not death. I want it to be truth-filled, raw, and real. This is what I told her:

"If you would look at it with worldly eyes, you would see that it was a total shit show. Terrible. But, if you were to look at it with spiritual eyes, you would have been amazed!"

Last weekend, I reconnected, in a HUGE way, to my inner Woman Warrior. She has always been there. In fact, she is a huge part of me. I am feisty. I realize there are those who don't appreciate that in a woman, but THAT is who I am. IT has served me well. My inner Woman Warrior rocks the party. Seriously she is something else. Among the softness of my feminine, there lies a rock of great strength and commitment and knowledge and focus. This rock was given to me by the Supernatural.

When I look back at the path we have been walking in our home, it is unbelievably gnarly and rough. I am amazed that we were able to walk through it with no injury. When I look down, I see myself carefully placing my feet, choosing my steps wisely, one step at a time. Breathing…Breathing…Breathing.

When I look too far ahead, all I can see is more gnarly roots trying to trip us up. I feel overwhelmed, discouraged, and lost, so I stop looking ahead. I am in the here and now, this moment, for it is all I have. By staying in the moment, those feelings of discouragement leave me, and I no longer feel lost. I am here, in this moment, with everything it has to offer.

A slow burn fight

A prayer: "This home belongs to Love and Light."

Running Away.
Running After.
No shoes.
Cold feet.
Heart beating out of my chest.
Warrior Woman in command.
Searching in the Dark.

A prayer: "Please go to a friend's."

Go to the other home.
Fill them in.
Back searching in the dark.
How many red jackets are there?

A prayer: "Even though I walk through the valley of the shadow of death I fear nothing for God is with me…always."

Search out a possibility.
Truth is told.
"My son is a good kid. He just has some struggles."
A kindred mother who knows.
Hugs and complete understanding.

A Prayer of Gratitude.

Not Found.
Home.
Waiting.
The Call.
Afraid to come back home.
Tears.

Story of the Prodigal's Son comes to mind.

Do not be afraid.
Come home.
The Door opens.
Run to him.
Hug him.
Hold him.
Love him.
Resolve to follow.
This was the night when I once again became a Warrior.
This time for different reasons.

I realized that I cannot come in and out of The Storm. I have to stay here with my Young Blood. I have to do things that go against the norm. I have to be a Spiritual Warrior for my son. The child that was given to me to care for. I was picked for this reason. My feistiness, my determination, and my spiritual gifts were all given to me for a time such as now.

Today the Light shines through the trees. The week has been peace-filled. Full of affirmations, apology, time together, love, forgiveness, and freedom.

The battle is far from over.

I know my place. I know what I am capable of. I know how far I am willing to go.

I am not afraid.
I do not fight out of Fear.
I am not afraid.
I fight for Love.
I am not afraid.
I will die for Love.
I am not afraid.

February 26,2011 The Season of The Storm – Part 3

"Spiritual Parenting"

~a story of a mother's journey to be her son's light

This has been such a time of Supernatural Interventions. I cannot begin to tell you the amazing things that have been shifting and shaping in my world as a parent and as a Warrior Mother. For example, last week I was at an amazing Spiritual Gathering were among other things I received an image of my Young Blood. While a storm whipped around us, I stood in a boat. Now this is not too new of a scene for these days, but the boat was a new entity.

The talk at the Gathering was about faith being an action word. Unless you put your faith or beliefs into action, you are not doing much to impact yourself or the world around you. Victory requires action, so shout victory even before you have it! Live as you have already attained your heart's desire. Be bold and take the risk that is acting upon your beliefs.

I see myself in this boat, in a storm with the Young Blood. I hear the words,

"Step out of the boat." My first reaction is literal. I think I need to step out of the boat. As soon as I move to do this, I know that is not what I am to do. I see my heart glowing. I see the warmth that it gives. It is giving comfort to the Young Blood, but it is not enough. I realize that I am to take him down into the cabin of the boat. There it is safe, warm, quiet, and far more secure than standing out on the deck.

What a gift.

If I believe in Love as I do…why would Love or the God of Love want us to be in a dangerous or frightening place? Does that make sense?

The fact is that refuge is always provided. Sometimes we just miss it. Sometimes we are so distracted by the hardship that we do not see the Loving relief that is so readily given. I took my Young Blood inside, where we ate warm food and drank a warm drink. This is where I was a mother who gave comfort and security that my child needed…

…and I received the comfort and security I needed as well. For though I am a Warrior Mother, Love is there for me as well. I was reminded that I am not holding my sword or my shield alone. My purpose is to nurture and be nurtured. It was an amazing awakening within myself in that vision.

In turn, as I allow myself to be nurtured and lead, I become strong and more effective in my role of Warrior Mother. My vision gets clearer. My love glows quickly and easily. I am no longer quick to judge. Instead, I am quick to Love. The feeling of loneliness diminishes. I begin to understand a deeper sense of how turning my eyes to the Spiritual free me, even in my parenting.

Spiritual Parenting.

Within the parameters of my thoughts, we are all spiritual beings, created by One Source and intertwined with one another. I have Faith in spiritual help and guidance along my way. I have experienced that there is purpose in everything. Even when I am unable to see or understand that purpose

I have learned in this "Season of The Storm" that the thought of my deeper purpose needs to be an active part of my parenting. The mountain may look big. As a Warrior Mother, I look small. But the truth, it is all an illusion, because I am larger than life, as is everyone. In my Faith, I can and do move mountains.

So can you friends.

So can you!

Yesterday I journeyed back to that boat, with the Young Blood and me still sitting in the cabin. I did not go in to see how we were doing. Instead, I looked around and had the most astonishing realization. The storm did not exist. The storm was something only in my Young Blood's perception. I realized that it did not have to be mine. The storm was not real. I stood there stunned and thrilled by this offering of clarity from Spirit.

Through this "Season of The Storm," I learned that God, The Great Mystery held sacred wisdom that went deep into the interior of purpose. It was not the latest thing or new age. It was age old and has been around long before us and will remain even after our time ends.

Spirit does not skim the surface, but dives deep into Love and brings out the best of each of us. We only need to allow and invite it in. Love knows what Love is thinking and wants you to know as well. Each of us has this Love within us. It was stitched inside of us when we were formed. No book, teacher, or education can give the Love to you. Education and knowledge along with life experiences and living whole-heartedly and awake will help you find the Love that you instinctively know exists.

On its own, the unspiritual self does not have the capacity to recognize these gifts of Spirit. To the unspiritual self, these things appear to be unnecessary. In many cases, they seem stupid or even silly. Spirit is only known when our Spirit is ignited within us and together we join in communion with The Great Mystery, God, The Universe, or whatever word you choose to use. We join together as One.

I hold fast to my new-found knowledge and walk as a Warrior Mother within a Spiritual context, see everything as a Spiritual Source, and know that all is Spiritual. I keep in mind that the grace I have been given needs to be passed on and given wings to touch others, as I have been touched. My son, my Young Blood is one such gift. He is beautiful, bright, alive, and exciting. I will continue to stand in this invisible storm with him as long as he needs. I am grateful and honoured to do so.

I will write it here again, one of my greatest teachers has been my Young Blood. No one could take me to these places of learning like him. During these times of struggle, he taught me how to love in the unconditional way that love was intended. The love I learned about had so many conditions. This relationship with my Young Blood was breaking that way of loving off my heart piece-by-piece. It wasn't like Love had not tried before. Often, I heard Love whisper in my ear, but I ignored it, blocked it out, or even hid from its voice. But now, because of my son, I could see that no matter what, I have Love, an endless supply flowing into me, through me, and out of me. Love is a full life of freedom. I learned that Love longs for me, for us, to be free. Freedom doesn't mean that the challenges of the journey disappear, but it means I could see them, accept them, and make sure that they did not take my power, my focus, or my love for the life I was living. Loving the life I was living was key, and now I was living that life in Love.

March 9, 2011

I have a friend whose name is Gail. She has decided to do something today that is quite out of character. She decided to love on herself and not only that, but she invited her friends to tagalong to the love party! Always one to enjoy a party, I have decided to join in.

5 Things I LOVE about ME!

#1 I love how committed I am to my husband and boys. They mean the world to me. I am willing to ebb and flow, even if it stings, in order to be the best I can be for them. Those of you who are in committed relationships know this road has many ups and downs. I love that I am willing to go the extra mile to keep our marriage healthy. I love that at the end of the night the last thing I say to myself is "I love my husband" and I mean it, and like him, too.

#2 I love the kind of friend that I am. I live from the heart in this area. I am loyal, giving, supportive, and not afraid to go out on a limb for a friend.

#3 I love my spunk and my not-so-conventional ways. I am a little quirky, peculiar, and march to the beat of my own drum. I have really come to love that about myself. I love the Light that shines from within. I used to try to hide it, but not anymore.

#4 I love my passion for all things Spiritual. This is the essence of my being. I love the gifts that come along with this journey. I am honoured and humbled by all that has been given to me by Spirit.

#5 I love my hair.

Seems so simple now. Back then, I struggled and felt challenged by self-love. Along with everything else, I was healing and determined to heal my relationship with myself. I was committed to do what was needed to change how I saw myself and how I loved myself. Years before, I would have shied away from such a prompt, but no more. I was always ready to shout from the mountaintops for others. It was time I did the same thing for myself.

I expressed this love for myself in other ways. I was still cultivating a healthier relationship with my body and doing so by entering a variety of running events with my best friend. Completing these events gave me a great sense of accomplishment and kept me focused on caring for my body in a healthy way during training. I enjoyed the training and preparation so I could finish well, mentally and physically.

While in training, I learned valuable lessons about life. We don't train for life, though there was a time when I subscribed to the thought that life was about planning and preparing for what was around the corner. I discovered through my healing journey that Life was in the here and now, this moment. This moment meant more that anything from the past or anything in the future.

The breath
The blink
The movement
The beat of my heart
The ripple of my hair
The bend of my finger
The touch of my love
The pain
The emptiness
The sadness
The joy
Each moment is THE moment.

I discovered that it took <u>practice</u> to live like that. It took commitment, perseverance, and a willingness to fail over, and over, and over again. The failing wasn't the tragedy, like I had thought. The tragedy was in the not living. Life unfolded as something alive and now, not something for which to wait. I already knew that living a life "alive" as opposed to "dead" brought with it not only joy, but sadness as well. There was contentment and restlessness, too. Finally, I understood the practice of living.

I unleashed a deep hunger, to learn, grow, and move forward. I dropped lies about myself and took on truths about who I was. Even when it was uncomfortable, I put myself out there as this renewed me. Sometimes it was very uncomfortable. Being out on a limb can leave one feeling very exposed. I got over the hiding I had done. I felt more and more ready to expose myself for the person that I truly was, and step-by-step I made it happen.

April 10, 2011...Blog writing

I am sitting on the back deck. Something I have forgotten to do for a while. It is early morning, 7:30 AM on Sunday. The rain is coming down. After a fun night with friends, I am in reflection mode. There has been so much placed on my heart as of late. Things I know to be true but of which I am still afraid. No I will not be afraid of who I am to be. Am I prophetess, an Oracle, or a fortune-teller? Even as I say it, a battle goes on within me. I know it to be true, but the ego doesn't want it. There is fear. I am doing "Hearts Restored" again. It is not what I had intended. When I put it out there for others, one of my Moon Sisters was interested and is coming in each week from the city to go with me. We have a sleep over, which makes it so worth it! I continue on a path of living without fear, anxiety, and their faithful friend, depression, who always seems to tagalong for the ride. There is also the shame of admitting that I have fear and anxiety. Silly really. But definitely time to address these things. Time to go in and start a fire.

I went into this session of "Hearts Restored" feeling that it would probably be my last. I felt that all the Christian-eeze that needed to be rewired in my head and healed in my heart had gone as far as it could within this circle. I would forever be grateful to Jodie and her offering of this space for those caught up in the chains of Religious Law instead of living free in Divine Love. But for me, this path was done. I knew there was more. There was a thought inside me that I had found such a place through a blogger friend of mine.

Her name was Pixie, and her blog was called Pink Coyote. She was starting a woman's online community, which she called SouLodge. It was a place for women to gather, a safe container for like-hearted souls on a journey to heal. Much of what she taught and held swirled around the shamanic beliefs of her First Nation's heritage. This attracted me on a deep level. I had walked with her already in the blog world for a year or so, and appreciated her language and her ways. I felt a kindred spirit in her words, so I timidly signed up and remained in the shadows, watching and waiting.

April 27, 2011 "Deeper"...Blog writing

Last week, when my girlfriend and I returned home from "Hearts Restored," we enjoyed a dainty glass of red wine and some evening reflection time. This session, we were placed into our small groups, so we can go deeper into our journey if we choose to do so. The "homework" was to give a five-minute testimony or story as to why you were there. We each fumbled through, opened our hearts to the strangers that sat around us, and hoped that it was indeed as safe as it was set up to be.

At home, Sofia asked me what it was like to share my story as it was "very emotional", as she put it. Truly it is an honour, and a privilege to look where I had been and where I am now...amazing! We chatted about our families, shared our hearts, and eventually had to succumb to the tiredness of our minds and bodies.

The next day, "The Great Sadness" came on again, as it always does when I reflect on The Brokenness that was my life and still is for some of my loved ones.

I texted Sofia:

"You asked me last night how I felt about telling my story...it is an honour and so exciting to share the freedom Love has given me. It is always a day or two later when the sadness and the brokenness bubbles up and washes over me. It is so sad. And so, this morning, I cried for my family and handed it over, once again, to that which is bigger than me, and hope one day for healing and wholeness for my entire family. But until then, I stay on my course of LOVE and FREEDOM... FREEDOM to feel all the Love and Goodness that is around me."

It has been hard to leave what I know, especially when there are loved ones who I also leave behind. It is hard to hear "it's easy for you." When clearly looking at the scars I bare, it has not been at all "easy."

But...
This life has been given to me.
I have children,
a husband,
and deep meaningful relationships...
...so meaningful that merely thinking about them brings tears to my eyes. I am so overflowing with gratefulness, abundance, and Love for

this life.
Is this the one I chose?
This life is the one I was born to live.

I do not walk a religious path nor do I belong to an organized church.

I belong to The Creator and The Earth. My church is the community of diverse humans that have been placed in my life by Love.

It is neither church nor religion that brought me here.

It was Love, which took hold of my heart when I cried out in my darkest hour,

and does so over, and over, and over again.

That is my Truth, the one I need to remind myself of from time-to-time.

Love that was within me from the start and is within all of us.

And because of this Love, I choose to live Free from a past that tried to devour me and all that was within me.

Love said "Behold I stand at Hearts door and knock…If anyone hears my voice and opens the door I will come in to them."

When May came, it brought me to my knees as my Young Blood took himself to the edge. He had come to the end of his rope and could see no other way. He felt everyone would be better off without him. I am forever grateful that he failed. But it broke me. I felt like I had been dragged across the pavement. My heart was raw with the reality of just how close we came to not having his precious face to look at anymore, his beautiful voice, and even his frustrating teenage ways. All would have been gone. It was close, too close. I had to find my way so I could heal, so he could heal.

In the shock, the terror, and the darkness of it all, there came a beauty.

A deep, rich, and unexpected beauty. With deep intention, I practiced the beautiful art of unconditional love, exercised boundaries, and learned not to take things personally. The weeks following what happened with The Young Blood were so open and soft. It was the ideal time to pour in love, truth and affirmations, and in his vulnerability, he actually received it. My strategy, or the better words to use would be "my lifestyle," choice was to pour divine truths into him, over, and over, and over again. To take all that I had learned and had been given, and put it into practice.

May 9, 2011 "a thought"...Blog writing

~Transformation
~Renewal
~Restoration
~Rebirth

Life has taught me that every negative experience holds the seed of transformation.

This knowing gives me...
Freedom to smile through my tears
Joy in the heartbreak
Abundance in a time of drought
Peace in the face of the storm
Stillness in the chaos
Purpose in the hopeless
Meaning in the abyss
Warmth in the cold
Light in the dark
Knowing I'm never alone even when I am lonely
Knowing when nothing makes sense
Wholeness when I feel broken
Beauty when things look ugly
Water where the well is dry
Food in a time of famine
Triumph when I feel defeated
Certainty when things aren't certain
Truth in the midst of lies
And the greatest of these
LOVE
Love that is constantly around me
Holding me
Lifting me up
Surrounding me
Within me and without
It leaves me breathless...

May 18, 2011 "Somewhere in Between"...Blog writing

Wife: How are you? Where are you with all of this?

Husband: pauses...

"Not hopeful...not hopeless...somewhere in between."

This was the exchange between The Horticulturist and me one morning...

I thought what he said was so profoundly beautiful, I had to write it down.

Not hopeful
No hopeless
Somewhere In Between

Have you ever been in the in between?

It is a strange place, still and seemingly lifeless.

A place where you have walked through a traumatic "main event" and are completely stripped of knowing what's to come. You're still trying to grasp what has happened, and make sense of this new look of your life, while longing to hold onto the life you knew and stay engaged and functioning in a life that keeps moving, no matter what happens all at the same time.
This is the place where I am learning to put on the Blanket of Trust and carry the Light of Faith.
In this place of nothingness, there is something.
*The **Anticipation** of what is to come*
*The **Cleansing** of Refiners Fire*
*The **Freedom** of layers dropped*
*The **Gift** of Rebirth*
Saying those things only matter when I live them.
They are just empty words without the life living them out.
It's not easy when all emotions seem lost,
and yet, I just can't help but feel the beauty of this in between.
This is a place of peace and stillness
where clarity is not lacking
because you know you are there.
*It is a place to **regroup, reflect, and rejuvenate.***
The In-Between is...
*... a place to be **Still** and **Know**.*

"How Many Times?"
How many times
How many times can a clay pot be broken?
How many times can you put it back together
with the hope of it functioning the same?
Can you fill it as full?
Will what it contains seep out?
Does it not lose its value?
Does it not lose its beauty?
Really
How many times can a clay pot be broken and put back together,
before it is time to just throw it away?

Coming out of a very difficult month,
these are the things I ponder.
Dark days took me, and I wondered just how much I could take.
Words whispered
"You're Alone!"
"This is Hopeless!"
"You can't do this!"

They were only lies.

Exhausted I lay my broken self out
Piece-by-piece
They are all there,
each piece.
I am broken...yes...
but each part of me remains
intact
contrary to what the whispering voices
would have me believe
They would have me convinced
that I am lost
that I am not whole
But clearly
Through tear-filled eyes
I can see all of me
every piece.

I let emotions wave over me
Again, and again, and again.
I will not run from them.

I will not hide.
The worst has already happened.
I am already lying in pieces.
There is nothing more to fear.

What would light be if there was not the darkness?
What is it that it should bring such fear?
For is there not beauty found in the night,

The comfort found in a lovers touch,
The quiet breathing of children sleeping,
The stillness of a summer's night,
The showcase of the starry sky,
The brilliance of the waning moon,
The songs of the night creatures,
The joy of being awake, while the
rest of the world sleeps.

After a hard day,
the darkness can actually
bring relief and
the knowing that tomorrow is a new day,
and this one is done.
And for now in the dim, we can
Rest
Reflect
Rejuvenate
Restore

Every piece is there
Each accounted for
And with the help of the Potter
I place each piece back together...
...and they fit perfectly.

How many times can a clay pot be
broken and put back together?
As many times as is needed!

Reflections of me, and my life as a mother to a beautiful, gifted Young Blood whose wiring leaves him wondering if life is worth living...

It is my son. It is! Each piece is perfect...I love you.

I have a new command for you. As I have loved you, so you must love others.
~Jesus

10
Returning to Love - Part Two

June 5, 2011 "When a Mole comes to visit" ...Blog writing

A mole came to visit us last week...

It must have fallen down our basement stairwell with no way to get back out.

It was small.

Could have fit in the palm of my hand.

When I opened the door to let the Pup out for his morning business, it was there curled up into a ball.

At first, I thought it was dead, since it did not move.

But I think it was playing dead because the Pup sniffed at it.

So small.

It remained still as I pulled the Pup back while calling the rest of the family to come and see.

The Pup went in for another sniff. The mole had had enough at this point and went on the defensive.

Puppy did not know what to do with this squealing little creature.

"Back off!" said Mole.

Ruger stepped back.

With that the tables turned, and the mole was now on the offensive swatting up at Ruger's nose as he came in for another sniff. This bewildered the Pup, and he backed off.

We decided to get the mole out of there with the use of a shovel and put it into the ravine behind the house.

There was a message in that little guy...one I reflected on later that day when I was out walking on the dykes taking to a friend.

I saw that little mole as helpless.

He was lost, stuck, small, and blind. Things were looking very bleak for him.

His first defense was to play dead.

But after a time, he chose to change his strategy.

He actually came out and got aggressive with the big black pup.

When Ruger went down for a sniff and a nudge, Mole would lie on his back, squeal, and swat at Ruger with his very large digging paws. He meant business!

Even though Mole is small and blind his other senses are very sharp.

Mole knows what he needs to do just by touch. He puts his faith in what he has instead of what he doesn't have. This causes him to become even stronger. As he uses his energy to make the most of what he has, he strengthens his other senses and sees his world differently. He is able to "see" things that others cannot. He knows about hidden treasures and mysterious places. He is always searching for his treasures, which he ultimately finds.

There have been times in my life when I focused on what I did not have and would even feel sorry for myself. In truth as I look back, those very things are what made me grow and focus on what I do have, and what is right in front of me. It gave me strength where there seemed to be only weakness and vision when I felt blind.

Perspective on a situation can change everything.
I really love that.
My life.
My choice.
My freedom.

August 12, 2011 "Friends"...Blog writing

I am losing old skin...exfoliating if you will
up...and then down
emotions so strong my whole body hurts
while gently moving myself forward
gingerly
I have slowed down
it takes time to shed skin...to peel back layers

but it's been a while
and it's so easy to forget. Patience is my friend.

Unconsciously, or now what I would see as consciously, my focus was shifting around my "self care" intention. During the previous couple years, I invested time and money intentionally into physical health, taking part in ½ marathons and small triathlons. The physical health was still a priority but my intention was turning toward deeper spiritual, heart, and soul work.

Again, through blogging, I met a woman named Cathy Hardy. She was sharing a journey of grief on her blog, one that I related to and I saw myself in her words. Through this connection, I found out that not only was she a singer, but also co-created a silent retreat, which happened, locally, in November. It was close to my home. Purely on heart faith, her writing, and her response to my comments on her blog, I signed up for her Silent Retreat. It would be my first time entering into intentional silence, and I felt that I was ready.

Another retreat coming up was one with "The Wisdom Club," my book club at the time. We were heading up country to delve deeper into our latest read, *The Wishing Year* by Noell Oxenhandler. This book is a memoir, which takes the reader on a journey with the author to fulfill three wishes. To fulfill these three wishes, Noell embarks on different rituals and ceremony for an entire year. Our plan was to do the same over a weekend, using some of the rituals and ceremony from the book. As it ended up, only six of the twelve could make the weekend retreat. For the six of us, the weekend was more than any of us could have imagined. We unleashed a power and experienced an awakening that was undeniable.

It was during this weekend retreat that I experience the full power of what happens when women gather with intention. I always knew it was there, but had yet to experience it on such a level, and it was mind-blowing. I was given the name "The Messenger," which I found humorous, as one of my biggest fears is not being heard. I wept and laughed when it came to me. I was introduced to more animal guides and fully engaged in the energy centers of my body, my chakras, for the first time. Above all, I experienced a rebirth.

Sept. 11, 2011 "ReBirth"
(first entry of my new Blog...Love and Light)

I have been reborn...again.

This has happened before...

And I know it will happen again, but, I have to say, this time, was like no other.

When I look back at the past few months...the year

I can see the pattern emerging

Nine months

Nine months to get to this place of Rebirth

Not an awakening.

Not an A-HA moment.

Not a shift.

It was full on, pushing my way through the canal of life and being reborn.

Envision a grown woman being born. It's a little uncomfortable. *smile*

I will bring you back to the beginning of this nine-month gestation.

Without even realizing it, I had set the tone for the year.

I had welcomed Owl as my guide this year and was taken into the dark, where she dwells to find the treasures of the shadow, the night, and those things that scare me.

After many promptings from my Spirit, I had decided to start living in the courage of who I am. Owl had come to reveal herself to me as an important part of who I was in the spiritual realm.

The time seemed right to answer the invitation with a "Yes, I am ready."

Of course, we are never truly prepared for what is given when we ask for it. Are we?

But I asked, and it was given...this is how the story began.

It started with the Seed of Realization.

It was the realization that I could live in true joy and a peace that surpassed all understanding, even while standing in the storm.
We talk about living in Joy and Peace.
We are told it can happen.
We desire to attain it.
But true surrender to this Truth is different.
Bringing it from head to heart takes intention and time.
Things began to change and a seed was planted, one that was eager to grow.

I had put Power on a shelf. Then I reconnected with it.
The Truth was I put it on a shelf, abandoned and forgotten. Things started to become clearer as to why I felt a longing and restlessness inside. With the Power being poured into that seed so quickly, the foundation was laid for this new life within me. The seed that was planted had a chance, a real chance to grow into what it was meant to be.

After these awakenings, Truth began to quickly unravel, like fishing line being taken deep into the lake by its prey. The Truth unravelled.

I have not looked back.
It was the Truth about what I feared…the fear of not being enough, being too much, or being too damaged.

The Truth I uncovered was what I feared existed because of me…my doubts and insecurities. I had control over these aspects of me, I only had to apply it.

Truthfully, Fear has no hold on me, unless I allow it.
When I ask Fear to come along side and walk with me instead of me running from it, everything changed. The seed inside continued to grow at a rapid pace with great strength and assurance.

Then a near tragedy happened just before the season changed to summer.

A family crisis deep within.
I easily could have lost that life inside of me. Something had exploded in my chest and tried to rip out my heart.
But it was not meant to be.
I would not let my heart be taken.
Broken it was, but not taken.

I don't tell you this for you to feel sorry for me.

No.

Instead I tell you this because of all the beauty that comes from such tragedies. During our lifetime here on Earth, all of us face tragedies.

We walked through this time as a family.

We did not run or hide, deny, or blame.

This was our Truth, and we were in it together.

With the life that was growing inside of me, and the Truth of a Love that was beyond all loves, I allowed every emotion to pour over me. I marinated in the pain of what could have been, cried for joy and relief of what was, and treasured... treasured every scrape and bruise this season had given me. I was living a real life. I AM living a real life where challenges and grace walk as good friends, hand- in-hand...

And the seed grew.

Now I could feel it.

I knew it was there. I knew it was real, and I surrendered to it.

The next season was like a nesting season, but I saw it more as an exfoliation. I was beginning transition, getting ready to emerge as something new. I was a butterfly getting ready to break from her cocoon. Have you watched that? It takes time, and she cannot have help. It is all a part of her process to develop into all that she needs to be to live fully through her next stage of life...

...the final stage.

A spiritually infused, intentional weekend away with five other women was where I was able to give birth to myself.

It was safe.

God...well God was there in a way I had never experienced before. He was in every fiber of our beings, in every molecule, cell, and atom. In every vibration, God, Love, or The Source of all things danced, sang, and breathed Life into us as we journeyed into ourselves and back out again.

We laid down our regrets and fears, and drew in our dreams and prayers.

We walked this journey together and became intertwined with one another. The Love that manifested from us was insurmountable, unexplainable, and bigger than we each imagined it could be. It was good and all was well with our souls.

With these five amazing women around me, I birthed a new life for myself,

a life that I knew had been waiting for me.

This Blog will be a reflection of that life.

Not just for me because I did not get here on my own.

This space is for other travellers like myself, who seek the Truth, Grace, Love, and Light.

I hope you will join me...as we are not meant to walk alone.

We are women.
We are meant to gather.
It is The Way.
Gather here with me...
...and let us become Traveling Sisters who are discovering our Truths.
I am a Messenger, who has come to bring Good News, plant seeds, and open doors to all those who seek it.
Love and Light

I was fully and completely stepping into my rebirthed self. Looking back, I wonder if this has to happen for healing. I spent years showing up again, and again, and again, stumbling around in the dark, and hoping for something that I did not know, but hoping none-the-less. Through the process, I was given a chance to take the healing and transfer it into a rebirthed self.

Next came a weekend workshop with a woman named Monique MacDonald, Author, Trainer, and Shift Disturber. The workshop was called "Discover Your Sacred Gifts." The weekend workshop was insightful and filled my spirit. I found a lot of verification, validation, and appreciated Monique's refreshing directness and straightforward talk. However, the really big hit came when I had a one-on-one session over the phone with Monique. It proved to be another propelling event. In the session, I brought her my self-doubt and challenges that I had with letting go. She immediately shifted my perspective to the fact that if I doubted myself, then I doubted God. If there is a lack of letting go, then I did not trust God. I heard it and got it. Ninety minutes later, my mind expanded and my power grew. I made a very detailed list of what I wanted to do next.

Things I want to do:

- Surrender into the Trust
- Voice my Desire:
- Ask God for everything
- Place all things before Spirit
- Ask directly for what it is I want
- Welcome conflict:
- See this as an exciting opportunity to move through this and watch myself move into my sacred purpose
- Stop being Lazy
- Seek out my spiritual maturity
- I seek because I know it is in the Spiritual that I will find my Truth, Peace, and Oneness with The Creator, my Protector, and my Love
- Push passed the desire of my flesh, which tells me:
- It's too hard
- This hurts too much
- I don't want to do this
- Can't someone else do this?
- Why is this my life?
- Be Bold:
- Go boldly to Spirit
- Be bold about what I require
- Be bold, and be clear
- Die to my old self:
- Die to the old wounds
- Be healed and live the life of the new me

We discussed my birth path at which time Monique told me about my connection to "magic." She told me that I came from a history of magical people with unique gifts. She verified the conflict within me about this due to the perception of my upbringing. She also said that in ancient times there were those who used their powers for the wrong reasons creating an "evil" around these gifts, which left those who followed feeling very uncertain about their own gifts to the point of leaving them dormant for many generations. This deeply resonated with me.

Then toward the end of our 90 minutes came the biggest revelation of all. This is what I came to see as a huge block on my healing path. Monique touched a Pandora's Box within me. With that one gentle touch, she unravelled a whole package of items. This was around disappointment and my judgment of my sister. Behind that judgement was anger and hurt that was feeding my struggles, holding me back, and affecting my healing path. Monique stressed how <u>important</u> it was that I look at and address this. This was not the first time I had been told about my anger, but it was the first time I decided to hear it without taking it personally.

It was absolutely true. I was in total judgement of my sister. Not only was I judging, but also on further reflection on the anger, I saw that I had transferred my anger around my dad onto her. WOW! That was huge! I also saw that every hurt and disappointment that I had with whom I was in relationship, was filtered through that anger and that old remaining piece of my family wound. It was why things hit me so deep, why it was so hard to let go and move on, and why it was so hard for me to forgive. Though I had managed all the crap with my dad well, I had missed the most important thing, Forgiveness. I had not forgiven him.

October 18, 2011...Love and Light

So my letting go process began immediately. And it all came down to Trusting Spirit and handing it over to Spirit.

At first, I got all caught up in my head and worked up about having to go up to see my sister. This was something that I did not feel good about doing. I did not see it going well. I was a bit all over the place with my emotions. At 1:30am, I lay in my bed trying to visualize myself free of this anger. I wrestled with myself for almost an hour until I finally got on my knees at the side of my bed and laid it all out before God. It was then that I heard the reply "I did not ask you to go to your sisters." hmmmmm, yeah...true haha.

October 20, 2011...Love and Light

A vision was given to me about my anger. The anger and pain are hard balls of packed clay that sit in the middle of my solar plexus. At first, I thought I would pass it like a gallstone, or something painful. But Spirit has other plans for me. There is water and God's hands are turning it over and over, like a potter's hands. The water is melting the anger away into liquid. This liquid lines my body. It does not go away. It takes on a new form. I have also been given four things to do to complete the releasing process. And these I will carry out. There will be no more filtering hurt through that old wound, no more anger that is rock hard in my gut. No more doubt. I will rest when I need to rest and not feel guilty. I will shine when I need to shine. I will say what I need to say, and live how I need to live. I have had some negative feedback from a close friend about my journey. It put me to the test. I trust the guidance that has been given. I know this path is the right one. It feels like home.

I must say that the breaking down of that hard ball of clay, my anger, did not happen in one night. This was a process over many nights, where I would lay in bed as the hands of God came inside me and gently, along with healing water, transformed it bit-by-bit.

October 23, 2011...Love and Light

This morning we went for a family walk to one of our favorite spots. It ended up being a piece of my healing. I know there was a lot of emotion packed into that ball of clay.

Confusion
Hurt

Confusion was a big one. Knowing something inside me but seeing something else outside. While God is emulsifying that hard ball of clay, I am realizing part of this journey will be me letting go of the emotions. Needless to say the tears flowed. Even writing about those emotions is difficult. I am willing to forgive. If the emotions come with that, then I am willing to feel. The aftermath of such encounters is what I need to address here today. On the walk, I was trying to share with The Horticulturist all that has been going on. Of course, talking to him opened my heart and gave those emotions a chance to come to the surface. Now, as I sit in the backyard by the fire, I feel like I have been crying all day. I feel deeply wounded crying with buckets of pain emptying out of my chest. I want it to be over, but I understand the outcome and necessity of this purge. I am safe and loved, and it is okay for me to fall apart and clean out these emotions, and release the emotions of the past that I have held onto for so long. Though I moved the emotions from place-to-place, they got smaller with every move, but they never entirely left me. They came to rest in my middle and formed a clay ball about the size of a baseball, hard and dry.

Seeing Cathy Hardy perform last night for the first time really started all of this for me. She moves me deeply with her sacred singing. Many times I found tears streaming down my face. I felt the words she sang come from deep within her. I felt opened up and "preached to" in such a beautiful, gentle, and organic way. God showed me the beginning and the end, leaving the middle to my heart as it unfolds. I think it is perfect...

I am willing to forgive.

Wherever you are Dad...I'm coming home.

November 5, 2011...Love and Light

Today I will be going to the graveyard with my new heart. I will go with a forgiving heart, not an angry heart. This is all part of my journey to healing and learning forgiveness.

Forgiveness
I could have never known how it looked
Until I invited it in...
It was nothing I could have imagined

in my limiting flesh}
As everything God...it was quiet and simple
As simple as saying~
I am willing...
I am willing to forgive.

As there was healing and forgiveness happening so was there a breaking down and a breaking up of a treasured sisterhood and friendship. A dear sister-friend of mine chose to voice her concern about my walk. As she put it, I was being tricked by the devil. I was being fooled by my sin-filled choices. She let me know that I was not the right kind of Christian, and she could not longer be in relationship with me.

I knew, and understood, where she was coming from. In the religious world, which we were both brought up in, there is only one way. That way is right while all other ways are wrong. However, I no longer believed that and had not for a while now. I just did not have the courage to say it, let alone live it. But it was true, my view of God had changed, had shifted and expanded. It hurt deeply to have this friendship end over a difference of beliefs.

Once again, it was tough to let go. It took me a long time to grieve the ending of that friendship. I loved her so. I know the guidance and motivation behind her actions and knew how she justified them to herself, because I had lived in that world. But, I had been reborn and all was renewed in my life. Looking back, I can see it was another aspect of the journey. I will say it was a very painful part of my journey. She emailed me numerous times sighting scripture that in some way, she felt, proved the path I was on was wrong. I chose not to respond to the emails. There was no point. I knew all too well the story of "there is only one way." After time passed, she let me know she missed our friendship and me. I could not step back into a relationship with her. I was no longer able to trust her with my heart and that truth caused me great sadness.

November 21, 2011...journal writing

I have entered into Silence – 60 hours of it to be exact. I have taken myself out of my life to spend some intentional time with God. My hope is "She" will guide me through all my journals and writings. That She will make clear the path of this first book that I write.

I am at The Mark Center in Abbotsford. Two hours ago, The Horticulturist and The Ginger dropped me off. We opened the retreat with a meet and greet and an orientation of the weekend. When it came time to introduce ourselves, we were asked to say where we were born, where we hoped to die, what we hoped to meet in the Silence, and what did God have waiting for us.

Where I hoped to die is in Tofino, sitting on the beach, wrapped in blankets with the ocean calling out to me and her salty mist on my face. My boys are there with their families and whatever close friends I have left. With the time I have left, we celebrate together.

What I think God has for me this weekend is CARE. God wants to care for me this weekend. My heart really ached this afternoon with the pain of my friendship breakup. It hurts. I feel judged. I feel forgotten. I feel shut out, and yet, I know all this must happen right now. I trust the bigger plan and must get out of the way. My heart hurts, but I will trust.

I will trust.
I will trust.

> *"Silence creates awareness of a depth of conversation,*
> *us listening and receiving, and then becoming more and*
> *more willing to expose the hidden places of our hearts*
> *as we come into greater and greater trust."*
> *~ Cathy Hardy*

Into the Silence I went, and inside it, I flourished. After a very big year, this gentle walk into silence was exactly what my Spirit needed. I ended up filling an entire journal that weekend. Words poured out of me, affirmations, prayers, and songs came from The Divine, through me and out onto the pages. It was a fantastic, amazing event.

> *"We need to find God, and He cannot be found in noise and*
> *restlessness. God is the friend of Silence. See how nature – trees,*
> *flowers, grass – flows in silence; see the stars, the moon, and the*
> *sun, how they move in silence. We need silence to be able to touch*
> *souls." ~ Mother Teresa*

In my journal I wrote:

Silence evokes awareness
In the Silence I have become aware of the abundance,
the love, the life.
In the Silence I have become aware of Blessings.

In the Silence I have become aware of the need to Trust fully.

In this Silence I hear the song that God hums over me:

Shalom daughter
Shalom
Mighty are you with wisdom from within
The ages are yours to speak of
In your hands you hold my Truth
When the time is right
You will set it free

Daughter,
you are a wild woman
of the wood
the ocean is your Sister
and caresses your cheeks
She gives you the courage
to return to the forest
again and again
walking the paths
finding the souls
bringing the Hope

Daughter,
My Light goes before you
and behind
My Love pours into you
Your spirit is wild
Just as I have meant it to be
You walk with the ancients
and your gifts are from Me.

Do not be afraid
Smell the earth
See the sky
Know that I am here in it all
The darkness of the forest
is nothing to fear, my Daughter
I have armed you
Stitched into you secret armor
made by own hands
Trust me, daughter
Trust Me.

Back at the beginning of this year, I had dubbed it "The Year of the Owl." I discovered that Owl had always been a part of my life. This was not just something for this year, but for the years that had past, and the years that are to come. The beginning of this year brought storms and through those challenges came the understanding that storms are relative to perception. Within each storm lies The Light and within each storm comes a Shelter provided for all. This year we found a new rhythm in our family, just in time. This year brought this mother to her knees as I almost lost my Young Blood to darkness and despair. I found myself broken apart and shattered from within. I also remembered that mountains could be moved with Faith. It was a year where Mother Earth's beauty spoke to me, every day that I stepped out into her Grace. Conversations flowed from the heart filling the rooms in which we sat, enlightening one another's hearts with our Spiritual Truths and Journeys. Grace shone brightly over us this year as I felt the loss of friends, the blessings of new ones, and the gift of the Creator's Creatures blessed me every day.

This year, an old, familiar seed began to grow, one that was rooted deep within me. That seed grew strong without my help and continued to do so. I have responded to this growth. I have embraced it and all it has come to mean to me. I am filled with gratitude for this year's gifts brought to my family and me. It brought me many more steps closer to Me.

"You don't have a soul.
You are a Soul. You have a body."
~Walter Miller, Jr.

11
Vulnerability - Part One

Vulnerability was the word given to me for the year. When it came to me, my rib cage opened and emotions churned and fluttered about. It felt painful and uncertain. I felt scared and exposed. But I also felt uplifted, free, and so excited. Vulnerability made herself known to me at the Silent Retreat in November of the year before. The retreat made it very clear that Vulnerability had come to stay and would not be leaving anytime soon. When she revealed herself to me, I asked that my wounds be deepened into wisdom and my soul find rest in loving grace.

I stepped out even further and exposed myself even more, not just to others, but to myself as well.

I am Vulnerable to the Elements of Life
A tree...exposed to
The Heat of Summer
The Winds of Autumn
The Cold of Winter
The Rains of Spring
I embrace it all
The Truth of Life
and what it holds for me
The revealing of each Season
The Death and Rebirth
The Rotting away and the Revival
I stand
firmly rooted and open
I do not hide
I say "Here I am"
I may offend
but if you try to cut me down
you will see your axe has no power over me.
I stand in the Truth of the "Great Magic"
The Great Source of all life
Only when It decides will I crumble back to the earth
from which I grew
Ashes to Ashes- Dust to Dust
Until that happens
I remain

Light Shining
Love Flowing
Truth Living
I remain.

~CBB

Vulnerability felt like another step in the direction of sharing my voice, speaking my truth, offering love, and living as my teachers did: living whole-heartedly and resiliently. Slowly, I was learning to cut the crap and shovel out the shit. It was all to reveal the undiscovered diamonds in my own life. I prayed that others would do the same. Because as I saw it, when we all did this, we could stand together, each holding our diamonds, and the shit just wouldn't matter anymore. For me, there was a lot of shame around that "shit." There was an abundance of shame. My hope was that living in vulnerability would help shift that shame into something less debilitating.

Perfect timing struck again as an amazing read came into this year with me. The Wisdom Club was reading Brene Brown's *The Gift of Imperfection: Let Go of Who You Think You're Supposed to Be and Embrace Who You Are, YOUR GUIDE TO A WHOLEHEARTED LIFE.*

This read soon became a holy scripture for me. It revealed what it looked like when I spent my time trying to be what I was not and the effects long term. In this book, Brene brings the reader, the straight goods about guilt and shame, and how those two "feelings" separate us, not only from ourselves but also from Universal Love. She does this by sharing ten guideposts on the power of wholehearted living and learning how to engage with the rest of the world and yourself from a place of worthiness, as opposed to engaging from a place of guilt or shame.

To move through shame constructively really appealed to me. Shame had been a burden I carried since I was a young girl. The shame of being a "bad girl," participating in bulimic practices and self-harm, promiscuity as a young adult, being a "party girl," being an unwed mother... shame, shame, shame! Even though I was years away from the days of my youth and childhood, shame had worked its way into my being, vocabulary, view of myself, and my way of life. I consciously and unconsciously lived a life that reflected the shame I felt.

Through all the work I was doing, I learned that it was most important to love myself, and embrace all of me, even my imperfections. Growing up in a world of perfection, I had taken on some of that outlook. I saw the imperfections in others, but I especially saw them in myself. The feeling of not being enough, or being "too much" was ever-present. This was why it was so easy for depression to lay heavy on my world. By reading Brene's words, I learned even more skills on how to keep the depression from taking over, as it once had. Self-love and acceptance impacted my depressed mind patterns in a big way.

I felt and still feel very strongly that it was because of my spiritual practice that I had come so far. I was seeing myself less and less as damaged goods and more and more as a loved and loving human being, filled with purpose and something to offer. God, and how I saw God had changed tremendously over the years. It was becoming clearer that the God I was taught about in church barely skimmed the surface of the God I now knew. The Creator, The Great Mystery, The Universe was so diverse, so vast, and so full of wonder and abundance that the little boxed God of church paled in comparison.

Reading Brene's words went deep and fit perfecting alongside my own words and views on the part spirituality plays in each of our lives. And so it was that I stepped up my spiritual practice, entering fully into the teepee that was SouLodge, held by the dear Pixie Lighthorse. The call to fully engage was strong, as the indigenous ways from which Pixie taught resonated deeply with my soul and my being. It was as if I was awakening memories within myself as I ventured farther inside this Sanctuary for Wild Women. My intention being that I wanted to open myself further to The Divine's Truth and plan for my life.

The format of SouLodge was an interactive online classroom offering two- to four-week sessions, which contained daily and weekly prompts and activities designed to take you deep within to unravel your own truths. Engagement was up to the individual. For me, there was no other way but to be fully engaged, everything touched, all things over-turned. What was meant for me was embraced, and what was not was left for others.

It was in the shamanic journeywork that I found the most healing, the most revealing, and the most guidance and support. Journeywork was relatively new to me. As I became familiar with it, I realized that I had been partaking in my own kind of journeywork my whole life. It was raw and untaught, but it had always been there.

Shamanic Journeying is a form of meditation, a way to go inward and engage with you inner or Spirit Self with the intent of retrieving information or receiving healing. It is also a way to communicate with your Spirit and Animal Guides. In Christian terms, it was similar to entering prayer and meditation with the intention to engage with The Holy Spirit. My language was changing at a rapid rate, my views broadened, and my understanding sharpened. My new language was taking me farther and farther away from those early-childhood teachings.

I wasn't in Kansas anymore.

January 23, 2012 * Conversations with Arlene (Spirit)

"All those things you find a burden in your person, in your "makeup" and your "wiring" are in fact the very things that bring you closer to your Sacred Gifts. The time has come to fully embrace those things, to see them as friends, not foes, and to look at them through God's eyes. These "challenges" of the flesh are exactly what keeps you in The Spirit. In the sense that if there were not these challenges, would you have sought out the real face of God as you have? Would it even be as important to you to know God as you do? The Gift gives you the gifts of insight, compassion, vulnerability, and simplicity. With a shift of perspective, these gifts and many more, will come forth and flourish. The Divine will be there to help you do this and make this shift of perspective about these struggles and challenges. When you fully embrace all that is within, even that which you find hard to face, come to fullness through Love and Light. God shines through us brighter and bigger, and there is more impact on those around you."
A message for self and others.

January 24, 2012 "The Journey"

The second house I lived in, as a child, was on 18th Avenue.
At the end of our short, partially gravelled road was the town graveyard.
The going joke was that we lived on a dead end.

One might think that living by a cemetery would be creepy, but I spent a lot of time there as a young girl. I loved walking up and down the rows, getting to know those who resided there. They were mysterious neighbours, and I felt a sense of peace when I walked among them. The only place that slightly disturbed me was one area where the cement grave covers had sunken deep into the ground causing it to crack open. The children's section made me sad. I can still remember some of their names.

Part of the graveyard's perimeter gave way to a steep embankment that went down to a forest line, and beyond that was the industrial section of town. This made a great toboggan hill in the winter and a great hideout place in the summer. This is where my journey begins.

I am there, on the back hill walking the trails when I see a hole in the side of the hill. I know this is the place I enter to start my journey. I am a child as I enter the hole. Immediately my subconscious wants to know what is going on, so it tries to take me somewhere familiar, but I resist. I have come to learn. I don't need familiar to feel safe. Both places flash before my eyes as if there is a battle of wills. But I want to learn new things. I want to embrace the part of me that is the "Trusting Fool." I want to be here in a new space and be okay with that. I find myself in a rich, green forest. Trees tower above me and giant ferns grow all around me. The colours are alive.

The forest is still and peaceful. The Great Magic can be felt in this place.

I stand on a hillside. At the bottom of the hill I see a small sparkling lake into which a waterfall is pouring. There beside the lake, I see a white unicorn and above it five white doves fly in a circle. I shake my head in disbelief. "Really?" I say out loud to whomever is listening. I look again and now, not only are the Unicorn and doves still there, but I notice there is an arched rainbow over the waterfall.

I am feeling so much. I can hear the drums. They are calling me to run. But all I can think about is getting down to the lake and down to business. I realize the lake is my destination.
Suddenly the Unicorn is there with me.
"Are you really here for me?" I ask.
"Yes, I am. Now, go. Run and play!" He nudges me with his nose to go and run on the trails.
Fun? Fun? I think to myself, but I have so many questions. I have come here with a purpose. I have medicine to gather, things to figure out.
But, of course, He already knows all this and so much more.

The drums carry me, and I run like the wind.

At this point, I am an essence of myself and much too serious. I want to be the full me running. I want to feel the fullness of my person now. It takes some time, but it eventually comes as I run through the trails, not an essence of me, not the child in me, but the whole of me running, running, running in complete freedom and joy.

*

I catch a glimpse of a Grizzly Bear watching me from the ferns. A little while later, I see a Wolf.

I still have a strong desire to get down to the lake, but the Unicorn tells me this is my time to have fun to run free of all burdens, all that weighs on my heart, and all that I insist on carrying around with me. And so I do. A smile is on my face. I feel a wonderful sense of lightness and freedom. I feel giddy.

Suddenly, the Grizzly is in my pathway. He stops me in my tracks - not to frighten me but to give me medicine and guidance. He tells me to Trust the Stillness and my strength. He is firm and direct with me, his medicine being of the utmost importance. Though he is firm, he is loving and kind, too. He pours into me for quite some time.

After he is finished, he releases me back to the drums, the forest, and the running with the wind. Before I know it, I am running with a pack of female Wolves.

They are beautiful, strong, intuitive, and committed. They are committed to me. They are my pack. I belong to them. They know one another. They know who they are, and so it is with me in their presence. What they feel, I feel. I need not be afraid of what's inside me, and they challenge me in this. They push me to go deeper, run faster, keep going, and so we run together.

Suddenly someone steps out into the path and I abruptly stop. It is Jesus. A feeling of dread comes over me. I feel a sudden surge of shame. I don't want to look up but I cannot help myself. Jesus is smiling down at me and in his eyes is a love so warm and pure I catch my breath. I ask him, like a child would, if I am on the right path, and what I am doing is okay. His head falls back as he laughs and says in a full, joyous voice, "Of course you are Catherine!" Then I looked behind him and saw many Spiritual leaders from throughout time, men and women. Some whom I knew and many whom I did not. On one side of him stood Buddha. On the other side stood Martin

Luther King Junior. There was also an Indigenous Spiritual leader standing in close with this threesome, but I did not recognize him.

Jesus said this to me, "When you walk your Spiritual path actively, you honour all of us and all that we have gone through for our cause, our movement for Spiritual Freedom. Some of us have died for this. You honour us when you live out your Spiritual Practice, whatever that practice looks like. We are not so concerned with how you practice, our concern is that you do. Whether it is one prayer a month or a daily practice, you honour Spirit, God, your selves, and us. And we in turn have the pleasure of blessing you through this connection." I was stunned, in shock, and also so grateful.

Jesus could see my bewilderment and held me close. Then he encouraged me on my way, running once again with the wolf pack, feeling the awe and wonder of it all. I was believing it, but not quite believing it. This one would take some time.

*

As the elder plays the drum, I am not sure how much time passes, but eventually I find myself at the lakeside. I am there with the Unicorn, the Doves, and someone I have been looking for. There is my dad.

My conscious self wants to see him in the familiar, but he has other plans.

He comes to me as a "close to" middle-aged man, the same age as me. It is an emotional exchange with the Unicorn looking on. He tells me it was not his plan to become the father he became. That he too had plans to be something different, as we all do. "The best laid plans," he says. He is sorry. He is crying. He is on his knees.

"I have forgiven you," I tell him.

"I know this." He says to me, "but I wanted you to see me like this. I wanted you to see that I was young once, too, with Hopes and Dreams. I wanted you to see the side of me you did not know." Again I try to reassure him, but this is not at all what he needs. He has come to give me this. He came to further my forgiveness, so I can be completely Free and grow in Trust.

He tells me this with his eyes and his heart.

I still feel a bit confused and overwhelmed. The pouring out of this medicine is a huge gift. It is nothing I expected or could have *dreamed. I tell him I need him.*

He gets up from his knees and says to me, "No you don't."

He looks out to all who have gathered and sweeps his arms wide to show me.

The Unicorn
The Doves
The Grizzly
The Wolf Pack

He says to me, "You never did....not in the way I wanted you to anyways and that was hard for me."

There is a stirring among the animals, I feel it.
More life reveals itself around me. Frogs start coming out of the lake.

Up above there is movement.
A Griffon comes down. I feel a host of birds that are about to follow. This is where I ask Spirit to slow things down. Right now, I need to keep it simple. There is so much inside me. I am not sure I can handle much more. I feel the thousands of birds of prey circling in the sky above. I don't look up. I don't see them, but I feel them and hear them calling out.

They are waiting for me to call them in.

But for now,
just for now,
what I have been given feels like enough,
more than enough.

A fire was lit and we danced to the sound of the drum. The Native Indian Elder from the trails was there to provide the drum and chant. There was buffalo to eat, which had been provided by the White Buffalo who made a brief appearance at the forest's edge.
My sisters were dancing and celebrating with me around the fire. They were women from all aspects of my life.
We danced and feasted into the night.
When it was time to leave, Ruger, my black lab pup, came to get me. His tail was wagging. He told me with his eyes that it was time to go.

I gave thanks and followed the pup back up the hillside and through the hole. This was the same hole into which I entered as a child. Now I come out as an adult, myself, complete, and fully who I am.

With puppy beside me, I came back to myself, home with a full heart, and much to ponder.

Let there be no doubt. This kind of medicine takes time to absorb and has a way of crashing your world apart. Learning to live with vulnerability had already taken me to my deepest depths. It was only one month into the new year! I was feeling it deep. Later, I would come to experience that these shifts happen on a cellular level, but I had not yet come to that place. I only saw and felt my entire spiritual world morphing into something else

January 20, 2012

In life there are many variables and a lot of uncertainty. This is a gift.

Our challenge is to accept all those variables, choose one, and then walk it out in Faith.

"The opposite of Faith is not doubt, but uncertainty." ~Anne Lamott

So in Faith we step out and choose a variable. We have Faith that it is the one for us. If we find later that our choice doesn't fit, we can change out mind.

Dear January

I will be honest
I am not sad to see you go
|You've pressed upon me this year
I've felt the shadows closing in
Emotions bubbled up my throat
Often leaving it hard to breathe
I have felt the cold of your breath
on the back of my naked neck
The isolation that
Cold Winters can bring
I have, at times, felt lost in the abyss
of silence that would seem to
steal my voice
You've walked me down
The Winter Path
and pulled me

through my Flesh
not to suffer
but for Freedom
And there
you showed me Light
Your challenge I rose to
and have been revealed in Truth
and
Discoveries
otherwise
left unfolded
New beginnings have taken root
Unexpected visitors
have come to call
And again my heart
has been opened wide
No, I am not sad
To see you go
Yet, I do say thank you
for all you gave
the challenge
the darkness
the growing
the lightness
But mostly I thank you
for my boys who both came to me this month
as they really are the best part of you
they lead me to be a better person
they both hold a key to what I need
Thank you and Good bye
Until we meet again, next year.

~CBB

February 2, 2012

They do not go willingly
They don't want to be transformed
They cling to my ribcage for dear life
Not understanding that the life they cling to is already dead
Not understanding that they are being invited into a living Life
I have to be still

So they can be moved
My skin feels delicate and thin
And so I walk
Becoming a messenger to myself
And it is here
Mother Mary comes to me...

Besides finding support, teachings, and guidance in SouLodge, I was also getting sacred sisterhood support from my circle, The Sisters of Light. The Sisters of Light came to be after our book club weekend retreat in September of 2011. We were all so impacted and impressed by what had transpired during the weekend that we decided to continue meeting as a way of supporting one another. We designed our sisterhood around the concept of Evolutionary Relationships found in the Feminine Power seven-week telecourse created and hosted by Claire Zammit and Katherine Woodward Thomas. We committed ourselves to being more than just girlfriends, but to move past that place and go deeper into a sisterhood. It was to be a "true partnership" of standing for and with one another in a new way; a way in which we realized we could not become our true selves by ourselves. We needed to be together to co-create interdependent ways of being and knowing.

We met twice a month to set intentions, expose our challenges, and stand in support of one another. In this place, as well as SouLodge, I began to learn a new way of seeing and being with the women in my life. I had longed for this way but was unable to see or manifest it, because I had yet to discover the tools. This place of meeting and intention with these five other women was a place of safety and support. It was sacred, and we all felt it. We all knew it. We were all hungry for this deeper connection and willing to take the steps to go deeper.

For me, it was like a dream come true. It was a step back to a memory I had once experienced in another time and had been searching for during this life. I learned so much.

In March of this year, I was blessed, again, to take a trip down to Colombia with Seeds of Love and Hope International Society. My plan was to set up a hair studio for the week and do some much-needed grooming on our kids. This time a dear sister-friend was going to join me on this pilgrimage for her first time. There had not been another team since our last visit because of safety reasons. The local gangs had been trying to press in to get their hands on some of the money that was coming to the center from Canada. They had offered protection for a payment and a warning that if this offer was not taken someone was going to die. One of our leaders at the time, Pastor Javier, called up to Canada relaying the events that were happening and let it be known that in no way should we be bowing to their requests. Instead, from his home, Javier called the gang leader, gave him his address, and told him that he was home alone if he wanted to come and kill him. He told the gang leader that there was no way any of the money to support the center and the children would be going to the gang...ever. Pastor Javier is still with us, alive and well.

Our presence on the hill had ruffled feathers. Thus Jorge, our founder, felt that a group of "gringos" would not be safe to visit the center. Also during the year in between visits, there had been a lot of political upheaval and gang leaders were getting taken down. In one way this was good, and yet it caused war within and between the gangs. Things had settled down in the community around the center, as well as in the city political forum, enough for Jorge to feel it was time for us to go back and give our support.

This visit was very different from the first in so many ways. The group was much smaller than the first, allowing a certain intimacy to happen between some of us. Also the trust was slowly beginning to build between those in the community we served and our group. So often organizations came into the ghetto communities making promises, but soon realized the enormity of the challenge and disappeared without fulfilling what they had promised to do. We had now been a presence for a few years and were proving we were in it for the long haul. We were not looking for the happily ever after as much as let's heal what has been broken and begin again one step at a time.

In my journal I wrote *"This place opens me up. I think that is why I love it so much. It is all about moving out of comfort and familiarity. This is good for me. It is a gift to be totally in a place of giving of myself. It is challenging, intense, and fulfilling...."*

One story that really stands out on this trip, and there are many, is one from a pastor who came to see us one night. He shared with us the work he and his wife were doing in the city. From the moment I first hugged him, I could feel his open heart.

His work was getting girls and women out of prostitution, a huge industry in the impoverished areas of this region. Girls who were willing to go with the pastor were put into safe houses and educated in a trade. The work was grueling and slow. His wife would approach the girls in the bars. The pastor would wait and watch. Pimps were not happy with them interfering with their girls, so there was always a level of danger. As he spoke to us, with Jorge interpreting, his honest passion could be felt. We were all very moved by him. This is another thing I noticed about being there. In a place in which there was a language barrier, other senses were ignited and expression became noticeable. Without being a master of the language, I was even that much more sensitive to the emotions that accompanied the conversations.

As he spoke, tears began to stream down my face. I could not control them. Karen had some money for him and those of us who could, added to the offering. He was so grateful and was moved to tears when we gathered as a group and prayed over him. The raw emotion of the situation and his story were heavy in the room. Hearts were opened and words were hard-to-find. After we prayed, I left the room to go to the washroom where I began to sob. I wrote that night in my journal: *"My heart is big here. I realize that a piece of me will remain here forever in this unexpected place."*

"Happiness is not dependant on happenings. But on relationships within the happenings." Corrie TenBoom

During this trip, I was reading "Jesus" by Deepak Chopra. This book was a stunning read for me. Thank you Mr. Chopra. The stories of Jesus, his reluctance, and the challenges he faced to take up the calling of his spiritual purpose stood out and spoke to me. This book told about Jesus in the human view of his life, presenting me another perspective causing yet another shift in my realities and concepts. Reading this book in a place where Jesus was ever-present was powerful indeed.

On the Sunday, we attended the sister church that supported the center. They had asked that some of us speak. This is what I shared…

"Jesus said there are two great laws for us to follow…Love God and love your neighbour as yourself. In Corinthians 12, we read about the unity and diversity in the body, just as there is unity and diversity in the world community. I believe that we are all connected. I believe that what happens to another affects me-sometimes directly-sometimes indirectly, but we affect each other none-the-less. We are like threads in a great tapestry. Together we weave something

beautiful, something handcrafted by The Creator. When one of us is fed, we all are fed. When one of us is healed, we all heal. To come to this place is my heart. To come here, helps me learn more about The One from which we all originate. To give of myself here is easy. What I receive from that giving is great. This is not about saving one another. It is about coming together, working together, coming alongside one another as Brothers and Sisters. When we do this, God's great Love is shown. When we journey together as people from different worlds, we show the abundant Love of Divinity, which does not see us by the country we live in, by the home we have, nor by our standard of living. Instead we show a Love that surpasses all these things, a Love that sees the heart and true reflection of a person. When we come together, that Love grows. It crossed miles, countries, and continents. It brings hope to those who are lost or think they are alone. When we feel alone and separate from others, hope, faith, and love are easily lost. When we stand together, we become strong and our hope and faith grows. When faith grows, Love flows forth. It is Divine Love that flows through us, that can, does, and will change this world."

Those words still resonate deep within me. And each time I return to Medellin, they are re-ignited again.

May1, 2012

I have been fooled by the immediate.
Tricked by the obvious.
Distracted by the initial.

Like the maiden swept off her feet,
I've been carried away by romance,
Intoxicated by fancy and smitten with flattery.

I've seen the blood and been afraid.
Heard the screams and felt terror.
Felt the cold hand of darkness creep in,
Leaving me unable to move

I now know beyond the immediate lies my future.
Passed the obvious awaits the mystery.
And on the other side of initial, there is what comes next.

Now as a woman, my feet are firmly planted.
I am carried away by Wonder.
I am intoxicated with Love and smitten in Grace.

I've seen the blood and know the soul remains.
Heard the screams and know they are battle cries.
Felt the cold hands of darkness and let them embrace me.
Telling them, they will be all right.

I have learned to walk in the twilight of morning,
And there I find my strength.
Seeing beyond the immediate, I see what I am truly made of.
I see the woman I was born to be,
No longer a captive of "Blue Beard." I find my strengths in my
weaknesses.
I find my truth in the lies.
I find my womanhood in the catastrophes of life.

~CBB

I had started reading *Women Who Run With The Wolves* by Clarissa Pinkola Estes, Ph.D. It was influencing my wild heart hard! This book would become like another bible for me. It was a source for guidance and unraveling, and a map to look beyond what was on the surface of my life and find deeper meaning in every breath and every movement. Looking back, I was embracing the thought that all was spiritual. There was becoming less and less of a gap between day-to-day life, the mundane so to speak, and my spiritual life. Both were intertwined with each other now. By reading books such as *Women Who Run With Wolves*, I learned just how true that was. Within every story in my life, mine and the ones that were told to me, held a key and further understanding into the psyche of my Self, as a woman. I am a woman with power, strength, and wisdom, and a woman in charge of her destiny and the sacred divine that is within.

The month of May brought with it more challenges around The Young Blood. In a whirlwind of discontent, he left home. All children must leave home as some point, but when the leaving is premature, when they are still in school, when they have nothing in place, and when they leave in anger, it is not easy to let go. My mama heart was again brought to a deep place of sadness.

May 9, 2012

This morning I woke up feeling sick, the reality of The Young Blood's absence weighing on me. So off for an early morning run I went. The moon on one side of me and the sun on the other. Then low and behold an owl. It flew up from a low bush, due to Ruger bolting toward the bush upon catching the owl's scent, and flew low in front of me. I realized in that moment, it was the same bird I had seen the day before, but had not seen its face and had taken it for a hawk. An owl is a rarity for me to see. I figured out why in SouLodge. It was amazing and no accident to see one today. I took that gift. I ran and prayed, and the sickness left me. Today is a new day. The LadyBug card came to me today, indicating a time of good fortune and abundance. It is inviting me to give gratitude for the joy and abundance around me. For a week, I pulled Camel who called me to trust that I had the resources to get through the challenge before me. Even in this time of unrest, I have this undeniable peace around me. I weep for my child who has left too soon, but maybe it is not soon enough. I feel the Divine holding us all. I see the steps laid out. I know we are not alone as we walk this out. Trust walks by my side. Faith lights my way. Hope keeps my back. To feel such things in a time of seeming darkness, I feel blessed and grateful. Sometimes one must walk in the deepest darkness to discover the brightest light.

Again, it would be my Young Blood teaching me the lessons of letting go and trusting what could not be seen. Being in this place of grief kept me focused on my various spiritual practices. Each day began with pulling a card from one of my decks. This season there were a lot of cards pulled from my Animal Medicine cards. This kept me grounded and focused on the bigger picture. Keeping me from getting caught up in the worry and anxiety of what was happening in my family. Pulling a card also offered time for prayer and reflection. Daily I took myself out to commune with nature and the animals that would show up for me. This place in nature had now become my "church." These daily visits deeply fed my soul. There was loving support from wise sisters, *"Don't push. Don't fight. Don't struggle. All you can do is release...release and hold tight."*

During this month, I also participated in a all-day retreat at a local monastery held by two dear sisters Cathy Hardy and Lori Martin. The theme of the day was

"The Art of Being Still." During this day of stillness, I wrote the following:

May 11, 2012

"I have a simple philosophy: Fill what is empty. Empty what is full. Scratch where it itches." ~Alice Roosevelt-Longsworth

Card Pulled: Cat – It's time to strike out on your own and relinquish your over dependence on others – it's easy to slip into a comfortable dependency with anything or anyone – to make truly autonomous decisions, don't get caught up in the polarities of being dependent or independent.

Yesterday was a tender day, one of great expansion and transformation. Though I feel the rawness of stretching, I also feel the blessing of it. It started with yoga class with Antje (Hope). She opened my right side and revealed to me the deep sadness within, not just about the Young Blood, but an even deeper sadness- the sadness of rejection and not being enough. There was one point where I know that if Antje had pushed me physically or even merely touched me the floodgates would have burst open. But it was not the time for that. It was a time to pay attention, be aware, and learn. What is happening with the Young Blood is bringing up other emotions. It is time to look at those things so I can respond to this season with clarity and truth. I will not fall into conditioning or old patterns. My desire is to learn from this season as a mother and a woman.

It is spring.
A time for new growth.

When I left the class yesterday, I carried the class experience with me. I felt the heaviness of grief and have accepted that it will be with me for a while. It is only a reflection of my love. It does not need to consume me. It just needs to be with me.

The workday was a busy one. There was no time to indulge in my feelings or reflections – though one did come to mind while eating my breakfast…

Learning to live sad without being mad

Being a year of Vulnerability this is a reaction, a learned pattern. Sadness either brought me to the dark halls of depression or to anger. BUT, I choose to change and transform this into a response, and one that I will become comfortable with so I can feel sad without being mad.

What am I mad at?

The Vulnerability brings Sadness. The revelation of a "weak spot" came to me. There is a fear that if someone sees this weak spot, they might use it against me. Also there is the vulnerability of feeling weak. This is an old thought. The fear of weakness is being transformed within me. I know it is in that weakness that I will find my strength.

Then there is the learning of how to express that sadness in a healthy way. Again not having it is all-consuming or the darkness of depression, but also acknowledging it so that it feels heard and validated.

So I will continue to explore what has been brought to my attention and learning to be sad without being mad.

Of course it is not an accident that I signed up for this event. This is what I needed after the past week, a time for instructional worship, reflection, and stillness. The Abby offers this.

There is an invitation to continue. This is the gift of being still. Here is the fullness of this practice:

I am...
I am one.
I am many.
I am Earth.
I am sky.
I am mountain.
I am tree.
All the things I worship are a part of me.
All that I honour on the outside
Lives inside of me.

The Young Blood has left home
And I am learning to be sad
I miss him

"Come, come, whoever you are, wanderer, worshiper, lover of leaving,

it doesn't matter. Ours is not a caravan of despair.

Come, even if you have broken your vow a hundred times.

Come, come again, come."

~Rumi

12
Vulnerability - Part Two

SouLodge, was a place that truly was becoming a sanctuary. The language was so familiar to my bones and the container a place of integrity and honour. With question prompts from Pixie Lighthorse, I was being led out and then back inward for the answers.

What do you feel you learn or are faced with again and again?
The practice of letting go and opening the way for my faithful companions to join me: Trust, Faith, and Hope.

How can you reframe your thinking around the pattern in order to bring a new perspective? *My former pattern was to allow the darkness to consume me. I let it have its way with me. The food that has come out of this is that I am deeply familiar with the darkness. We go way back. But now, in my transformed self, I befriend the dark, embrace it, but never let it become bigger than me. I realize now through my journeywork that this serves no one, not the darkness nor myself.*

What are the undeniable aspects of you that call for your attention? *To not be a victim, to stand tall, even when I don't know the way. Even if I don't have the words, I have myself and only I can keep myself rooted. Only I can keep myself stranding tall. Only I can be true to me. Everything else will follow…*

This is so beautiful to be reading on such a day as today, but there are no accidents are there, sweet Pixie. I welcome these words of truth and am grateful for the prompt to reflect. Love to you beautiful sister. Love and light.

Vulnerability had taken me to a deep place, and along with that, it had bought me to great elation. One of my Sisters of Light and I were embarking together as co-creators of daylong workshops for women. A container in which to assist them in establishing deeper and more authentic connections with themselves and others. "You Matter" was our theme. Back in September of 2008, I had a premonition about Sylvie and me working together. I saw us standing side-by-side being part of the revolution of awakening the Sacred Feminine. I was shown that through our own diversity, we would bring together worlds. We would represent the diversity within creation, human life, and Mother Nature. We had both sat with it and waited until the time seemed right and that time had come. The workshop was a beautiful success. Through the nervousness of it all, I could feel that this was a place I was being called. I had brought women together all my life. But now, more than ever before as I was coming back to myself, I was becoming clearer about my own gifts and the vision of the sacred space I wanted to hold for other women was coming clearer.

There was a lot of death within me that needed to happen and through Dr. Pinkola Estes words in *Women Who Run with the Wolves*, it had been brought to me in a way that I finally understood. I had never been afraid of death. I had not been afraid of the dark for a very long time as I spent a lot of time there. But I was still holding on. Now was a time to understand the natural life-death-life cycle that was a part of this earthly experience. Up until this point, I had not fully appreciated the ways of the seasons, and how they pertained to me in such a personal and relational way. The Seasons of Life, Seasons of Death, Seasons of Stillness, and Seasons of Renewed Life were coming clearly into view within and around me.

May 29, 2012

Death Mother
Let it die
I hear the words
I understand it is part of the work I do
Great Work
The Creation Mother
The Death Mother
They both live inside me
And now...
...Now is the time of death
Allowing what must die to die
And then in turn...
Creation Mother can create
from that which has died
The double-sided archetype
a two-edged sword
In this death,

It is hard to see
Creation Mother
In this darkness,
It is difficult to see Her light
I look but I cannot find
I listen but I cannot hear
I don't know what lies ahead
The dark is thick with uncertainty,
And yet, I know what needs to be done
I know beauty comes out of the ashes
But I am unsure of how to let something die
That means so much to me.
How do I begin to let it go?
Watch it fall to the ground and broken pieces it becomes
Only you...

...Only you can help me,
Great Spirit
Walk with me in this place
This place of darkness and death
Help me do what it is I must
Help me see The Great Work
That is mine to do
Protect my Creator Mother
And give her peace, as she must wait...

...Wait for her time to soar
Great Spirit,
Open my eyes,
Open my heart,
Open my hands,
So I am able
To do the Great Work
That I can be Death Mother
That I can be...

...Complete

~CBB

The summer of this year was spent beside a creek in a forested, non-traditional campground. We tucked our little 15 ft. travel trailer in a back spot, away from the residents of the campground, beside a little creek in a grove of trees and thick-bushed forest. Here I "moved in," as The Horticulturist observed. We would go back and forth from our home to here. Often The Ginger and I would camp out for a few days on our own until The Horticulturist joined us after his workweek was done. I also had a lot of opportunity to be out there alone, which gave me long days of solitude in which to read, paint, write, and invite the Death Mother to sit with me. When I was by myself, there was a lot of grieving going on in that little camp. There was a lot of releasing and letting go, while the creek rippled by, taking my tears with it. The trees swayed overhead and kept watch. Raccoon, Woodpecker, and Heron were frequent visitors. I loved this hideaway in this very peculiar place. Here I was the "Roots of the Earth," "Winds in the Sky," "Stars of the Night," and "Light in the Love."

July 2, 2012 My Summer Prayer

Guide me Mother
Protect me Father
Remind me who I am
Open my heart
To Your Love and Light
Keep Grace and Understanding
Close by my side
Let me be slow to anger
Quick to Joy
Help me see what I need to see
Help me learn what I need to learn
Help me be what I need to be
Speak to me in this place
Guide me...Mold me...Make me
Jesus...
Be my constant companion as I walk this road
Whisper your wisdom in my ears
Radiate your love all around
And above all,
Bask me in your Infinite Joy
May this book reflect
All that You Are
The Great I Am
May it reflect your Abundant Love,

Your Abundant Wisdom,
Your Abundant Understanding.
For without You,
I am nothing
Without You, I am lost in the Abyss
Without You, I am not me.
I am Grateful for this time
I am Grateful for this space
I am Grateful for Strength
I am Grateful for Truth
I am Grateful for Love
I am Grateful, and I am Willing
To be used by You.
So it shall be…

It was a good summer for my soul. Even though the exfoliation went deep, I knew and was continually reminded that I was exactly where I needed to be. Slowly and methodically, I studied my way through *Women Who Run With the Wolves*. Through Dr. Pinkola Estes' words, I became recognizable to myself. I began to see that healing was not always about finding a cure or a remedy to "fix" what was infected or broken. More and more, I found myself in a place of wanting nothing more than full acceptance of my Self, to live, accept, and embrace all that made me…Me. The Spirit of Mother Nature beckoned me into transformation and yet invited me to take my time. I was learning the character of The Creator and seeing the movement of Spirit through new eyes. I knew that there was so much more ahead.

September 12, 2012

To Abide
To dig deep
To care fully for oneself
To listen to the deep stirrings within
To listen for the whisper
To take in the sun
To sleep with the moon
To twinkle beside the stars
To Be
As the grass is
As the flowers bloom

As the birds sing
Not because they have to
But because it is what they do
It is how they "Be"
Following their nature
Humans
Complicated with flaws and brokenness
We forget
We forget ourselves
The journey is to go back to that
The place where Creation began
In our Hearts
In our Souls
When we stood with God,
And He/She said,
"It Is Good"

Then it happened, a day of days. It was one full day in which I was broken down, broken open, and broken free. It was on this day that my world cracked open and the levy broke. Whatever had a hold of me or whatever I had a hold of, let go, and a new normal came into being. It started as a good day. I had a day of errands to do with the first one being a trip to the hair supply store to pick up goodies for the hair studio. The woman working that day was one I had known for years. We had a lovely chat, and as I turned to leave she asked me to wait. She had remembered that I pilgrimaged down to Colombia so she wanted to give me some samples to bring down with me. I was touched that she remembered and grateful for her contribution, which ended up being a big bag of sample bottles. As I drove away, I felt so blessed by her generosity. The smile would not leave my face.

Next, I had to go to a government office to renew some important legal documents. This office had not been open for more than 15 minutes and already the air was thick with negativity. **Could people really be this unhappy right at the start of their day?** was the thought going through my head. Apparently, they could. It went from bad to worse as I felt boxed in. My efforts to stay in my place of Joy were no match for what was in this place. I spoke with two different women. Both were cut from the same piece of cardboard. They were flat, no colour, and lacked any depth whatsoever in this environment. It was all I could do to not slide down their rabbit hole with them. I could not get out of there quick enough.

As the door to my car closed, cocooning me into this familiar space I *broke down.* Waves and waves of uncontrollable emotions poured out of me. I could no longer contain it. The time of "holding it together" had ended. The cards scattered as my body shook. There was more that I had to do that morning, but there was no way to do them. I drove straight home, Angels carrying me as I went. I should not have been driving.

I burst into the house where The Horticulturist was waiting for me. My words were unrecognizable. My voice barely a whisper. My body was shaking. I wanted to disappear. I longed to sink into the Blackness. I had not felt this way for a very long time, and the last time I did I "went away" for awhile.

It took me some time to get clear in this state, as my first reaction to such deep emotions was flight. But then I remembered and recognized my own *broken open*.

Broken Open was exactly how it sounds. It is like glass hitting a tile floor. The sound is startling, the impact painful, and the dismemberment frightening. But in my memories, lay the Truth. In those moments, I was uncertain about facing my day, unsure if I could face clients, work, or the world. My memories took me to the bottom of the ocean, where stillness and calm reigned. In this place, there was nothing to fear, confuse, or hurt. In that Cathedral, God came and sat with me until I was ready to resurface. In those memories, I found strength enough to walk through my day, courage enough to not give into Fear and truth enough to know it was all happening, as it should. My heart broke wide open and was exposed, yet covered and held. In the morning of the next day, the world was renewed and everything had transformed. I had *broken free.*

I was not completely clear on what happened that day. As I remember the year, I see clearly what happened. This was my last stand with Depression. This was the day Depression and I disconnected and were no longer one. Up until this point, I believed that it would be with me forever, because I had little, or next to no memory of it not being with me. It was time for me to notice and believe that depression truly was no longer attached to me. That story continued to unfold into the New Year. But I wanted to remember so I wrote: *"Whatever had a hold of me or whatever I had a hold of, let go."* This is so key. When I did figure it out a few months later, I would say that my Depression had released me. But now, a number of year later, I say it was I who released the Depression.

(Mic drop)

I know that for some this will be hard to hear and might even piss you off. I'm sorry for that. This is my story and every word of it is true. If someone had told me that I had power over my depression, enough power to set myself free of it, first, I would have argued with full conviction that it had a hold of me. I would have felt offended, or maybe even angry that someone would imply that I wasn't doing all that I could do. When I was in that place, I was so unable to see it any other way, as it is with depression. With depression comes a fog of self-doubt and feelings of worthlessness and unworthiness. It is so debilitating and only those who have experienced depression can understand the brokenness of the mind in that state. I had learned to manage it, medicate it in a healthy way, but the thought of being free of it was not something I could not wrap my head around. But the truth is, unbeknownst to me, I had done just that. It was about me letting go of it.

This was also the year I learned about a man named Stephen Jenkinson. He was a Canadian with an impressive list of education credentials and a career within the health industry. He calls himself a Death-Trade Worker and was featured in a riveting documentary in 2008 called, "The Grief Walker." A dear sister-friend of mine had directed me to it, and I was hooked. The documentary stirred so many things in me. I immediately began to look up information about him. Low and behold, he was speaking in a town just a few hours away from me. I was going, and so I did. It was amazing.

Stephen was a straight-talker, speaking the truth as he knew and experienced it. He told me everything I didn't want to hear, but already knew. He also told me things I did want to hear. He greatly impacted me. It became a dream of mine to one day study with him at his Orphan Wisdom School. I consider him to be one of the great teachers of this time, and definitely a teacher to whom I looked and paid attention. The following are a few things I jotted down in my journal:

*Death is the cradle of your Love for Life...your love for life is because *of the fact that it ends.*

*The depression does not come from the fact that we are dying. It comes from the fact that we are dying here...now.

*Why is dying such a surprise? Indeed!

*If you can't participate in your own death, then how strongly are you in your own life?

*It is not human to fear death.

*Grief is the sign of awakening.

*Grief is the sign of Life going toward itself.

*Grief is not personal.

*Grief is a skill...Grief and the Praise of Life...side-by-side

*Until the time comes, Live Well.

In my own words and thoughts, death and grief offer a place to open the vents of your heart and soul. It is a time to release, not to hold it together. In the release, we find freedom, the freedom to allow the river to take us where we need to go. Maybe it is a place we don't want to go or a place we've been avoiding. However, there are places that hold Sacred Answers. In my language, I would say Sacred Medicine for us on our journey. And these places hold a peace that passes all understanding. There is a blessing in this place.

September 28th through October 1st, the Sisters of Light were having a retreat in the mountains, facilitated by me, but with everyone making a contribution. It was another shifting weekend as we dove into Prayers, Stillness, and Love. One of the big things that came out of this weekend for me was the promise I made to myself that the bulimic behaviour I still indulged in now and again would stop. During our work that weekend, I went to some core places of when I began to believe it was okay to treat my body with such disregard. In those places, with the help of my guides, I brought in healing. Part of that healing was standing naked in front of the mirror and really, really looking at myself. This was not an easy practice, but I wanted to move through this. Furthermore, I was ready to stop the abuse. My life and reality had far surpassed the life in which I began the abuse, and quitting was way overdue. I made a promise and commitment to myself, and I have stayed committed. There have been moments of temptation, but that is all. As soon as they come, they go. Now the temptations barely come at all. I am so grateful for a space to which I could come and do good things for my body and me.

October brought me back into the SouLodge TeePee where we were goldmining our shadows with Panther. The biggest message she brought me: When going into the darker parts of the soul, Trust. This came up again and again for the entire month. Another thing that stood out from this session was a question from one of the prompt sessions.

What betrayal am I still feeling the result of, if any?

My Betrayer
Religion
Saw in me the light it longed for
Saw in me the love it needed and wanted
Saw in me the pure innocence of being
Saw in me the long to be connected with something bigger than myself
Saw in me the hunger to be free
Saw in me the determination to live...not hidden, but out in the open, for all to see.
Saw in me Compassion and Hope
Saw in me the Deep Magic that was there before time began
Saw in me a life times of freedom fighting...a soul that was constant and true
Saw in me all that it feared
Saw in me all that would transform it to something else
It tried to steal my essence
It tried to trample my being
It tried to stomp out my Hope
It tried to break my Spirit
It tried to take my Freedom
It tried
It tried
And it tried again...and sometimes
I conceded...tired, exhausted, and longing for peace
I would give in
So it would stop slamming up against me
But it never lasted

Soon my bright eyes would shine
My heart would long to soar
My feet had roots, and they needed to be places
And I needed to respond. I could not deny the pull
I would have to follow…
The Voice that called my name
The Voice that knew me
The Voice that held me, molded me. Shaped me.
The Voice that came in stillness that holds the Love of the World
Would gently guide me
Back to my place of Holy
Back to the place prepared for me
Back to my Spiritual Home
Where there is no one hanging on a cross
And where the blood and honour have been replaced by Love and Light
Back to the place where I was created to serve
Back
Back
Back
The Voice is forever calling us back
Religion
My betrayer
Born by man
Fed by fear
Nurtured by control
I forgive you
As we stand now
Face-to-face
You my Shadow
Me your Light
I forgive you
And Thank You
For it was you who pushed me back
You who sharpened my edge
You who kept my longing alive
You
You are not what I long for…and yet
Because of you
I know what it is I am going back to.

~CBB

My voice was becoming bold. To finally and fully leave the world I knew was both terrifying and exhilarating. I knew there would be ramifications and backlash. I had already experienced the death of friendships that I had loved and valued. I was sure there would be more. Knowing the place of religion from the inside out, I knew what was to come. Even if things were not said to my face, there would be "talk." But it no longer mattered. I didn't like it, but it wasn't enough to cause me hesitation. For the entire year, I had been gently called to take my place with my guides, the ancestors, and the Earth. I had rooted deep into all that was rekindled inside me. Now, I was reaching my branches high. I lived in a time when I did not have to hide, so I was not going to.

The following is my last entry for 2012 on my blog...Love and Light:

Reflections of a year living with Vulnerability...

It is the last morning of 2012. The snow is gently falling outside my window. The woodstove is crackling and all the boys, including The Horticulturist, are playing Skate 3 on the PS3, and enjoying each other's company. I am still in my PJs at 10:51am, sipping on a Starbucks with nowhere to be. It sounds like perfection.

Doesn't it?

Perfection, what does that word really mean? Truth is I live a real life, not a postcard life. I would say moments like this one are moments that I treasure, because at any given moment it could totally turn upside-down, or go severely sideways!

*But, I have come to learn perfection can be found even in those upside-down moments, too. Perfection is a state of mind. Perfection is objective. Perfection is a choice, which means **perfection is what you choose it to be.***

Vulnerability was the word that I travelled with this year. I did not complete and publish my book as I had hoped. However, I did complete the first five chapters and will continue that journey in the coming year.

There was a lot to learn living with Vulnerability and there were happenings. In order to bring that vulnerability to my story, I now know, I had to live through these happenings. There was amazing growth that came out of this year. I could not have imagined or anticipated this growth. The allies that vulnerability brought, I would never have known had I not trusted her, followed her, and allowed myself to be drawn into her. The road was challenging. At times, I felt stretched to the max, like I had been dragged across the pavement. Sometimes I just wasn't sure it was all worth it, but I chose to continue on.

This path of Vulnerability brought me closer to Trust and Faith. It brought me closer to the Life/Death/Life cycle and brought me closer to myself. That is my Soul Purpose—to journey back to myself—my Spiritual Self and the place from which I came. Vulnerability walked with me as I travelled deep within. She invited me to go places I did not want to go, but places I needed to walk through. More often than not, I could not clearly see my way, except for the very step I was on. There were times when I had no idea where that path would lead, and many times there seemed to be more darkness than light.

Vulnerability taught me that seeing clearly is not what is important. Continuing the journey, in spite of clouded vision AND learning to ask for clear guidance through such times, is essential for a HEALTHY Spiritual Journey. Having enough light for the step I was on was enough, more than enough. I also learned that I did not need to know where the path led. It was more important to know where I was than where I was going. She showed me that sometimes seeing around the corner affected the gifts on the path in front of me. She showed me how to accept where I was, and not only accept it, but sink into it, embrace it, love it, and cherish it.

This year taught me to further embrace the dark, the struggle, and the fire of Life. Vulnerability taught me to feel. By feeling all, I could embrace all. By embracing all, I found freedom to Love all. Vulnerability taught me the importance of Death and allowing something you love to end and something new to begin. She revealed the loving side of grief and journeyed me through the place of letting go, release, and rebirth. She showed me the path is there for all. She told me about the choice we all have. She made it clear that in here there is untold power, treasure, and gifts.

Walking with Vulnerability has allowed me to release my shame, guilt, and struggles. These were all important for me to write from my heart honestly, authentically, and openly with no attachment to outcome. Releasing allowed space for new Life, and allowed the Life I already had to grow much bigger and stronger.

Space had been created within and without. Coming to the end of *this year, I made a big decision. After 25 years of being a hairstylist and 12 years of running my own, very successful hair studio, I am closing my doors.*

It was a difficult decision to make, as I know what I offer to the women who come. However, it is no longer enough for me. My soaring needs more.

It's a chance I am taking, giving up a steady income, and walking away from something that has been such a huge part of me. I do not know what the coming year will look like. I am measuring my success spiritually. This is what walking with Vulnerability gave me.

I have found courage to follow my heart, bear the fruit, and grow the leaves. The Courage to reach my branches high with no fear of judgment found me in the vulnerability where there were no chains of oppression. There is only Love wrapped around my soul.

This year has been a deep, difficult blessing to my life. I am grateful for all it offered, for every soul it offered and for every gift.

I am filled with Trust beyond measure.

I have no idea what the future holds.

But I am ready...ready to step out into the Sun.

*"Humankind has not woven the web of life.
We are but one thread within it.
Whatever we do to the web, we do to ourselves.
All things are bound together.
All things connected."*

~Chief Seattle, 1854

13
Sunrise - Part One

A new season had come. A renewed light seemed to be shining on my path. Words like "rejuvenation" and "exhilaration" were lingering in my reality. It had been a long winter residing in my being. While it befriended my soul, this winter was a companion, one that brought me to what seemed like my breaking point. Winter offered me a place of stillness, a time to reflect, and a place to hibernate in the wisdom of The North. It was a time of Purification, Renewal, and Cleansing. It had been a long season, one that I saw as both treacherous and beautiful. The coldness was lifting like the thaw in Narnia. I could see my path was looking new. Frozen lakes were melting and the green of new life was once again returning. There was much beauty where I had been. I was grateful for all that winter offered. The Silence there is like no other. It brought cooling to the hot fire flames of transformation and refinement.

I was ready and willing to cross over to something new. The Sun was beckoning me to come and bask in its warmth. I wasn't rejecting its invitation to do so. I knew that with Spirit there was a season for everything. My Soul was ready for what was next.

The word given to me for this year was HUMILITY. I had felt it press upon me as 2012 came to a close. I sat with it and waited. The word remained.

It had been a full year. I was humbled by the Love that had been freely given. A God, a Spirit of such goodness and grace, humbled me. Even in the darkest times and the greatest of loss, I lived in a knowing that there was more that I couldn't see and that all things would find purpose. Through it all I was loved and cherished for who I was, not what I did. My heart had grown so much bigger than I ever thought possible. My dreams had come to life. Love was in such great abundance. It took my breath away. These days were filled with many things new, including a new rhythm and a new beat. There was a readjusting of space and time.

In SouLodge, we were embarking on a different format. We were still following The Medicine Wheel, but this year we would have a new guide to walk and work with every month. For the month of January, it would be Bear. She came to us as a nurturing Grandmother. Taking us into a loving embrace for protection, while we replenished ourselves for the year ahead. This nurturing was welcoming to my renewed heart, as it was still unsure of the shift that was taking place.

The phrase "It is time" was showing up in my meditative journey work and my soul reflections. I was being called to continue to turn inward, recognizing and utilizing my own God given strength. I was being pressed to trust my strength and trust that I was not alone. What I had been learning since my father's death, needed to be put into practice. My voice needed to be used and the messages from my guides needed to be shared.

January 18, 2013

What if I told you that everything you ever needed
Was already inside of you?
What if I told you that you were loved and cared for
Beyond your own thought of Love?
What if I told you that inside of you lay a purpose
Deeper and bigger than what you are able to imagine?
What if I told you
that you are beautiful beyond compare
and special beyond words?
What if I told you that without you, this world would not be complete?
What if I told you that life is so much more than what you see?
What if I told you worldly success is not success at all,
But that real success can only be found in Love?
What if I told you that magic is real?
What if I told you that you are magic?
What if I told you all of these things and more...
...Would you believe?

~CBB

It was only February. I felt like the year had already been a whirlwind. My hair studio was now morphing into a sacred space, and I loved it. There was a twinge of grief in closing down the studio. There were so many faces I would miss seeing, but there was no doubt that it was the right choice for me. The Young Blood had moved on, and was now living with his dad and step-mom for the first time. What an adjustment for my mama heart. But it was clear that it was time. I felt that his relationship with his dad was important. Even when we know we are doing what is needed, it can still cause the heart to grieve.

There seemed to be a Spiritual Simplification going on, one that was not intentional but happening anyway. The direction of my "work" was taking shape. Doing workshops with Sylvie was coming to an end. We had one more coming up, but we would be presenting for the last time together. Another area in which to work and share my gifts was calling. I wanted to be able to give this area the attention it needed. When there is too much "on the plate," I believe that one cannot savour the different flavours and they begin to run into one another. So, simplification was necessary. My intention was to be present, so I could be clear.

The direction that was calling to me was Stillness in Nature Retreats, now called Shaenalach Healing and Retreats. This was where my heart was being called. It is a place and experience where women can begin a journey, nurture self, and come back home. More specifically, it is a place of listening, learning, and healing. All of this is within the space of communing with Spirit, Mother Nature, and each other. I heard a call to create and hold this space. By doing so I stepped into my life purpose and spiritual role.

So many shifts happened and so many things came to life. I was feeling more and more engaged. Funny thing, I always thought I was engaged, and to a certain extent, I was. But something had shifted. It was something that I could not put my finger on and quite honestly, did not even think to give it a name. What I did know was that there was an excitement for what was coming. I felt the peace of surrender and trust as I was being guided into, what felt like, a new life. I found myself constantly asking, "Is this really MY life?" I felt the blessing of love and light. I felt myself more than I ever had. I was rooted into who I was. Of course, there were challenges. There would always be challenges. But the truth was far out weighing the uncertainty, and that was something new.

February 10, 2013

My Song of Surrender
Surrender came when I fully understood the Love that was all around me.

Surrender came when I saw, with my own eyes, my place in the tapestry

211

And believed I was meant to be there.

Surrender came when the journey began...
...when I was tired,
...when I was done,
...when I was over it,
...and ready to live free

Surrender came when I dared to go within,
when I walked my valley of death,
when I turned to face my Blue-Beard,
when I walked along the lakes of fire,
and when I went to the places of shadow and saw
that there too was God.

Surrender came when I handed it all over, and when I invited The Divine
to guide me, nurture me, and lead me to the sacred place prepared for me.

Surrender came...
...as a willing friend and
a loving companion.
Surrender came
and continues to do so....

For the month of February, we were working with Cardinal and giving attention to the sacred masculine and sacred feminine within each of us. We were being invited to go inward to see where the balance or imbalance was between these two sacred aspects of ourselves. Two beautiful messages came out of this session. One message was found in how these two aspects worked with one another and how they balanced each other; much like a couple in a loving and healthy relationship. I was shown a three-strand braid. Spirit was the center strand. On one side was the sacred masculine and on the other was the sacred feminine. They all came together into a beautiful braid—balancing each other out—bringing balance into element and thought. Nothing could break this bond for it was sacred. All is a woven tapestry: Masculine and Feminine, life and death, and joy and grief. They are all woven together, and it is in their diversity of each other that balance is found. The other message was: "There is no rush. Life knows what it is doing. There is always time to stop and enjoy the present moment." Good Medicine indeed.

February 28, 2013 A Time to Every Purpose

There was a song I listened to as a child that I loved.
It was called "Turn, Turn, Turn" sung by Sheila Walsh.
She had the voice of an angel...still does.
I loved that song.
And I can remember singing it at the top of my lungs in my bedroom,
another light in darker times.
She sings about a time and season for all things.

This I believe.

In this culture, where we are under constant pressure to grab the brass
ring,
I want to say that there is a time to ALL things,
Not just the things we want,
Or think we want,
Or think we deserve,
Or feel it should be.
There is a time for all things
And sometimes that means we have to dig down deep
Within ourselves and find Grace for others.
Granting Amnesty...Giving Grace

This is not always easy.
Forgiveness can be hard work.
Grace can be a costly gift.
And it is most needed when it is least deserved.
That is why it is Grace
To live as common threads in the same tapestry,
We must be willing to exude Grace.
To others and ourselves,
We are all connected.
We all matter and could use a little Grace.

In SouLodge to conclude this month, I wrote the following:

A marriage to self...

This month has been a rollercoaster. It has been a time of feeling,
both the sacred masculine and sacred feminine, distinctly within. I
realize my feminine side is afraid-timid. She has depended a great

deal on my masculine side to protect her, and yet at times, it has been too much for the masculine side of me. Too much for me to handle. It is long overdue that there be a balance between the two. Much of my life, I felt like a warrior on the battlefield. Then, when my father passed, the battlefield changed. I learned to allow myself to fall back. This took time. Then came a season of being taken right off the field. This was a season of refinement and anointing. Then I came back to the field, but only as an onlooker, until I became rooted enough to stand with my own convictions, my own staff. Now had come the time to walk back on to the field, but I am so changed, so transformed. I no longer carry a sword or wear armour. I come as a robed woman with staff in hand, wings grow from my back and roots from my feet. My hands are made of fire. My eyes are black as night. A stream of divine light pours into the top of my head and out of my chest. I am different, but my feminine-self is sure and unsure. She was battered and deeply wounded on that field and does not fully trust herself to be able to live this transformation. She sees the shift in her mind but has yet to feel transformed in her heart. This month has brought that fear and doubt to the surface. For all is not as a fairytale.

We are wed, she and I. Bound together. I know her, but in order for her to know her own power, she must go back down to the battlefield and so we go.

For me, walking with the animals, nature, and creation was a way of getting to know myself better. What better way to get to know my Creator than immersing myself into relationships with creation: The animals, the plants, and the stones? All of which hold sacred medicine, sacred knowing, just as each of us do. In the understanding that we are all connected and come from the same source, it made sense for me to live in this Shamanic Way. I did not hold myself separate, but I am one thread of many. I am me. I am part of many.

We had begun reading *Women Who Run With the Wolves* in my book club. It was causing quite the stir. Some were loving it, a few were mildly liking it, and others wanted nothing to do with it. But, as a group, we decided to take the year to read it in segments; After each segment, we would come back together and discuss.

I had already started reading through it last year and was one who loved it and fully related to its teachings. The other book that came my way at this time was *Everything that is Bitter and Sweet* by Ashley Judd. A sister-friend of mine had read it and felt the desire to pass it on to me. She was right. Ashley's story touched me deeply, not because she was an actress, but because she was a woman. I could relate to much of her story. The outcome of her story deeply resonated. By the time I finished reading her book, I felt like I needed to call her up and chat.

Ashley's words reflected on her childhood and how those around her saw what they wanted to see. They never saw the depressed child that she really was. This cut into familiar places in my heart. The places where a little girl would hide in the back of her closet, hit her head with her fists, and wonder what was wrong with her. As I read her words, tears fell from my eyes and bore witness to her story. I felt like I knew her intimately. She was a sister, and I wanted her to know I heard her words. I understood. I had lived it, too. I am sure if I had actually made contact with Miss Judd, I may have come across like a crazy fan, which wasn't my desire. So, I resigned to asking The Universe to send her my love, witness, and compassion.

March brought with it Buffalo and the ebb and flow of walking with strength and vulnerability. Buffalo also brought in the awareness to the abundance that was all around and the need for heartfelt gratitude. Which coincided greatly with a trip that was happening this month. This trip would take me back down to Medellin, Colombia with SOLAHIS. I was thrilled! This time things were going to be a little bit different as far as what I was going to be doing.

During the last summer, I had read another book that had deeply inspired me. After reading it, I thought to myself, I could do that! The book was called *A Thousand Sisters: My journey into the worst place on earth to be a woman* by Lisa J. Shannon. It is Lisa's memoir of how she became aware of what was happening to women in the Congo and what happened when she decided she was going to raise money to sponsor Congolese women. By taking action, she founded her own national organization, "Run for Congo Woman." She also found herself visiting the Congo to meet the women her run sponsored. While she was there, she gathered their incredible stories and placed them in her book. She inspired me to do the same.

So the goal for this next trip to Colombia, was to find an interpreter, which I did. She is a very special young woman, Tania, who would end up being my translator for future visits as well. My intention in getting a translator was to gather the stories of the children, women, and other staff who worked in our kitchen. I wanted to find out more about them and their lives. I was going to write their stories and share

them with my people. I won't go too far into it. It needs a book of
its own. I will tell you that this journey touched my heart, soul, and
being. There were times when I did not know if I was up or down. The
stories that spilled out in my little office room were more than I could
have imagined. When I shared them with my group at night, we all sat
in breathless awe. I could feel myself becoming more invested and
more intertwined with the community of the center. I could see myself
connecting further to each soul and they with me. So many familiar
faces, children whom I had watched grow, and women who had visibly
taken back their power. This was where I wanted to be. This was
where I needed to be. The following was written the day I returned
home from my "other" home, Colombia.

April 1, 2013

I have returned a weary traveler, back to my home
and to that which is familiar.
I return from a place of the most amazing beauty and most terrible
stories.
A place where innocence is fleeting
A place where such things are taken not lost
A place deep within the mountains of despair and helplessness
Where mothers are not mothers and fathers do not stand strong
Where brothers know not their place and sisters scream in silence
I bore witness to stories given by those brave enough to give
And by those who held the stories for the children who speak in
secret
I am forever changed
Not ready to be home and yet here I am, raw and tender.
Willing to stay on the battlefield
Willing to stand on blood-soaked soil
Not fully knowing the protocol but willing
ever so willing to be used in any way I can
Today upon my return
I entered the forest's waiting arms and breathed in the familiar Earth
The spring sun was warm upon my skin…
I felt the balm of Mother Earth as she wrapped herself around me
Helping me linger in the scent of yesterday,
Helping me saturate my mind with all that I experienced.
I hold onto the tear-stained cheeks,
mapping out their routes on dirty faces
the clinging hugs,

the gazes that never end,
and the smiles at the moment of joy
Holding tight to what they have
It is here that I linger
Hoping to wash myself of all that is unclean
And brand myself deep with the mark that says
I was there.
I heard you.
I see you.
I love you.
I miss you.
And as my own tears make their marks on my face,
I remain whole and broken,
In deep silence and reflection,
Heart aching,
Ready to charge...

*

April 8, 2013 Gratitude to Buffalo

I have a deep gratitude for what was given me
Strength awoken deep within
Strength that gave way to Freedom
The freedom to roam
Freedom
Found in the knowing of who I am
Though big and powerful
I am also gentle and quiet
I can run like the wind
My feet shaking the earth, and yet
Through gentleness I find my food
My soul's nourishment
I can be both
The gentle and
The strong
For that is the Abundant Song
Being all we can be
With more than enough for all...

We were stepping into Spring with Rabbit in SouLodge. As we were getting ready for the session, Pixie sent out some prompts to "warm us up."

She asked us to tune into Rabbit and connect with her in a way that would wake our senses. What did we want to leap forward to and what did we want to get away from fast? What was it that we were creating and how was that serving our healing?

My response was: ...so good to read this prompt in my inbox this morning. I had carved out this morning to spend some time with Rabbit so this is a great way to start. This has been a beautiful weekend for me. I attended a Shamanic Healing Circle on Friday evening, taking two journeys guided by a Metis Wisdom Keeper and Teacher of mine, Leonard Howell. Then last night, I attended a CD release party for a dear sister of mine, Cathy Hardy. Cathy's music comes straight from within and moves me in the deep. I feel myself fully integrating the male and female aspects of my psyche, leaping toward wholeness and a fuller understanding of myself. Leaping toward the warrior within, the strong tree, the priestess, the medicine woman, the healer, the lover, the light, and the powerhouse that is me.

I am leaping away from resentment. When it came time for the healing during my shamanic journeys on Friday, I could feel the resentment dwelling in my ego. It seemed to be in my spine, so I released it to the rattles, allowing it to be loosened, shaken up, and transformed, It is not the emotion I wish to feel or have cloud my judgement, I want to walk only in and through Love...Love and Light.

And what I am creating is a life of openness, healing, and love. A home that lends to self-expression, open communication, and unconditional love. I have my own space in my home in which I can express myself fully, where I do my hearts work and through that work reach out and touch those around me and the world...sending Love ad Light in all that I do. This is what I strive for. Some days are prettier than others, but there is always beauty. Thank you sweet Pixie and my sister of the Lodge...you are all beautiful...xox.

April 25, 2013

peel back
crumble
expose
taking me to that place
where not everyone is willing to go

listen
breathe

step within

there I find the deadliest of sin

It's not what I thought
not what I was told
it is sacred Truth
that was lost
in the dark times of old...

the layer
beyond the layer
and deeper still
vapour
breath
light as a feather
touching it
you can barely feel...
but you know it is there
like a brick
a cinder block
making itself known
gentle
quiet
Truth

Truth
the word so empty
to the freedom that it is
Truth
relative
yet universal
Truth
I stood tall
feet planted
roots strong
I said
"I am ready"
and the gates of heaven opened

pouring down all that I needed
to be whole

giving me a place to stand
giving me a cause to stand for
and fight
Courage Sister
Courage
stay your course
while the rocks crumble around you
the earth thunders and shakes
and as the darkness creeps over the land
know this
the sun WILL rise
the sun in all its glory
with the tapestry of colour
it brings
splashing across the sky
beautiful chorus of love and light
exposing all Truth
Courage Sister,
Courage
this is the beyond.
this is the enlightenment.
this is the awakening.
step into the wonder of it all
and look around.
to see
others
like you
others
like me

~CBB

Then May came with the duality of unexpected Joy and unexpected Grief. With them came a realization on the wings of Hummingbird. This was the month a dear sister-friend was diagnosed with Stage 4 colon cancer and another dear older friend, a surrogate mother to me, was also diagnosed with cancer. This one was a very rare form of blood cancer, only 23 cases in North America. These diagnoses were blows to my heart and radically changed how I showed up in life. There was also the launch of my retreats, my web page, my "coming out," which made my heart soar. And, there was something else. It had been there for a while, but I dare not put word to the thought.

This shift, this transformation had brought with it the unthinkable, the unbelievable, and yet here I was in a completely new state, one that did not include my long-time companion, depression.

I noticed it at the beginning of the year, but I was scared, scared of saying I had "been healed" for fear of it coming back to consume me. So, I became still, watched, and waited. I watched for the familiar signs, the familiar feelings, but found none. Even with the sad, heart-wrenching news about two people I loved, there was nothing. Usually something like that would plunge me into the darkness for at least a few days, if not longer. There was nothing. I decided to share in my Sisters of Light Circle. I told them I was feeling something I had not felt in a very, very long time, if ever. I was feeling sadness. Now for most people that doesn't sound great. But for one who totally found herself skipping sadness all together and falling into the depths of despair, sadness was looking really, really good. My sisters celebrated with me and heard my words, honouring where I was, and their belief in me was just what I needed.

Next, I went to one of my best sources, The Horticulturist. A man who had willingly walked with me, waited for me, was always there when I "came back," and someone who had really watched it all. I asked him if he had noticed anything different about me in the last few months. He said that he had, but had assumed I was on an extended up-swing. When I told him what I thought had happened, tears filled his eyes. I shared with him how I was feeling scared, but also felt convinced that it was so. He held me close and told me that he believed it could be so.

I warned myself not to be naive about it. I felt like I could feel the depression lingering around me. It felt like it was waiting, waiting for a chance in which it could latch back on. I thought it wasn't completely over, and I proceeded accordingly.

Now months later, I was beginning to see that what had been released was the depression. I had held onto the depression like an addiction. In my world, this was a true miracle.

Years later in January of 2016, while sitting in a Soul Care woman's circle led by Cathy Hardy and Lori Martin, I was paired up with a woman named Jodi for a heart exchange. She was asking some things about me. I told her that I was a Medicine Woman. She shared with me some information that she had recently read in a book by Martha Beck, *Finding Your Way in a Wild New World*. She had read that often people who are Healers or Medicine People are often "sick" until they claim their true purpose. Jodi had no idea about my story or journey, but this divine appointment and exchange gave me much clarity around my healing of depression.

During this time, Hummingbird came alongside me, and offered healing and guidance. Within my spiritual practice connecting with Earth and all her inhabitants is a key element and that includes the animals. My animal guides and helpers assist me in cleaning my energy field. As a human, I am full of, what I call, fleshy responses and feelings. It is easy to filter through past wounds or scars to replay old stories and get caught up on the hamster wheel of my mind. My animal guides help me move passed the trappings and distractions of my flesh and move into pure-awareness without "ego cloudiness."

They allow me to filter my own wild, instinctual nature, through theirs. By doing so, things become easier to see. It becomes easier to hear, and it brings me closer to my spiritual self and to The Great Mystery. Walking the Earth Medicine walk resonates deeply with my Being and assists me on my journey. Feelings are not bad, they have a way of telling us what we need, but feelings are only part of the medicine, especially when feelings are influenced by our stories. Sometimes we are in need of something clearer, so we can make the best decisions possible with the best kind of results.

Hummingbird opened my heart, released my expectations, and replaced it with the sweetness of life. She showed me how to gather the nectar and taste life. Her message was to keep the nectar for myself. If I could accept the sweet things in life, those around me would do the same. All sweetness needs to be brought to self before giving it to others, is what I learned from Hummingbird. A clear message that went straight to my heart.

May 22, 2013 In the Stillness that Is...

In the stillness that Is, I can breathe.
In the stillness that Is, I find truth.
The Sacred Truth of rock and bone, tear and blood, earth and sky,
root and paw,
a place in which I bare witness.
The stillness that Is, never falters, never fails, never crumbles.
It always Is.
And it is in that stillness where I am reminded of who I am.

That no matter what befalls, all is well and as it should be.
Here I am reminded to embrace this journey, yet not hold on too
tight
As it is one piece of something bigger, a stop over of sorts,
The journey within a Journey.
I am reminded to let my blood flow, and my bones creak,
Allow my tears to fall, and feel my feet take root,
Hands on fire, raised up high
I am willing
For it is in the stillness that Is
that I find You...and know...

I am not alone. ~ CBB

June was a month of flying with Creator's messenger, Eagle. I was being asked if I could surrender the way things are for the way they can be. My answer was, "Yes."

"Aaah, Eagle. How familiar you are to me-like coming home. After huge shifts in my life, you have come to reinforce my connection to Creator. My unlimited access. For this, I am grateful."

June 3, 2013 Creators Beauty

Today is the holiest of days and
You are the most precious of God's Children.
There is nothing you need to fix.
There is nothing you need to do,
*Other than **BE**.*
And sink into the miracles
That every moment brings.

~CBB

Even though I often felt the need to soldier on, I was invited to enjoy and be a part of the gentleness and peace that is. This is not always easy for the walking wounded, but I was hungry for more, and so I asked. I was told that I do not need to go charging in. All will unfold when it is meant to. I can wait and sit in the abundance of Creator and Be. Still, I am a living breathing effective part of the unit that is the human race. I was told that when I am given messages, I don't have to run out and "save the day." This way that I was shown was the old way, a fear-based way. Strength is found in patience, trust, and waiting for the right moment. Eagles are like that. They are powerful creatures that don't dive, dive, and dive. They sit and wait, and wait. Then, they glide in.

Through Eagle's eyes, I could see myself as strong and gifted. Now was the time to cultivate these gifts in a healthy way that was for my greatest good. They gave me a word in my language which was Love. They also gave me a work in their language, which was Hukthe, "A New Way."

It was during this time that a most amazing thing happened. It will forever solidify this spiritual practice of which I have chosen to be a part, this way of life that I have chosen to live. During this month with Eagle, we did a segment called "Seven Journeys, Seven Days." Each day we took a journey, (went into meditation) with Eagle as our guide. The following are two of those journeys, ones I still see as clearly as the day they were given.

June 14, 2013 Journey #1 The Wolf and I

I am on Eagle's back. We soar downward into the blackness. He leaves me in a dark forest. Around this forest, I see the glowing opalescent colours of greens, oranges, and purples. I start to walk but immediately have the sense that I need to stay within this clearing. I ask: **"Who will guide me through this journey for Angela?"**

(Angela being my sister-friend with Stage 4 cancer. Angela being the mother of Josef and Zofia, wife to Steve, Daughter to Nina and Sister to Arthur and Suzie.)

Wolf comes out of the darkness toward me. She is Angela's wolf. She turns and I see a tumour growing on the side of her torso. I think to myself, Is this Angela? Yes, I feel it is and walk beside her, and hear myself saying, "She is teaching me." As soon as the Wolf enters back into the forest, I can no longer walk with her. I turn around. Now, there is a fire at which I sit. I ask for a message, "Does anyone have anything to give me?" Another Wolf appears. He is a big male on the opposite side of the fire. He aggressively lunges toward me through the fire. Eagle comes down indicating to him to back off. I do not feel afraid of Wolf, but I do feel his aggression. Eagle made it clear that now is not the time....

June 15, 2013 Journey #2 Embodiment

Again, I am on Eagle's back. We fly for quite some time before he leaves me in a new spot. I am hiking a canyon trail heading toward the high lands and a Wolf appears. It is the same She-wolf from yesterday's journey, as she has the same tumour. I follow her but lose track of her. I hike on for a while, hoping that I am going in her direction. Now and again my vision changes from walking the trail to watching myself walking the trail. I realize that I'm watching myself through Eagle's eyes. A Red-tail Hawk comes and lands on my arm. We stand like this for a while, looking over the land. Then, he turns to me and starts flapping his wings in my face. I try to block him but by doing so I fall to the ground. There are now three Wolves standing around me. It feels like they want to eat me , but I am not afraid. They begin to eat my lower abdomen but then the dominant Male, the same one from the journey yesterday, growls at the other two, indicating for them to back off. He swallows me whole. Now, I am looking through Wolf's eyes. We run the trails until we come upon the female with the tumour. I/We bite off the tumour, tearing it from her side with our teeth. We don't consume it, but instead, we tear it apart to nothing. A wave of tiredness comes over me, and I find myself back in my human form – traveller – being welcomed into a First Nations Village.

What you need to know is that against all odds Angela did come to a place of healing. With faith, a fierce desire to live, and by using both modern and holistic medicine, she shrank her tumour into none existence. After enduring 23 rounds of chemotherapy, and using a variety of holistic healing techniques from utilizing a Naturopath, to Reiki, hypnosis and many things in between, she was able to reverse her ileostomy in less then two years after her first major surgery and diagnosis. After an intense recovery from her ileostomy reversal surgery, she is stable. Her tumour markers are in the "normal" range, and she is living a full and active life with her children and husband. In my mind, she is a walking miracle. After going through so much, her immune system and her body were forever compromised, but she is alive and thriving. She is a different woman from the one she was before this began. But if you were to ask her if it was worth it, she would tell you, "Yes!"

So, the journey's prophesy came true. It was through Wolf that I could communicate and "see" where Angela was in her healing process. Sometimes when things were not good, a pack of four to five male Wolves stood around her, not letting me in to see her. There were times that I would be able to visit her. It was always me in my Wolf form and her in her Wolf form. After these encounters, I would relay them to her. She was always so moved as to how the Wolf in my journey reflected her authentically.

I realize to some this may sound strange, and a little Woo Woo. And perhaps it is, but what I know, what we know, is that this happened. What was being shown spiritually was happening in real time. Right up until the day of my final journey, her and I both turned into our human form and left the Wolf village hand-and-hand. That was just before she was given the okay to have her ileostomy reversed because they could no longer find the tumour that was in her colon.

During her journey with cancer, I felt a deep call to walk closely with Angela. I did not always know how to show up for her, and her first couple years were tough. Sometimes I felt at a loss for what to do, but when I went to that place of loss, words would come, guiding me to come from my heart, and walk the road of a medicine woman.

July 11, 2013 A text to Angela

"Love transcends all things...there is nothing that can break its power.

Not illness, not poverty, not even death.

Love is what moves us passed our human flesh and allows us to believe in the deep magic that IS. Love...simple, yet complicated... easy, yet hard;

It covers all seasons, holds light and dark.

It is the key to all that is beautiful and good.

Sink into the Love that flows in and out of you. In abundance, you are just that...

Not a vessel for Love

No

You are Love.

You can do this...whatever "this" is; you were born to do it.

Dig deep, go passed the immediate, and find out what is going on behind the scenes.

Everything has a purpose, and there is a season for all things.

Take off/Let go of your Super Girl cape.

Hold onto the Heavenly Truth and Love that surrounds you.

Go into the eye of the storm.

It is there that we all meet God.

It is there we all find Peace."

~CBB

Make no mistake about it—enlightenment is a destructive process.
It has nothing to do with becoming better or being happier.
Enlightenment is the crumbling away of untruth.
It's seeing through the façade of pretense.
It's the complete eradication of everything we imagined to be true."

~ Adyashanti

14
Sunrise - Part Two

The summer of this year was hot and dry, as were my emotions.
I glided through it as best I could one-day-at-a-time. I am not a
summer person. It's my least favourite season, unless I am by a water
source. Summer is hard on me. It is not that I hate it, but the heat
really knows how to kick my butt. Summer brings with it "the hot
emotions of summer," as a sister-friend and I like to put it. This would
be my first summer without the fog and distraction of depression,
so other emotions had room to rise. One of those emotions was the
lingering shame of some of my past choices. Though I had come to
a place of forgiving myself, time and time again, there remained a
residue that left me feeling somewhat trapped. The gift of knowing
these things is that we get to go in and apply a necessary remedy or
needed medicine.

July 11, 2013 Honouring the Ebb and Flow in The Great Magic

Life is a beautiful experience
A gift full of wonder and magic
There was a time when those words would not have been mine.
I was unable to see passed the darkness that surrounded me.
No longer is that so.
I believe in the Ebb and Flow that Life offers.
I believe that Ebb and Flow is the Deep Essence of Life
I believe that Ebb and Flow is Sacred and Divine
And you cannot have one without the other
When one is brave enough to willingly embrace the darkness,
the light shines even brighter, and the Deep Magic comes to life.
That is the gift to those who venture deep within…

The Ebb

In uncertainty I walk
the pushing
the pulling
taking its toll
finding my voice
when lips have been stitched shut
not by Spirit
but by man
treated like a wound
that needs tending to
for fear of power and strength
that would come forth
slowly I cut the threads
I loosen the shackles
Realizing I hold the key
A time of darkness is here
I cannot see where this path leads
I call out
Where are you Spiritual Guides?
Where are you Lover of my Soul?
They answer…
"We are here…I AM here
You must Trust
Use that which you have been given
Do not wait idly
all you need, you have
within you
remember
and
believe
And so, I continue to walk
staff in hand
into an unknown land
it is barren and lonely
it would appear
nothing here grows
I pour into it
Only emptiness comes back
I lay my love down
and the cracked earth
sucks it dry

the winds strain my roots
trying to force me down
it draws me in only to
spit me out
but I remain
warrior
maiden
warrior mother
warrior crone
I will not be shaken.
I will not be moved.
I am not afraid.

The Flow

Within your Valley of Peace
I am held
cared for
loved
chosen
Songs fill the trees
As the Sun filters through
Dancing leaves upon my page
as the breeze tickles the branches
Golden Light
Transparent Greens
Beauty beyond measure
A babbling brook
Life water it gives
not a care in the world
no worry
no strife
it continues
No beginning
No end
and yet
sure of its direction
A stillness is found
in such Valleys
the gift of peace
the gift of calm
the gift of knowing

The Deep Magic
is visible here.
Felt by those
who choose to see.
A Magic
that we are all part of
a Magic deep within
each of us
That comes from the place
from which all things come.
It rumbles beneath the Earth.
It flies among the trees.
It lingers on the wind.
The beautiful Magic of Life.
Here in the valley
I find you
Lover of my Soul
Always You

~CBB

This was the summer that I went back home to a place in the north that once held me, molded me, and gave me life. When I was 16 years old, I moved away. I had not been home for more than 12 years, and only something as special as my niece getting married could draw me back there. Not that I did not have good memories, I had some wonderful memories growing up in a small northern town. But there were also the bad memories—those were the ones that I wondered about. I was well aware that a pilgrimage back home in my rebirthed self was going to be important.

I was always one who held on tight to relationships, almost like a hoarder, finding my worth in those around me and living in the concept of lack. I lived with a sense that as a relationship ended, there would be nothing to replace it. This was no longer the way for me. I was finding my worth in a place within my own being, a sacred place where divinity lives. A Home for my Soul where it gathers strength and knowing. So when I began the pilgrimage back home, back to a land of rich First Nations Blood, to the place of the Raven Clan, the Frog Clan, and the Wolf Clan, I was already on my way. I drank it in, as if it were life-giving water. This place was the dirt in my skin, the leaves in my hair, and the tone of my voice. To share it with the ones I love was a gift. The Horticulturist had been here once before, but The Ginger had not. It felt so right to be there with them.

On one of the mornings, I spent time with those who had passed on to the next life. When you grow up in a small town, going to the graveyard can be a reunion of sorts. Many family members had passed on since I moved away, and many with whom I grew up. I grieved for the old and wept for the young. It cleansed my Being. I walked through each row of head stones, seeking those I loved and finding those I knew. A sense of connection walked with me as I made my rounds and laid my offerings of cut flowers and allowed grief and sweet memories to wash over me.

Being in this place where I grew up, reminded me that there was much struggle and confusion. There was also an idyllic aspect to a childhood surrounded by so much family and in an environment and time when children had so much freedom. My many cousins and I were children of immigrants. Six siblings immigrated to the same small town. While the other eight remained in the "old country" along with my grandparents, Paka and Pepe, as we called them. We all grew up together enjoying Rockwell-style Christmases in the deep snow, the vast farmlands, and the high mountains. So many memories made as we spent a lot of time together. There were so many of us. Picnics at the lake, birthdays, holidays, sleepovers, and caregiving when parents went out of town. The smallest family had three kids and the largest had eight. There was never a shortage of companions in that kind of equation.

While we were there, a small family reunion was arranged for whoever could make it. In each of their eyes, I saw my own reflection. I don't look like them, because of being adopted and all. It was more about me seeing how they saw me, how they knew me, and in those eyes I saw home.

We camped out at my cousins for a few nights. Many stories were remembered and many seasons given homage to and witness paid to that which had faded. We talked about those who had passed on and missed their presence as we came together. The grief of missing them was still so real. Now I smile thinking about it. Home was and is a place that houses the reflection of Self. This visit was so good for my soul and my own homecoming to my Self. I was filled with gratitude and love as we headed back south to our home.

In SouLodge, I was in a gentle flow of healing with Dolphin, shedding skin with Snake, and going deep into forgiveness with Octopus. I was doing Yoga a few times a week and making sure I was continuing with my intentional self-care. My spiritual life was rich, full, and active. As the year went on, I sank into the reality that indeed the shift had happened, though I needed to be mindful. I was still tender in spots and wanted to take care.

Years ago when I was a club kid, party girl, I got pneumonia really bad. Ever since then, I can clearly feel when it is time to slow down. My chest tells me with a tightening and a shortness of breath. Now, my Being responded in the same kind of way if I was not giving myself what I needed, pushing too hard, or expecting too much. It still does, and I am grateful. It is a little reminder that I am not a superhero in a cartoon, but a Spiritual Being having a Human experience; I am The Mindful Sage, a Peaceful Warrior, and a Medicine Woman.

Make no mistake about it, I will kick serious ass when it is needed, but it is done in a way that is much different than before. My body tells me when I need to pull in, sleep more, eat better, move less, move more, and especially spend more time with and in Spirit. The reminder of the past is still there, and I know I am not going back, but I do need to be mindful.

A big shift happened this year in my Sisters of Light Circle. We had been coming together twice a month in the upper room of a sister's home for two years. We shared, supported, and learned what it looked like to be in a sisterhood with one another. At the end of September, we had our 3rd Annual Weekend Retreat. It was here that one of our sisters announced she would be leaving the group at which time the group dissipated. It was a sudden and unexpected shift. The sister leaving was a surprise but what was unexpected was that because of one sister leaving, we would all disperse.

This was a sad and tough shift for us as a sisterhood. For myself, gathering as we did, grounded me, and kept me accountable. But I also sat in trust of the ebb and flow. However, I did know that I needed to circle with other women. This was not something I was willing to give up. So, with that in mind, I decided to begin to pilgrimage down to Oregon to circle with Pixie and the Portland area sisters of SouLodge. This proved to be just what I needed to grow and learn.

I had also been seeking a teacher. One in the flesh, closer to home, and I was sure I had found him. Leonard Howell was a local Metis Wisdom Keeper and Teacher. I had done some work with him already and felt the connection. I felt that there was so much brewing for me, but unsure of the direction I needed to take. What I did know was that all would come in the right time. In the meantime, there was nothing to prove and plenty to do! It was my thought that all I needed was to step into the thoughts and dreams that came across my heart. Some of these thoughts and dreams would turn into something solid, and others would be for experience and not stay long.

One of the things that made its way into my dreams was to have my first art show featuring the imagery I collected of Mother Nature. Creativity was knocking loudly, and I decided to answer. Fall was my favourite time of year, so it seemed the perfect time to host such an event. I began making plans for it to happen in early November.

October 24, 2013 We Choose how we live...

On Friday last week, I was driving over the bridge heading to my sister-friend, Claire's place to do her hair. (There are still a few clients that I have kept...those who were more than clients) Claire lives just blocks from my dear Angela. I had hoped to pop over to Angela's place after I was done with Claire's hair. Angela was off to an appointment, one of many she attends these days. The appointment was special. This appointment would determine if the chemo treatments were doing what they were meant to do, which was to shrink the tumour that had taken up residence in her colon...So that morning, as I crossed over the bridge, Angela was on my mind, and I reminded myself that I would send her a text as soon as I arrived at Claire's. It was then that I went to my Spirit for guidance and the words I should write. As I came over the crest of the bridge, high above the river in the morning fog, I heard these words, "Catherine, you do not get to choose how you die, but you get to choose how you live." These were same words that came to me so many years ago, when I was ready to give up on life. Tears...Tears reflecting the knowing of the truth, the sacred truth in those words. Tears as I thought of Angela and her husband getting ready for this important appointment. Tears in the AWE of her spirit, her conviction, and her willingness to believe that all will be as it is meant to be, and no matter what the outcome, all will be okay. Tears because of the beauty and fragility of life. Tears because we are so held, so loved, so cared for, and we only need ask and believe. This is what she wrote on her blog after her appointment:

It has been a very long day and an even longer evening. I attended an informative session <u>tonight</u> on Cancer and Diet (specifically the Gerson Diet) and although a fruitful one, my head is exploding with new information and the task of doing more research. I am very tired, which always makes me emotional but also because the implication of what I "could" have heard today and what I heard instead is only hitting me now.

I was blessed with good news regarding the CT Scan results. The Cancer has not spread!

There is no measurable tumour remaining visible in my colon (this was the rascal that started it all). Unfortunately, even though it may have shrunk, it left behind a heck of a mess. But even the mess seems to have some positive results. The multiple masses on the lining of my abdominal cavity have decreased significantly in size, and the metastasis on my liver and right sacral bone (which is the large triangular bone at the base of the lower spine) have decreased in size as well. The accumulation of fluid that was in my abdominal cavity has also resolved itself.

The chemo has been exhausting and a struggle, but at least I know now that it is working. The juicing, the diet change, the exercise are also key to this success. What I need to do is incorporate additional holistic herbs and healing to help keep the good cells healthier and keep me strong. I will be scheduled for another CT Scan in 10 weeks, and we will see again how much progress is made.

Thank you for your love and prayers, and your unending support and positive motivation... I KNOW that I could not have gotten this far without them.

A very special friend told me "We don't get to choose how we die. But we do get to choose how we live." I made my choice, I am doing it now and I am ever so grateful and thankful. I may not be there yet, but I'm closer than I was yesterday.

Angela xox
(Sat. Oct. 19)

We don't get to choose how we die...
But we get to choose how we live.

My dear sister-friend is such a reflection of that reality.

Six months ago, the doctors told her to say goodbye to her kids. Today...who knows?

But the truth is she is alive and living and that is the happy ending...

The end of the month had come and that meant one of my favorite things....ROAD TRIP! It was my first trip to Portland, and I was not disappointed. I booked a hotel room close to the area of the city where we would gather. After settling into my room, I took a walk to find the studio where we would be meeting, and get a bite to eat. Another favorite of mine is to pick some little eatery in which I can enjoy a good glass of wine, some good food, and people watch and journal.

Portland was a beautiful city with eclectic qualities and reminded me a lot of parts of Vancouver. I was filled with nervous excitement for the next day. The gathering was more than I could have asked for. It reflected so much of what I found valuable in a circle and the sisterhood was ever present. Half of the women I knew only by name from SouLodge online. Some of the women, I did not know at all. Meeting Pixie was a definite highlight! After so many years of getting intimate in the cyber world, we were finally in the flesh with each other, face-to-face.

The day was surreal for me. The flow was beautiful, and the women who came to gather were amazing. I am still deeply connected with most of them today. I went away feeling so glad that I took the time to drive down and knew that when I was able, I would return. As I left Portland the next morning, Hawk was sitting on a lamppost by the city bridge, letting me know that I was right where I needed to be, in case I had any doubts!

On the way home, I connected with another dear blogging and SouLodge sister, Kelly Clark. We had been bloggy friends for a number of years. She had recently moved back to the Pacific Northwest. This would be our first face-to-face meeting, too. We indulged in a three-hour conversation about life, soul work, art, marriage, and sisterhood. We could have talked even longer.

Aaaaahhhhh! My heart was full as I crossed back into my homeland of CaNaDa. I could not help but wonder how I could bring all that goodness a little closer to home.

November brought my first imagery art show. It was to be at my sister-friend's yoga studio. It was a beautiful venue for my imagery. I was excited and slightly overwhelmed to be sharing my intuitive imagery collection.

The show would feature "The Hannah House Collection" along with other imagery. The Hannah House Collection was a series of imagery that was donated to a local woman's recovery center, called The Hannah House. The home was built by one of my sister-friend's husband. It was a project of The InnerVisions Recovery Society, a non-profit organization.

It was a cause close to our hearts for many reasons and for the last year or so, three of the sisters had been gathering to make personal supply bags for the women coming into the center. Many came in with only the clothing on their backs. A portion of the Art Shows profits would be going toward buying what was needed for those gift bags.

The night proved to be a success with a wonderful turn out and a lot of sales. Wow! Getting paid for what you love to do and raising funds for a good cause felt very good to me. It was amazing to see this full circle of the same photography that was part of my healing, was now going to others to add healing to their homes, and lives.

This month in SouLodge we were working with Owl as our guide. Owl would bring me into a time of honesty. She was inviting me to face my darkest fears and put to voice what I saw as my greatest failures. She asked me to talk to her about my addictions, obsession, and distractions. Those were the very things that kept me from spiritual intimacy. She wanted to help me shift the shame and implement the boundaries. The only way we could do that was if I exposed myself. This is what I wrote...

November 21, 2013

Darkest Fears: I have had many. The fear of rejection and not being accepted, but my greatest fear was always not being heard. I knew at a young age that I was being divinely spoken to, but the messages where not being heard. It has been interesting to me that I have been given the title "The Messenger," and Hawk is one of my totems. I am the messenger who fears not being heard. This fear does not have the strength that it once did, but I still feel it sometimes. When I do, I allow it to come and let it keep going. I do not allow it to attach itself to me.

Addictions? Obsessions? Distractions? The questions should be what haven't I been addicted to, what haven't I been obsessed with, and what hasn't distracted me! The addictions have ranged from alcohol and drugs, to food or lack thereof, partying, overthinking, perfectionism, over-achieving, sex, self-harm, and self-doubt. Honestly, you name it, and I've probably dabbled in it at some point in my life. I have observed, through my own travels, that addictions are a part of the human experience. Not one person on Earth has walked without one addiction or another. Some addictions are more socially acceptable, but this does not make them any less dangerous to one's psyche or the people around that person. I believe that if this truth were acknowledged so many would allow themselves to be released from whatever it is that clings to them, and in turn, what they themselves cling to. The shame that accompanies addictions, especially the socially unaccepted, can be the very thing that separates someone from realizing freedom, love, and acceptance are for everyone. Everyone has fallen short. Everyone has lost faith. Everyone has been addicted to something. A big realization has been my addiction to depression. As long as I can remember, depression has been a companion of mine. It did not start out that way. I believe it started as a protective shield for a sensitive child living in an unpredictable, insecure environment. The ability to check out and hide away within myself helped me cope and gave me a safe place to go. But over time, it became something else. I easily feel into this black pit and breezed passed any sort of "normal" response to situations that were triggering me.

Over the last 14 years, I journeyed high and low to return to myself. At the end of last year, I began to shift the depression. I had worked hard to maintain being balanced and live with it as best I could. Coming into 2013, I realized "the hold" was not what it was, so much so that I entertained thoughts that perhaps I was healed. After some time of observation, something came to the light. Something I could never have fathomed without a willingness to do the work. I realized that I was addicted to the depression. In that acknowledgement, I took back my power. I lifetime of depression clung to me, and I clung to depression. The outcome of this was a string of "symptom addictions," from which I was blessed that none of them took my life and all the wounds have been treatable. I had to be the one to let go. I had to show up for my Self. Neither God, nor Angels, nor my guides, nor those who love me could have done this for me. With their love and support, I was able to let go of the depression addiction for my Self. I find I am constantly dying to self to remain true, to move

passed "over-chewing," or to find my worth in what others think of
me. The road of addictions, obsession, and distraction is one of a
lifetime. As I travel forward, the season of addictions become shorter
lived. As I grow in wisdom, I recognize the signs and take action
for my heart. I get to decide how I want to show up...end of story.
Another distraction is putting other's needs before my own. So my
covenant with Owl is that I choose to put myself, my soul, my spiritual
well-being as a priority in my life. I honour my life, and honour the
medicine brought to me by Spirit.

And there it was, written out for all my SouLodge sisters to read, and
now written here for you to read. I am not claiming that this truth is
for everyone who walks with depression, but I am here to claim this as
my truth and my story. I was holding onto the depression, long after
it had let go of me. It had become an addiction, an attachment, and
something so familiar that in some ways, it felt safe.

November 1, 2013 exhale...

I did not know what to title this post
so I started it as I physically did...with an exhale.

an exhale of release and contentment
an exhale indicating that work has been happening
within and without

I have been feeling somewhat naked, raw, and vulnerable,
And yet all within the comfort of Love, Familiarity, and Beauty.
This month in SouLodge we have been journeying with Owl, who I
hold dear.

For me Owl is a reflection of my Self
She has vision in the dark.
She consumes only what she needs from the rodents and night
crawlers.

She feasts on
and expels what she does not.
She is a Shadow Stalker,
A Keeper of the Night,
Silent in her Wisdom,
Knowing the importance of Going Within

to those dark places of our psyche to set ourselves free.

This month's Soul-Work has been revealing and hard.
Facing those things within myself
that are not so pretty—the rodents of my soul, so to speak.

Not facing them in or with shame
but instead, facing them with love and acceptance
realizing what they have to teach me
and also challenging me to let go
of the addictions,
the obsessions,
and the distractions
that keep me from my soul purpose.

Moving me toward the freedoms to express
my soul truth,
my heart words,
my Self.

I have watched myself consume my fears
and spit out the pellets of what I no longer wish to carry.

Bringing up those pellets stung as they scraped up my throat. They
even cause sadness.

"All changes, even the most longed for, have their melancholy; for
what we leave behind us is a part of ourselves; we must die to one
life before we can enter another." ~Anatole France

And at the same time,
they gave me Freedom and Hope.
My wings have hardened,
and I am ready to fly.
I know this only happens
by going deep
there is no other way
but to trust in Spirit fully
and go where one is called…
not forced
but called gently
by the exhale
of the One.

My life intention was clear: To be healed and to heal. My heart's desire was to be a vessel for spiritual love and healing. This meant letting go of my own pain and moving through and passed my own heartache. I was meant to be within myself in complete fullness.

I am already given to the powers that rule my fate.
I attach myself to nothing so I have nothing to defend.
I have no thoughts so that I can see.
I have no fear, so that I can remember myself.
Detached and at ease
I dart passed the Eagle
To be Free ~Shamanic Prayer

We completed the year with Horse, which is very fitting. Horse carries vison, strength, passion, and freedom; representing flow and egoless progress. It felt appropriate to finish this amazing, refining year with this beautifully sensitive creature at my side. The message and gift I received from Horse was the freedom to live fully. It sounds so simple, but within my own restrictions and the chains that bound me, freedom was like a myth of old, passed on from generation-to-generation, getting thinner each time it was told. But Freedom was indeed mine.

That was one of the greatest gifts of being involved in SOLAHIS and spending time at the center in Colombia. I realized the absolute freedom that I live in.

I had the freedom to travel, explore, overcome, and nurture my soul.
I had the freedom to live in unity with my spiritual self.
I had the freedom of true authenticity.

I had the freedom to live out my life as my Soul desired and embrace all that came my way by filtering it all through a free heart, mind, soul, and body.

I was allowed to be free.

And now, what was I going to do with this freedom?

I was going to live outside of the shadows of my shame. I was no longer going to hide in the fear of rejection. Because, truly, who was I not to live in my full brilliance?

As I entered my 45th year of living on this Earth, I walked with a holy fierceness. So much so that I would walk into the New Year with "Fierce" being my word for 2014. It was not the word I wanted. I was looking for something softer and gentler. But after weeks of hearing it, I could do nothing but surrender to the face that this word was intended for me.

There was a lot to feel fierce about. I was fierce in that deep passionate, stand at attention kind of way. I stood fiercely for my place in this world, and what that represented, for the Spirit in which I dwell, and a deep, knowing need for all the causes that swell in this space, and all the souls that have yet to know their own voices. There was also the fierceness of love that I felt for those around me, including my boys, my marriage, my tribe, and me. Also, there was the fierceness of standing up with another.

Another one of my dear sister-friends had been diagnosed with cancer. It was her second round with this disease, and I was heartsick to hear this news. But beyond the grief, I felt the fierceness to stand

with her, whatever that took, and whatever that looked like.

Fierce.

After a year of growing accustomed and even comfortable in the Refiner's Fire, fierce did, indeed seem fitting.

I am She...
I am She!
the one who lives out loud.
the one who lives for stillness.
I am She!
the one who pours out
the one who wants to be poured into
I am She!

Fierce Maiden of the Night
not afraid of the darkness
for I know what treasures lie there
within the folds of the things that scare me
I am a tear,
an exhale,
a shout,
a whisper.

I am complicated,
Easy,
Simple,
Confusing.
I am loud,
Soft,
Gentle,
Rough.

I am
the sun and
the moon.

I wear the stars in my hair,
and dance with the mermaids in the seas.
Wolf is my Elder Guide and companion
Grandmother Bear nurtures and comforts me.

Eagle give me strength and knowing,
While Panther stalks the shadows
reminding me of who I am
winking at me in the dark.

I look to the trees, to the sky
And there I see Hawk watching over and
offering guidance and protection.
and when I look at my face
I see Owl and Her Sacred Wisdom.
I see what can't be seen.
I know death
and am not afraid.

I am She,
Naked,
Exposed,
Unsure,
Willing.

I am She!
Sister of the Woods!
Servant to the Mountains!
Keeper of the Night Lantern!
Dancer of the Seas!
I am She!

~Catherine Beerda-Basso, 2013

*"The world will know and understand me someday.
But if that day does not arrive, it does not greatly matter.
I shall have opened the way for other women."*

~ George Sands

15
Healing

Interestingly enough, yet somehow fitting, the end of this part of my story is the beginning. It would be here in the newness of 2014 that this story, one that took 14 years to mature and that I began to write about so many years ago, has decided its time had come to be laid out in word. Or did I decide this. Maybe my heart, my soul, and my being are ready. I am ready to share this very intimate, personal, and vulnerable part of myself. I would walk through it all again, and release it out into the world with the hope that it might be a lantern for those walking a similar path. Perhaps it will be a reflection of light back to them, so they might find their way back to themselves, too. I am finally ready for what is to come after writing and binding this story. Then again, maybe I am not ready but feeling the passion burn deep enough to do it anyway. Whatever it is, here I am writing. After much guidance and healing from Spirit, my guides, my angels, my ancestors, along with my amazing, and extensive tribe of Soul-Sisters, I am ready. The story was always ready and would always be ready. Me on the other hand...well... I needed some time, and what a time it has been.

In January of this year, I started setting a strong, focused spiritual intention around my life and me. Writing out what I wanted to draw in for my family, my Self, spiritually, physically, mentally, creatively, and financially. I pulled cards from my sacred decks and did an Angel reading for myself to cover the year. And the word I had been given for the year was "Fierce," a word I was not particularly jazzed about. As I was being told to be Fierce, I was also being given the mantra "Do without Doing." I was being told to sink into stillness, find a steady rhythm, set boundaries, seek self-discipline, and enforce willpower. It was clear that this stillness represented the stillness of solitude and writing. On the other hand, the word "stillness" with the word "fierce" felt completely opposite from each other. I sat with both in prayer and meditation to find out what they wanted to give me. It was within this duality that I realized that they were the reflection of each other. Fierce is not always loud and aggressive. There is fierceness in being still and in surrendering to the unknown of solitude, especially for one who surrounded herself with others her entire life, and whose purpose had been to "plug in" and be "plugged into."

The more I sat with all that had been given to me to take into the new year, the more I felt an excitement grow within me. My story was going to be told and not only would it take my healing even deeper, it would be heard, received, and assist others in healing! I could definitely unleash Fierce for healing and freedom. I could do this and enter fiercely into the solitude that would be a big part of my life in the coming year. So I spent much of January "cleaning things up," which, at times, felt a little like procrastination. I had a vision in my mind as to how it was supposed to look. I envisioned being able to give full attention to writing, with no other distractions. That was not happening. I assumed I must have been failing because I was not fulfilling that vision.

Even with a powerful word like "Fierce," all the blessings and signs I had been given, and knowing full well that this year was offering me an opportunity to surrender to the writer within, (something I had longer for), I still felt I was finding things to distract me. These were good things, meaningful things, spiritual things, but I felt that I was using them to distract myself from the scared, vulnerable feeling of my heart. Fortunately, Spirit is patient and waited for me to play out my human game of back and forth. On the last Monday of January, I went to see my Light Sister, Monica for a chakra aligning Reiki session. This was when Spirit came in and began the deeper healing work I needed to fully enter into the new year, renewed self, and new season of my life. This session gave me the courage and clarity of my process.

I went to Monica for help, knowing there was something blocking me, something holding me back, and I wanted to deal with it. I could feel it but could not identify it and was having a tough time moving it. I needed to move passed the feeling of procrastination and distraction and the back and forth hamster wheel game that was playing out in my mind. I knew Monica would be able to shift things around, break things up, and perhaps even identify "it."

Having a good healing practitioner in your life is such a gift. Just walking into her apartment began the healing process. The intention was so clearly laid out. It was hard not to feel Spirit and all those who were there to greet me. This included her little Chihuahua, Toby, who by the way, "has been waiting for you for the last 20 minutes," Monica told me.

Our session went beautifully. I am given a word from The Father... Abundance. I am told that I am in a time of abundance, an abundance that wants to be enjoyed, and an abundance that needs and should be celebrated. I hear the word whispered in my ear, as its truth bursts from my heart chakra. Then after some time, I was enveloped in the colour blue. It was ice blue with sparkles floating through it. I felt as if my entire body was being folded in half. I watched it happen and physically felt it, too. Angels push on my back as I fold over my legs. My spine was straight and unaffected, as were my legs. This was something that would never happen in "real time." They continued to push on me, firmly but gently. There was nothing evasive about the process. There was no feeling of violation or fear, I was completely at peace and knew I was in good hands.

After some time, they let me go and my body sprang back into a laying position. As this happened, a murder of crows flew out of my Sacral Chakra, my abdomen. They carried the poison away and took what did not belong inside me. They assisted in my healing. I felt the tears stream down my face. Later Monica told me that my body was convulsing when this occurred. She could see deep healing was happening and felt a strong energy around that part of my body.

Then The Mother came to me, Mama Earth. She showed up in such a peaceful manor. She was hardly even detectable. She began by speaking to me through Monica who let me know that She was there and had a message for me. These kind words always send a wave of excitement and nervousness through me. Silly ego questions came up like, "What if I can't hear her?" and "What if I don't recognize her voice?" and "Is that her speaking or my own mind?" and "What if it is bad news?" I am always amazed at how so many questions can fly through one's mind within a fraction of a second. As it was I let them all fly away and sank into this moment, opened my heart, stilled my mind, and listened for the voice I knew and trusted. It did not take long before she started speaking.

Vulnerability. This was the word that I heard, "vulnerable." Mama said to me, "I want more vulnerability from you Catherine." I cringed, "More? Really?" My conscious self, my ego thought how much more vulnerable could I be? As I rolled my eyes. She smiled, "Yes, more vulnerability". And I knew she was right. I knew there had been pieces of me that I was holding close, and that I wanted to bring back to life and set free, but had yet to gather the courage to do so. I talked about it, even started the process to do it, many times, but pulled back again and again. Of course, one of the pieces was this book, the story of coming back to myself. My story of grief, struggle, loss, and all the many rebirths along the way. Writing this story was my most vulnerable expression to date. Putting it out there, offering it up for anyone to read and form an opinion on it and me. It felt like putting my heart on display for anyone to poke and prod at their leisure. This idea was a little frightening and left me feeling intensely vulnerable.

When Monica brought things to a close, the smell of tobacco lingered in the air even though she was not burning tobacco. She told me a First Nations Chief came to speak to me. Using Monica, he told me a great healing had happened within me. He went on to say that the origin of the wound was not what was important. The important part was that I was healed and being healed. What needed to leave my body had left. He was happy with the work that I was doing and me. He blessed the healing within me. Then he was gone. His words about the origin of the wound deeply resonated with me. As I moved through this life journey, "the story" seemed less and less important. It had become more about how the story affected me—the medicine that the story held, and how I got to walk through the story and learn all I could. There was a time when the story was everything, so much so that the story was me, and I was the story. I was unable to separate the two. If this life journey had taught me anything, it was that the story actually holds the smallest part of importance. It was what followed the story that was where the real treasures were found. It was in the grief, the loss, the celebration, and the healing where the true story lay. It was in what followed the story that I found the tools and the medicine I needed for this life.

After the session was over I shared with Monica about all that had transpired, while I was on her table. All I told her resonated with her. I also told her about the place I was taken by The Mother. It was a new place, one I had not visited within myself on journey or vision. I was taken up the mountain, where the tree line runs thin. There were some trees but mostly rock with spots of grass. Here was where I was being called to be, in between two grand mountains at the edge of a cliff that drops into a large and very deep ravine. It was so deep that I barely saw the river that runs through it at the bottom. It might not even be a river, I can't be sure. Panther and Wolf were there with me but there was a deep sense of aloneness there. Not that I was lonely, but there was a level of solitude I felt being asked of me in this place. Companions will be few.

After our session, I felt intoxicated and weightless. This often happened after I go deep, or far from the now. Monica offered me some tea to help me ground myself, and I willingly accepted. This also gave us more time to chat, which I love, as her insight was a gift and the conversation was the kind I adore. We talked about painting, and

I noticed one in particular on her wall. It was a beautiful landscape image of the northern night sky with mountains, snow, and glitter. There it was, with one little sweep of the brush, the exact colour of blue with glitter that was part of my healing.

Walking away from that session, I felt like a significant blockage had been dissolved and transformed. I felt myself walking lighter and knew that I was that much closer to myself. These sessions are just the start. As I stepped back into the flow of my life the healing took hold. Now began an intention in which I applied all that had been given and lived actively in that intention of healing. If I went back to my old patterns and old ways, the healing would not have a chance to sink into my bones and become one with me and part of my DNA. In order for the healing to have its full potency realized, I had to do the work. I had to follow-through with active application. This was where things could bubble-up and challenge me. This was when I found it could get difficult.

Changing old ways felt uncomfortable and foreign. I learned to stay the course, sit in it. Even if it felt uncomfortable, I would just be. Sometimes I did this well. Sometimes it seemed I just did not have what it took to sit in it, but there was always another opportunity to do so. There is nothing fast-moving about Spirit work. God is not in the same rush that we live in. There are no time constraints with Divinity. One of my favourite verses from The Bible says, *"Don't overlook the obvious here, friends. With God one day is as good as a thousand years, a thousand years as a day. God isn't late with his promise as some measure lateness. God is restraining himself on account of you, holding back because he does not want any one lost. He's giving everyone space and time to grow."* (This translation is taken from The Message and found The New Testament in the book of 2 Peter 3:9.) These words of wisdom gave me peace when I felt I was not moving forward as quickly as I should be. I am reminded that all expectations are my own...not Creator's.

During my chakra yoga class on Wednesday, the healing continued. We were focusing on our throat chakra, the Vishuddha, the chakra whose prime function is that of communication and healing. Antje was taking us through poses to assist us in unblocking this area and letting go of any emotions that were causing the blockage. She always encouraged us to move through our practice with our eyes closed, thus eliminating distraction and the human condition of comparing ourselves to one another. I decided that throughout this practice, I would envision myself at my sacred place in the mountains, and allow the journey that started with Monica on Monday to continue. We were focusing on our hips, where we store a lot of our emotions. While we were doing a deep stretching pose, I was completely engulfed in the ice blue light with sparkles throughout it. Again a murder of crows flew out of me. This time they flew out of my hips. I felt them. I saw them. I watched them fly away. I am not exactly sure what they took with them, but it doesn't matter. I was just happy to know that they were with me, helping me on my journey back to myself. I am grateful for the Divinity that showed up again and again. As I laid in Savasana at the end of class, the tears rolled down and pooled in my ears. It was life giving water of gratitude and thanks.

Healing is continual. I know I have written that before, but I had to say it again. There have been many times that I met someone who believed that the healing process would end in this lifetime. I do not see it this way. I see this life as the healing process. When we raise our children, different stages bring different challenges, parental strategies, and joys. The ebb and flow of life is a continuum. We can choose to be a part of it or let it pass us by and stay in the safety of what we know and understand, regardless of whether it is best thing for our Spirit or not.

Now, I am at a point in my life where I see challenge and struggle very differently. I recognize that if there is challenge or struggle something big is going to happen within me. Divinity is going to show up big time. Things are going to be blown apart, once again. I still feel the feelings that come with challenge, but I am not stuck in those feelings. They do not rule me. I know there is more, and I know my higher self is being touched. It is not always easy. I am still a fleshy human, but it is doable.

And so it was, when I headed down to Portland on Friday, January 31, to gather with my circle of sisters there on February 1. My first stop was in Seattle to visit my dear sister friend, Kelly. It would be the first time seeing her after her being re-diagnosed with cancer. I was longing to spend some face time with her.

What a gift to spend soul time with likeminded people, particularly, likeminded women. My heart tribe has gone through so many changes so I am happy and feel blessed to have the stability of sister-friends like Kelly in my life. We had a lovely afternoon together. This was the first time I had gone to her home and met her kids...a male Boxer named Sancho and a female Doberman named Freyja. They were delightful. We sat in her cozy living room with hot tea in hand

and opened our hearts. We pulled spirit cards and dug deep into the reality of now. We went out for a meal, celebrated her slow, but evident healing, and glowed in each other's presence. These kinds of exchanges feed the soul and give joy to the spirit. They are sacred gifts to me. They remind me that I do not walk this Earth alone. There are others who think these matters of love, spirit, heart, and soul are valid and important. When we returned to her home after our late lunch, her husband was home. After a beautiful visit and exchange with him, it was time for me to continue my travels toward Portland. I left their home with my heart full, and the feeling that I had just spent time with two precious souls with whom I am so very blessed to know.

I continued on my journey south with no real plan in place, just knowing that I would like to be as close to Portland as possible before calling it a night and getting a hotel room. Looking for an adventure, I decided to stop at one of the roadside hotels. You know the ones that they depict in the movies that have some creepy past story of mystery and perhaps murder. I got as far as Castle Rock, a place that fits the criteria, and decide to call it a night. I grabbed a snack and drink, got a room, and settled in for a good night's sleep. At around 4:30am, some familiar voices and the feelings of old anxieties woke me.

My mind decided to take on some old demons. This was something that seemed to happen when I was on the edge of something big. I lay in my empty and still hotel room and listened to the voices tell me how I was not good enough, and how I was a fool to think I could write this book. They told me how I was completely off the mark thinking anyone would be interested in reading what I have to share. I sat with the negativity for a while, tried to let it go, and fall back to sleep. When this did not happen, I turned on the TV, hoping it would cause me to fall back to sleep. Instead I found myself watching a Reality Show in which the host reunites families who had lost each other along the way. The particular family he was following was one of tragedy and abuse. A family of children broken inside and from one another due to a mother who was unfit to care for the children she bore. Their story took me in. I sat and watched their reunion unfold. The tears rolled down my face. So many broken souls, so many people lost due to circumstances that were beyond their control, searched to find their way home.

Funny that it would be this very show that would cause the whispers of encouragement to drown out the yelling of negativity that was happening in my brain. The whispers let me know that my offering mattered. They told me that my words would bring healing. My story would change lives; the kind of lives I was watching right now on this TV show.

I did not fall back to sleep. After crying through the entire show, I felt emotionally beat up and raw. Looking back, that feeling was one of letting go, of deep release, and a time to let the voices come, but not react to them. I let them come and go.

I curled up in my blankets and watched some more TV, sitting in the emotions of the early morning. Eventually it was time to get up and get back on the road, which I was more than happy to do.

When I began to drive, I hoped to see Hawk, as I had seen so many of them the day before, along with Eagle. They marked my journey forward. The truth was, due to my raw and vulnerable state, I was looking for a sign that I was not alone. After those last few challenging hours, I needed to know that Spirit was still with me. I drove through the early morning light earnestly searching the trees on the side of highway for my Guides. The abundance of Spirit the day before could not have been seen in my hour of need.

And then the voice came:

Am I enough?
Am I enough for you?
Can it just be you and me?

Tears filled my eyes and rolled down my cheeks.
"Yes, yes you are more than enough," I say out loud.
"You are here with me, and you are more than enough."

No sooner had the words left my lips and Hawk was sitting in a tree on the roadside, my eyes easily caught his shape and laughter filled my car.

Part of my life purpose is to share this story. Not so much the story of my life, as much as I am meant to tell a story about personal redemption and coming home through spiritual freedom and love. The story that showed up: No matter what, you can always go home. No matter what you've been told, you matter. You are valued. The story of the in between, the story of what is behind the veil of flesh, and what we are truly made of, this is my purpose. I know it beyond the fleshy doubt I have.

I arrived early for the gathering, still feeling the rawness of the early morning, alongside the joy and gratitude of entering this time and space with likeminded, beautiful women. I had already met some of these women at the first circle, and some I only knew from cyber-world in the SouLodge group. I grabbed a coffee and got out my journal to write down the morning encounter with Spirit and Hawk but I am not alone for long. I could see familiar faces, those I have seen on screen, and they recognized me, and so the day of entwining hearts began.

Even now, I smile as I think about seeing the faces of Tiffanie, Nissa, and Twozdai for the first time. Hugging and knowing one another on a deep level even though there had been no physical meeting, we had moved passed a lot of formality that could waste precious time of soul connecting. The day moved into the ease of sisterhood and sacred exchange. In among these women, these beautiful souls, I found my strength once again. I saw the reality of what is. I saw myself in each of them, and they are beautiful, oh so beautiful. I felt the fire in the one that I sat beside. She made me feel unafraid to reveal my fire. I felt the honesty and the vulnerability of making hard decisions that we find ourselves having to make in the one who sat a few sisters down from me. I shared the struggle of balance with one, and I was moved by the sparkle and joy of another. The shared pain of feeling stuck is a feeling I related to and the joy of new life was one I know.

Each of their stories crossed with mine. I realized as I sat in this sacred circle with these amazing, vibrant creatures that I had truly found my home. Not one I felt compelled to hold tightly, but one I knew would remain forever. Even if the faces changed, this circle of sacredness among women would forever be with me. It had always been with me. I only needed this time and place to help me remember. I remembered that I belonged and still belong; and that I was and am one with these women, in all ways. They won't know, until they read these words, just how deep that day went for me. I walked away knowing that this book would be birthed, and they were my doulas, assisting me in doing so.

And so it is.

And now, as I sit in this still dark, early morning in February of 2016 with candles burning and prayers of gratitude on my lips, and abundant wonder and love in my heart. I make the finishing touches of this story. I have completed what I set out to do.

It is beyond words of explanation as to how I feel…how complete this feels.

Physically I feel like I gave birth after a weekend bender.
Emotionally, it feels strange and wonderful.
Spiritually, I feel rooted...strong...complete.

This year of 2014 brought fierce humility and gratitude. I was humbled by the gifts that were given to me, and the medicine that came my way so effortlessly. I began to gather medicine with intention, like I had never done before. I trusted that Mother Earth would supply all that I needed. My healing work grew to become Shaenalach Healing and Retreats. Within it, I created different offerings for healing. There would be one-on-one sessions and a variety of circles and retreats, some of which were collaborations with other wise souls. My photography became part of the healing I offered. It continued to be a source of joy and inspiration for others and myself. The book became more and more of a focus. It was a challenge at times to balance all that was happening around me, but somehow I managed. Even in the struggle, I managed to get the words out of me.

I gathered with the most amazing women this year. In April, I spent the day with two lovely sister-friends, Kelly and Marybeth in Bellingham. After catching up over lunch, we headed down to the ocean for an afternoon of cleansing, clearing, and letting go. I circled in Portland with Nissa Howard, of SoulCraft for Beltane, alongside a group of amazing women. These were days to remember. They were Soul days with sisters who were so sacred and so holy just as I knew it could be. I found myself back in the Soul Craft container with Nissa, in the fall with another group of amazing women and a dear sister-friend at my side, as we made our own elk drums. So many sacred circles that built me up and caused my branches to reach even higher and roots to go even deeper.

May 15, 2014

No longer am I a slave
For now I walk free
No longer bound down
I am free
No shackles on my feet.
No rope upon my wrist.
I am free to live
As I see fit.
No more do I answer to master.

I now hold my own destiny.
No more do I live in fear.
No more do I sleep in tears.
No more am I an animal.
For now, I walk upright
Knowing full well
That I am free.

~CBB

I turned old mantra's such as the one I had as a child *"Never let them know how much they hurt you."* to *"Never keep from them, what you want them to know about your heart."* I continued my spiritual practice with SouLodge and took on a few more spiritual studies with Leonard Howell, the Metis Elder and Wisdom Keeper. My journey to gather knowledge was an active one. The more I learned, the hungrier I seemed to become. With this time of learning, came many opportunities to apply and utilize what I had learned. My spirituality began to move passed being a practice and was becoming a way of life.

July 1, 2014

Warrior Woman
The road is rocky and dry
Dust kicks up as her boots hit the earth
The dry Earth of too many suns
And not enough rain…
Her armour weighs heavy
But she removes not a piece
For she is in battle, walking The Underworld
Calling out Demons and Exposing Shadows
Bringing them to submission and transformation
And those who do not comply
Must move onto the after life
Their place here is done
Her heart at times wavers
But her feet are forever sure.

Those she passes along the way
Can't always see her truth
They don't see the branches in her hair

On which the robin perches
They can't see the owl in her face or
That her large eyes see clearly in the dark.

They don't see the eagle that circles above her
Or
The bear that follows a few paces behind.
They don't recognize the grey wolf at her side.
They only see a mangy mutt of a dog.

And as for the black cat,
They cannot see it as the jungle panther that it is.
Some know there is something different about her.

Her face holds the beauty and the horror she has
seen
They see the lines etched into her face
Of one exposed to the elements
For far too long.

They can see her wild hair
Untamed
Like her spirit
And they know she has traveled far.
And for a brief moment,
They wonder what secrets she holds
That maybe – just maybe, she might know
something
Worth hearing.

But as soon as it comes
The moment is gone…
…they carry on their merry way
With not a second thought
Of the strange, wild woman
They passed on their way.

And then there are those who knew
They knew she had seen things
They need to hear about.

They see the earth move with her
As she breathes in and breathes out.

They long to come beside her
and take in her essence, and

Stepping into her world.

For it is a world that they long for,
But
They hold back...
...Afraid to be seen with such a creature
...Afraid of how knowing will change their world
...Afraid of the sins of desire and freedom
...Afraid to leave the containment of a world they know
And trust.

Even if his or her heart longs for it...
Even if his or her skin cries for it...
Even if his or her blood boils for it...
He or she will simmer it down,
Shut it out, and
Soothe it with words such as
Safe,
Conform,
and Obey.

But, finally
There are others who see her clearly.

Warrior Woman
Dry, Blood-crusted Wounds
Tended to by the Woodland Fairies
Eyes of Wisdom that come from outside
The human realm,
A wild passion bubbling up from deep within.

She is not one to tame,
But one to honour.

They see the trophies of the demons she has harnessed
As they sway on a rope
Strapped to her side.

She is not to be underestimated.

She will breathe dragon fire, if needed
And yet,
Will nurse the dying to life.

She is fierce in battle
And even fiercer in the way she loves.

She swam the seas of lava
And marinated in the mud of time.

She walked the corridors of endless darkness
And smelled the stench of hopelessness.

Her skin was saturated with the emptiness
Of a thousand bottomless wells.

She drank the waters of Life
And was blessed by Angels Divine
She witnessed the Dawn of Time.

When the Great Magic sang its first song,
She held purity in her hand
And swam in the Ocean of Love.

She needs no sword
And walks with but a staff in hand
And a lantern held high.

She has fear.

But stays on course in spite of it,
Ready to kick ass when needed.

She also soothes a babe to sleep
And makes a grown man cry
With the words of her heart.

She is All...
...Mother
...Warrior-ess
...Priestess
...Goddess
...Sister
...Daughter
...Friend
She is All.

Love her.
Treasure her.
Know her.

And if you are lucky enough to see her
And all those she walks with,
Step up and ask her the questions of your heart.

Walk with her,
Take her hand,
Eat with her,
Drink with her,
And you will soon see
Within her eyes
There You are.

~ CBB

And so, I bring this story to a close and allow the next part of my journey as Spiritual Activist, Earth Medicine Practitioner, Light Bringer to be as it is meant to be. I say to you, Dear Reader that more than anything I hope you experience this story as one that is about God and you. It is not only a story about me. It is a story of how *The Great Mystery* came to me in so many different ways. It guided me, healed me, redeemed me, and transformed me over, and over, and over again.

God, The Great Spirit, The Source, The Energy, The Love from which we all come is such a great mystery, as is this life that we live. It's been an awe-filled journey so far, terrible and beautiful. There is nothing I would change, which might be hard to understand. Let me put it like this. There is no light without the dark. There is no life without death. There is no transformation without exfoliation. I am grateful for the life I have led, because it has made me who I am. I don't like all that happened to me, especially as a child. Some of what I've experienced has been wrong, tragic and life long scars remain. But, out of those terrible things I emerged the woman that I am today, and I will not deny her...I will not deny mySelf, love and honour because of someone else's choices. Mine is a life filled with so much Love, Light, and Shadow.

Healing and living fully is a continual journey, one I will be on until my last breath leaves my body. There are many final chapters and many new beginnings. There is still much to learn, to unfold, and to heal. I was once a being who longed for death and wanted to leave this place. I was one who did not want this life. Now I am on fire for this life. That is how I know that this was all real, and I was meant to be a part of it. These many years of journeying out of my depression and eradicating the chains of my religious up-bringing have taught me how to utilize not only my gifts in the light but also in the shadows. It grew a heart of compassion and grace, not only for myself but for others as well. This journey brought me back to my Self.

More than anything, I want you to know that life is worth living awake and engaged. I want you to know that peace is not a dream, love is never-ending, and *The Great Mystery* will meet you wherever you are. If you ask, It will reveal Itself to you in a way that you can see and that resonates with you. If Spirit is not something to which you can subscribe, or wrap your head around, then I say to you, my brave reader, believe in Love. Believe in the goodness, the selflessness, the grace and compassion that You hold. Believe in Love and believe in You. You are sacred space. You are the medicine. You are a divine being. You are Love.

"The inferior teacher tells you that something is wrong with you and offers to fix it. The superior teacher tells you that something is right and offers a way to bring it forth."
~Alan Cohen

Gratitude

There were so many stories that happened during this journey that did not make it into the book. There were so many more people who affected me and helped me through. These words are but a glimpse into a full life. Truly, I could not have done this, as well as I have, without theses people...

My husband, Steve. Ours is a union built in reality. We love each other deeply, and like each other even more...most of the time. We honour our union and realize that we created it by choice and are responsible for it. I have always and will always describe you as an exceptional person. I used to wonder how I got so lucky, but the truth is, it was written in the stars, divinely placed. You challenge me to stay awake and alert. You fully accept all of me. Much of my journey, you did not understand, but you stood by me and honoured my process. I will forever be grateful for your commitment to me, to us, and to our family.

My boys. Truly, there are no words. My "Greatest Teacher" and my "Spirit Bear" ...without you I am half the woman that I am. I am so blessed by the both of you equally and so differently. I am honoured to be your mom. You are such a deep part of me, something that goes beyond blood and bone. Thank you , thank you, thank you, for being who you are. Bless you both. I have not been the perfect mother. I have made mistakes. I have not done it all "right." But I have loved you both; an incredible love that surpassed even my own self...truly, madly, deeply.

Without the three of you, being exactly who you are, I could not have taken this journey. My tribe of men and me, this was not how I saw it as a little girl, but it has been exactly what I needed. Thank you for all the love, for all the laughs, and for all the tears. I love you all in a way that words cannot explain.

I want to thank my parents, who raised me. They gave me the best they could, and there was a lot of goodness that I gleaned from the life they gave me. I want to thank my biological mother for giving me life, and enduring all she did, during the time I grew inside of her. A special thanks to my "surrogate parents" Bill and Yvonne, for being there...for always being there. A huge thank you to my amazing

Father and Mother-in-law. For how you loved The Young Blood as your own and accepted me as your daughter. You all played a part in making me who I am today and for that I am grateful. My siblings old and new, I love you. It's as simple as that. I love you and am grateful for the memories of the past and the ones we create today.

To Carolyn and Sonja. I'll keep it simple. I know neither of you like the spot light...thank you for believing in me, standing by me, loving me as you both do. You helped build the courage within me.

To all the many women who have woven their way in and out of my life. My childhood friends, my high school mates, friends from my twenties. You all made an impact, and left your mark. The Safeway Girls, The PUC-G Mamas, my blogging sister-friends, The Sisters of Light, The Moon Sisters, The Wapiti Sisters, The WWW Sisters, The Re-Wilding Sisters, The Sisters at The Well...our laughter and tears are forever etched in my heart. Thank you for the sisterhood, the friendship, the unfolding.

A special thank you to my SouLodge Sisters. SouLodge has ebbed and flowed, and we remain a sisterhood that I am forever blessed by. The list of soul-sisters is long; I trust you know who you are. xox

It's not all about the sisters. To those special men in my life. My brothers. Most of you husbands to my sisters...Thank you. Your wisdom, valor and man-love is appreciated and needed.

To my teachers and healers, thank you. Leonard Howell. For your healing, your wisdom, your heart. Thank you, Uncle for impacting my life as you have. Your beautiful spirit is a gift and your wisdom of the medicine vital. Thank you for sharing it with me. Pixie Lighthorse. My dear sister and friend, thank you for creating a space where so many powerful healers could come and be in each others presence to die, grow and come back to life along side one another. Your vision and teachings were instrumental in my journey back to myself. I am forever grateful. To Jodie, Monica, Angelaya, Lidia, Cathy and Lori, my healer sisters, thank you for your presence and wisdom in my life. You each brought/bring to me something unique and needed.

To those who write their stories so we can learn from them... thank you!

To all the authors mentioned in the book...thank you!

To all those who have crossed my path, be it positive or negative, you impacted me...

And finally, to my amazing, little, kick-ass publishing team. Heather Dakota and Twozdai Hulse. Sisters! I could not have done this without you...seriously! To my editor, Heather...thank you for helping me craft my words in a way that kept me raw and honest. Thank you for your calls to go even deeper. Thank you for your belief in me. Thank you for your encouragement and honesty. Thank you for holding my story in honour and respect. Thank you for you. To my designer and tech support, Twozdai...thank you for holding my hand and talking me down, when I felt overwhelmed. Thank you for your direct and straight forward guidance, it helped me breathe steady. Thank you for coming on board so willingly and sharing your talents with me. You were the even and steady flow. Thank you, thank you, thank you. Be Blessed, both of you!

About Catherine

Catherine Beerda-Basso lives in a suburb of Vancouver, Canada, with her husband, her youngest son and beloved Black Lab. Her oldest lives nearby, keeping the family close and connected. She strives to live a slower paced, simple life, while staying connected to all that she loves and all that sustains her.

Catherine manages a small healing practice from her home, while holding a variety of healing circles within her community. Her passion lies in one on one service, circle gatherings and weekend retreats. She identifies herself as an Earth Medicine Practitioner, Spiritual Activist, Word Smyth and Intuitive Photographer. Catherine is a midwife of deep soul awareness and healing. Her gifts allow her to take a woman on a journey to herself, held by the land, by sacred tools, and by her fiercely true presence. Founder of Shaenalach Healing and Retreats; Catherine's thought is that by giving women a safe container to connect to themselves in a spiritual, sacred way, allows them the opportunity to find the pieces that have been scattered, and to "re-struct" the beauty that is already there.

Catherine is a longtime volunteer at Seeds of Love and Hope International Society and is currently working on a book about her experiences with this non-profit society. The book, called "Flying with Clipped Wings", will hold the stories of those whose lives are impacted by the work of SOLAHIS, happening in Medellin, Colombia. She also volunteers at a local recovery home for women.

To find out more about Catherine and her work,
visit her web site www.catherinebeerdabasso.com

*"Out beyond ideas
of wrong-doing
and right-doing,
there is a field.
I'll meet you there."*

~Rumi

Made in the USA
Middletown, DE
09 September 2019